Gay Key West

Cruisin' Duval

The people,
history,
architecture,
gay bars, restaurants, and guesthouses

Complements of

Lee Dode', Ph.D.

and

BOOKS, ART & CARDS

830 Fleming Street • Key West, FL 33040
305-294-3931

Including *Memories of Key West,*
the sixties, seventies, eighties and into the nineties

Lee Dode', Ph.D.

ISBN 0-9663054 2 6
UPC 654725

Printed in the United States of America.
Solares Hill Design Group, Key West, Florida.
Cover Production, Dina Coyle, Dina Designs, Key West.
My thanks to Judy DeGraci.

Arete Publishing
Post Office Box 4382
Key West, Florida, 33041-4382

Author's note:

I was reared in the early days of the twentieth century and, being gay, found my associations with reality from books, plays and the motion pictures. I spent hours looking for a hero, someone with whom I could identify my life, someone on which I could base my personal values of who I am. Most values that I had were from my parents, many of which I still maintain. But, they could not meet all my demands. I was looking for for identity of being "someone", someone "different".

Hollywood, or specifically the motion picture industry, was my direction for escape. I found much idenity in the stereotypes of characters in films. Eventually the motion picture industry dominated a new concept called television. Hollywood and television denied the gay direction although their ranks were crowded with gays. The decision makers were backing themselves with lies about the gay lifestyle, and they were making judgments of reality so they could make more money. Their portrayal of a person could become a hero to those of us who were "different".

In this manner, the motion picture industry and eventuaollly television shaped our heros and even our values of being gay. We got some positive values, but none about being homosexual. We learned the "campy" lines that fit into our lifestyle. We adapted many of the mannerisms that we thought demonstrated us as a type or "different". As gays, we were misled, and we became part of the Hollywood mistique, the stereotypes of homosexuality. We quoted the characters and the stars. "The last time I read a book, I was raped. So, let that be a lesson to you" said Madeline Kahn in "Yellowbeard".

Escaping, as children and young adults, we saw all kinds of films. Some of the films were excellent, many were "less than excellent". Almost all created a character out of something that had made us, as gays, "different". I have used some of these quotes and stereotypes as a camp for "garlic on the hamburg", to bring out the flavor."
Regardless, the motion picture industry made the decisions of the image of an actor or actress in public and private. The image they should projected and the values of that image were the ilmpressions we got as the gays. We learned and projected that image.

My source has been a wonderful factual book, The Voyeur's Guide to Men and Women in the Movies, by Mart Martin, Contemporary Books, Chicago, 1994, a major source of whitty lines. He does not refer to the quality of the films. Neither did we as young movie goers. We saw the good and the bad, and an awful lot of the bad. These lines and stereotypes shaped our lives.

Lee Dode', Ph.D.

Introduction

I have been coming to Key West or lived here since 1960. About seven or eight years ago, I was asked to write my impressions of Key West, the gossip and the people. I wrote Memories of Key West, the Sixties, Seventies, Eighties, and into the Nineties., and I had 500 copies printed with profits going to AIDS Help. Copies went quickly and I have been encouraged to either republish the book or add to it.

When I travel to a new place, I want a comfortable place to stay. I'm interested in the history of the new area, its architecture, and its people. In the evening, I want to visit the restaurants and the gay bars. The seemingly unrelated qualities are all obvious on Duval Street, the one-mile stretch from the Atlantic Ocean to the Gulf of Mexico, called "the longest mile". This mile is ever-changing, charged with facts and fantasy, with real and unreal characters and events.

Some people say that Key West is not only a place, but also an attitude. It is an attitude that I love.

Lee Dode'

Restaurants, bars, and guesthouses

Most restaurants, bars and guesthouses are very liberal about serving the gay public. They really don't care so long as the gay man or lesbian behaves him/herself in their establishment. Obviously, in restaurants, the management is there to make money and they are limited in refusing to serve anyone. Almost all restaurants are mixed with gays and straights.

There are no completely gay restaurants with the possible exception of the restaurant at Lighthouse Court, which is there to service its guests. Outsiders are welcome. Even the pool bar of Atlantic Shores is predominantly gay but not Diner Shores, the restaurant in front on South Street.

1

Almost all restaurants are liberal. (There is always the exception of that couple of gay men or lesbians making a public display and insisting on having sex at the dinner table, an embarrassment to all.) Few of the restaurant advertise for gay clients; the town is simply not large enough to allow for a food business which is exclusively gay. Practically all are gay friendly.

However, there are certain restaurants that the gays repeatedly mention as being superior to others. The gay men and lesbians feel more comfortable in that atmosphere. These are mostly restaurants, and the listing does not include the dining rooms of large hotels which are always accommodating to anyone with money. Is the listing "all inclusive"? Absolutely not. There are currently about 185 restaurants in Key West. The restaurants mentioned are either on or within a block of Duval Street. The restaurants are also not categorized according to price. Some are more expensive than others, but the difference between an expensive meal in a small restaurant and an expensive meal in a first class restaurant is usually only a couple of dollars. Reservations are requested but not usually required.

During your afternoon walk on Duval Street, check the restaurant menus on display and select your preference for the evening. Practically all are "casual". All are gay friendly.

Restaurant suggestions are admittedly biased but are based on the experiences of locals. Florence Fabricant, writing in "The New York Times" makes some suggestions indicated by * on a following list.

As in any town, the bar scene is constantly changing, more so in Key West where rents are expensive and competition is fast. The following listing of bars is what most local gay men or lesbians believe to be the gay bars of Key West. Each seems to be of a little different flavor, and you'll have to decide what flavor you want. All of the listed gay bars are advertised as being gay, but they will not refuse anyone, not gay or straight couples. The unusual factor of Key West gay bars is that they are usually mixed bars. Some are restaurant bars, drag bars, a touch of leather bars. "Club International" on Simonton Street has a large lesbian patronage. Some are elegant like "Square One" and "La te da" and others more earthy like "Numbers" and "Saloon One". All have happy hours with happy hour prices.

The gay bars were identified as such if they have received comment from the local gays, advertise in predominantly gay magazines like The Advocate or Hot Spots, have previously been reviewed as being gay or have a historic reputation for being gay by previous owners. However, all bars in Key West are gay friendly and you are just as likely to see gay men and lesbians at the hotel bars as well as local popular hangouts like "Captain Tony's Saloon" or "Maragretaville".

The listing of guesthouses does not include hotel accommodations because the public knows the larger hotel chains. Most Marriot's are going to be around the same price, although Key West has a captured audience and the restaurants are very competitive. The price of the guest- houses differ greatly depending upon the season and the conveniences. Most of the guesthouses that cater to gays are run and/or owned by gays. The prices very.

The guesthouses are casual, many having unique surroundings for their guests. The "Rainbow House" is "for women only". Few of the other guesthouses are so restrictive. At "Deja Vie" clothing is optional, and the guests are mostly straight couples. At many of the predominantly gay male guesthouses, the guests can swim naked. Some have cocktail parties.

I talked with the front desk people to get the listing of gay guesthouses, and I searched the advertising of local gay magazines. This listing is, of course, only a few of the guesthouses in town, and many gay guesthouses have not been included, a listing filled with personal preferences. The clients and their reactions were the main source, but these reactions constantly change.

It is important to make your reservations at a guesthouse before you come down to Key West.   In l996, it was estimated that there were between 625,000 and 650,000 gay tourists in Key West (44%). The next year,1997, it was estimated that there were 650,000 gay tourists in Key West (43%). (1) Those who arrive without accommodations during Fantasy Fest (Halloween) have only themselves to blame. Being arrested while sleeping uncomfortably in a car is no way to enjoy a vacation.

GAY AND GAY FRIENDLY GUEST HOUSES - KEY WEST

Atlantic Shores Resort	510 South St	296 2491*+
Alexander's Guest house	lll8 Fleming St	294 9919*
Amsterdam-Curry Inn	5ll Caroline St	294 5349
Andrew's Inn	0 Walton Ln	294 7730
Coconut Grove	817 Fleming St	296 5107*
Colours Guest Mansion	410 Fleming St	294 6977*
Curry House	806 Fleming St	294 6777*+
Deja Vie Resort (clothing optional)	611 Truman St	292 9339
Duval House	8l5 Duval St	294 1666
Eden House	1015 Fleming	296 6868
Equator Resort	818 Fleming St	294 7775*
Heron House	512 Simonton St	294 9227
Island House	1129 Fleming St	292 0051*+
Key Lodge Motel	1004 Duval St	296 9750*+
Knowles House	1004 Eaton St	296 8132*
La te da	1125 Duval St	296 6706*
Lightbourne Inn	907 Truman Ave	296 5152+
Lighthouse Court Guest House	902 Whitehead St	294 9588*+
Lime House Inn	2l9 Elizabeth St	296 2978
Mangrove House	623 Southard St	294 1866
Mermaid and the Alligator	729 Truman St	294 1894
New Orleans House	724 up Duval St	293 9800

Newton Street Station	l4l4 Newton St	294 4288*+
Oasis Guest House	822 Fleming St	296 2131*+
Rainbow House (women only)	525 United S	292 1450
Ruby Guest House	409 Applerouth Ln	296 0281*
Sea Isle	915 Winsor Ln	294 5188*
Simonton Court	320 Simonton S	294 6386+
Tropical Inn	812Duval St	294 9977+
Wicker Guesthouse	913 Duval St	296 4275
William House	1317 Duval St	294 8233

* advertised in Hot Spots
+ advertised in Genre or Metropolitan Community Church News, Ap., 1998.

GAY FRIENDLY RESTAURANTS - KEY WEST

Alice's	1114 Duval St	292 4888 ++
Antonia's	615 Duval St	294 6565*
Brooklyn Boys Bar	610 Greene St	296 3002
Cafe Blue	1202 Simonton St	296 7500 ++
Cafe des Artistes	l007 Simonton St	294 7100
Cafe Marquesa	600 Fleming St	292 1244
Crabby Dicks'	712 Duval St	294 7229
Croissants de France	8l6 Duval St	294 2624

Diner Shores	510 South St	296 2491 ++
Duffy's Steak & Lobster House	Simonton and Truman	296 4900
Dynasty Chinese Restaurant	918 Duval St	294 2943
El Siboney Restaurant	900 Catherine St	296 4184*
Flamingo Crossing	1105 Duval St	296 6124 ++
Hukilau Inc	1990 N Roosevelt	296 7277 ++
La te da Restaurant	1125 Duval S	296 1075*
La Trattoria Restaurant	524 Duval St	296 1075++
Louie's Backyard	700 Waddell Avenue	294 1061*
Mangoes	700 Duval St	292 4806 ++
Orlgami	1075 Duval St	294 0092 ++
Palm Grill	1208 Simonton St	296 1744*
Southbeach Seafood & Raw Bar	l405 Duval St	294 2830
Square One	l075 Duval St	296 4300 ++
Rooftop Cafe	310 Front St	294 2042
Yo Sake	722 Duval St	294 2288*

Florance Fabricant, The New York Times, Jan I8, I998, p. 8 TR.
++ Listed in "What's Happening" , February I3-19, 1998.

GAY BARS - KEY WEST

Atlantic Shores Pool Bar 2491* ++	510 South St (on the ocean)	296
Bourbon Street Pub	730 Duval St	296 1992* ++
801 Bourbon Street	801 Duval St	294 4737* ++
Club International (lesbians)	900 Simonton St	296 9230++
Cafe Blue	1202 Simonton St	296 7500 ++
Coffee and Tea House	1100 Duval St	295 0788 ++
Diva's / Shag	71I Duval St	292 8500* ++
Donnie's 422	422 Applerouth Ln	294 2655 ++
Epoch	623 Duval St	296 8521* ++
Grand Vin	1107 Duval St	296 1020 ++
La te da	1125 Duval St	296 1075* ++
Limbo	700 Duval St	292 4606 ++
Numbers	1029 Truman St	296 0333 ++
Saloon 1	524 Duval St	296 8118* ++
Square One	1075 Duval St	296 4000*

*Advertised in the Advocate, Hot Spots and/or Southern Exposure.
++ Listed in "What's Happening", February I998.

From south to north, the Atlantic Ocean to the Gulf of Mexico

This book highlights not only the history of Key West, but also includes some of the past of our more famous buildings. It particularly spotlights the history of the town's gay bars, gay friendly bars, and restaurants in which the gay visitor can feel comfortable. It includes folklore and gossip, most of it thought to be true, but there are obvious lies.

The history of gay bars gives an understanding of the development of this city from a liberal fishing village to a thriving tourist mecca. Knowing the development of a bar in which you are having a drink helps you appreciate it. Even knowing some of the bars and restaurants, events that have passed, the humor of the city and the people helps you to understand why so many of us gay men and lesbians love Key West.

Some of the bars are no longer in operation, but their funny names and locations are fascinating. Many have been in operation for years and today are under a different ownership or different name. The current names of the gay bars, restaurants, and gay guesthouses have changed in time, but their history will not change.

[The book is organized from the history of Key West through a block by block walk down Duval Street, identifying some of the architectural features, pointing out the restaurants and bars, and telling some of the stories about the great people.

If you have just come to Key West and you have bought this book for direction, turn to page 34, and it will "get you out on the streets". Once you know the lay of the land, you can relax and then later read the history in the beginning pages.]

The very beginning ...

It was a flat plateau with a few ridges of coral only slightly higher than the water. When the Ice Age created the flooding of the oceans, a mere strip of half-underwater land reached between what is now the Atlantic Ocean and the Gulf of Mexico and wrapped around South America. It started a string of islands known as the Bahamas. Fed and growing from the ocean's rich life, the shells and corals added to the sand bars, and the islands stood free of the water with demanding shores. The Keys were born. As the ocean settled, they stood isolated and alone.

Birds flew over and dropped seeds onto the islands, and the seeds died. The waves carried twigs and nuts, but the exposed coral refused their growth. The fish and lobster carried sea life, but the island sand bars refused that too.

The winds began to blow carrying plants from other places, which died in the sands of the islands. Plants caught on the edges of the coral rocks of the shores and collected. The dying plants of the ocean created dirt.

A bird flew over and dropped a seed that started a plant on land. A nut floated ashore from the vast ocean, and another living thing was born to stay.

Time lingered on. Hundreds and thousands of years. The shrubs learned to grow close to the water line to avoid the winds. They became limber in swaying back and forth in the breezes. They went through long periods without rain, and many seasons where the sky would burst open and pour monstrous storms on them, hurricanes of rain. The islands survived, and they had plant life.

With this plant life came living creatures. Some were from the sea; the snails, the crabs, the sea oysters, and others hung around the shores of the islands inherently knowing that someday, somehow, they would learn and adapt. Some life floated onto the islands on twigs or small branches. Others were blown here by storms. The birds flew here by themselves. Turtles laid their eggs in the warm sand. The islands had life.

We like to imagine that one island of this chain was Key West, but we do not know for sure. It was a small island of only a mile or more squared. Our human presence on the island is only a fraction of the island's history, an amount of time so small that it can hardly be imagined, like a cup of water compared to the vast ocean.

Enter the Europeans

When the first European man landed on the sandy shores of Key West, it was inhabited by the Koalas Indians, a tribe driven south by the Tequesta Indians, but we really don't know how long the Indians had been here. As Ponce de Leon landed on the chain of islands and laid claim in the name of Spain, human bones were bleaching in the sun, supposedly the bones of the Koalas Indians.

This fact somehow got all mixed up with "Bone Island", "Bone Key", "Cayo Hueso" and settled to "West Island" or "Key West". Any talk of it being called "boner island" is false. It was 1513 when the Spanish explorers found the remaining Koalas Indians hunting some, but mostly fishing off the shores of Key West. The Seminole Indians were after them, and many of the Koalas Indians escaped capture by crossing the ocean in canoes to Cuba.

As man will do, some of the Spanish sailors stayed behind, married or had children with the Koalas Indian women, and these were the earliest white human settlers of Key West.

The English captured Havana, Cuba, and in 1763 Spain traded most of Florida for Cuba, which doesn't seem very logical, but since the English could not build a strong settlement in Key West, Spain took back Key West 20 years later, 1783.

At the time there was a little more human action in the keys. Much of it is not recorded, and certainly there is a lot of unsubstantiated history. Pirates.

Blackbeard. Sir Walter Raleigh after the Spanish gold. Captain Kidd. Black Caesar. The Caribbean pirates. There is no substantiation that one of the pirate boats was a gay cruise ship.

Don Juan de Estrada was the Spanish Governor of Florida in 1815, and he gave the legal deed of Key West to Juan P. Salas as an award for "unspecified" military service. (Wouldn't the tabloids have fun with that one?)

There were Indian settlements on the Keys, the last of which was 1743. They did not sell lottery tickets. The first white settlement was at Key Vaca (close to where the Seven Mile Bridge is now), in 1818, but it faded out of history. A second white settlement called Port Monroe was settled November 19, 1822, by a Joshua Appleby of Newport, Road Island, and John W. Fivash of Norfolk, Virginia. They found ways to distribute illegally gained wreckage without paying fees. Word of an Indian attack from the northern Indians made the people of the village flee to Key West for their personal safety, although there was never an attack.

The new city of Key West was recorded in history because it was the first case of a white man murdering a white man in the Keys. Nicholas Goulindo was accused of stabbing De la Stations as recorded and tried in St. Augustine, Florida. No one suggested it was a "lovers' fight".

The settlement had something called "privateers", privately owned ships which were allowed to conduct acts of war on an enemy, namely, the Colombians were allowed to capture Spanish ships and return the ships to the Spanish. Unfortunately, wrecked ships were not returned, and the privateers of Port Monroe found no ships that were not wrecked. The settlement of Port Monroe lasted only one year, 1823, but it was reportedly "a bed of thieves" who sold wreckage without fines.

Juan P. Salas must have been quite a guy. He sold his property of Key West to General John Geddes of South Carolina. In a Havana bar, he also sold the property for $2,000 to John W. Simonton of Mobile, Alabama, in 1821. Don't ask me how, but Simonton won out in court.

The names "Bone Island" became "Thompson's Island" because Simonton wanted to impress Lt. M. C. Perry, commander under the Secretary of the Navy Thompson. Others referred to Key West as "Allentown", but that didn't take. We were stuck with the name "Key West".

The Bahamian influence

The people of the islands were mostly Indians and Bahamians. When the country was still unpopulated by many white men, the Bahamian took the opportunity to homestead large plots of lands. The Bahamian were dark, thin lipped, often blue- eyed island people who found great stretches of beach and farm land in the flat lands of Florida and prepared the land for them to settle. Do not confuse the Bahamian with the African Black who came later in the history of the island.

The Bahamian were proud people, capable and conscientious about doing a hard day's work, a comical people of laughter and joking and a serious people without our Christian or Judaic God. Their religion was a mixture of spiritualism and one benevolent God that represented a strong basis of right and wrong. In 1789, there were more than 11,000 Bahamian settlers in the South, many of whom established homesteads and remained.

One of the earliest Bahamian settlements was in the Upper Keys in the late 1600s when Antonio Gomez opened a trading shop on Indian Key. The community grew to be a wrecker's paradise, with a general store, bar, post office, hotel and warehouses and about 40 homes in the village. Other Bahamian settlers arrived. The three families of Russels, Pinders, and Parkers bought Upper Matecumbe Key for a $20 grant and recording fee around 1870.

The Bahamian people from the islands mixed their knowledge of how to fish with the Indian people of the swamplands. The seas were plentiful with fish, conch, green turtles, clams, and crawfish. The fish included barracuda, jack crevalle, cobia, dolphin, the Spanish and the king mackerel, grouper, and, perhaps, marlin and sailfish. There were other products from the ocean and the bay, and someone always tried to farm whether or not it was on land or in the ocean. The turtle farmers sent slabs of meat north from their pens of captivity. Sponging became a business. The ocean and the bay supplied the people with food, and the farms of the ground area provided the harvesting of fruits and vegetables.

To give an example of how successful the farming business was, by 1882, one farm yielded 480,000 pineapples, which were shipped north. The biggest competition for the fruit growers was Cuba, who could boat their products to the cities. The major interference of farming was the mosquitoes. Fruits could be boated to Key West from Cuba, shuffled through the Keys, and on to New York less expensively than grown in southern Florida.

Long before Miami was settled, the little city of Cocoanut Grove, five miles south of what would someday become the downtown center of Miami, was established by Bahamian homesteaders. In 1821 the Bahamian families of Charles Lewis of Nassau and John Egan filed for his land claim through the Spanish government, both settled at the mouth of the Miami River when Florida became a United States territory. The assumption that two Indian bucks had created a gay bar named "The Hamlet" is false. They were a couple of the few families that created a shipping port while Key West was the major military and shipping city of the vast empty land of swamps and low- lands, the Everglades.

Wreckers

It was not unusual to see many ships passing by in the deep water shipping lanes. They were either on their way to Virginia on the eastern coast, or to Cuba and Mexico. Out of 150 ships, a few would stop in Key West.

Some stopped because they wanted to get provisions, some because they had to. Seven miles of shallow water and reefs lay between the Key West shore and the deeper ocean gulf lane; seven miles guarded only by a singular lighthouse built in 1826 after many a ship had wrecked in the shallows or on the pilings. Up to the time of building the lighthouse was the wrecker's period, but Congress passed a law the year before in 1825 outlining what was legal salvage. Up until this time, the first person to the boat claimed the rewards of the cargo. There was an old story ...

The preacher of a local church was giving the Sunday service to the few wreckers and their wives. He glanced out the window and saw a ship struggling to free itself from the coral rocks. He said to the congregation, "Let us pray. Let us put down our heads in prayer and close our eyes." The preacher walked from the front pulpit to the open front door while the congregation prayed with closed eyes, and finished his "amen" and announced "wreck in the harbor" and ran out the front door for his boat to be the first at the salvage.

You know that story is probably not true. Every seacoast town that had wreckers tells the same story of their town. It could have happened in Key West. The entire history of Key West is not necessarily accurate. All the stories about luring ships into the rocks from the porches of the widow's walks never made sense. It's like mermaids, I'd rather believe they exist.

Stories about the wreckers taking all the goods off the ships and selling them were probably false. True, a salvaged ship and its goods were put up to auction at the "wrecker's auction" and the salvager got a percentage of the profits. There was even federal wreckers' court and the court would decide what degree of danger, peril, or bad weather the wrecker had faced, and the court would establish the percentage based upon how difficult it was for the wrecker. First came the saving of lives.

In 1822 the President authorized Key West as a Port of Entry with a Customs- house and a tax collector. Key West was not a large city. In the early 1800s, there were fewer than a couple of hundred people on the island, and the island was much smaller. They had a saloon but no "gay bars". Well, maybe late on Saturday night.

The town was centered around the warehouses and the docks, and a new ship would come in every two or three days. Florida wasn't a state as yet. Its position at the end of the Keys of a vast new land that led to a thriving Havana was a place envied and desired by many.

The town was bordered by the lighthouse to the south, the military base and eventually another martello to the west. Front Street was to the north, and Simonton Street to the east. Most of the streets had names, usually the name of the person who lived on the street. But there was Grunt Bone Alley, Lover's Lane, Donkey Milk Alley, Seminary Street and Division Street.

It was swampy, hot and wet. There was a large shallow pond at the end of Simonton Street and the Gulf with a long wooden bridge, and another bridge on Duval ran from the St. James Hotel just about to the corner of Caroline Street and it was over 15 feet long. The land was alive with swamp vegetation, but there was little vegetation in the town around the houses. The small amount of soil was mostly crushed coral. Everything seemed to grow. Especially cocoanuts. Limes and lemons. Grapes and pomegranate. Guava and sapodilla, and mosquitoes. Bananas, oranges and mangoes and a few peaches. Citron, plum and figs and sugar cane, and mosquitoes. And salt.

Life in Key West
Once Key West started to get a reputation as a growing, commercial seaport, and once salvaging was outlawed in l825, we got a judge appointed and lawyers. Then we really started to see things happen. In l829, we had postal delivery which was brought by boat, the Post Boy from Charleston, and it arrived about every six weeks. The next year we got the salt business (not to be confused with saltpeter).

In l828 Monroe County and the "Island of Key West" was incorporated. In l833 the "City of Key West" was the richest city per capita in the South. A footnote: in l835 the population of Key West was " 582, including black, white and all other colors, lame, lazy and blind". But, not "gays".

Lucy Mallory was the first white woman to settle in Key West in l820, and in l835, she ran the boarding house. There are no records of what was happening before she got here; those lucky Indians. There are no figures for "bachelors" or for "run-away husbands". She had many rooms for men that had come from Boston and Savannah to help trace the boats and goods.

In l829 we had our own newspaper, "The Register", and in l831 we established our own burial grounds.   In l835 we had our own jail. We were a part of Monroe County named after President James Monroe.

Spain gave the Florida land to the United States and Andrew Jackson became the first United States Military Governor. Key West was a military base, the Navy was fighting the pirate boats traveling the Caribbean from St. Augustine to New Orleans. In l822 Key West had a customshouse.   Florida became a state 23 years later in 1845.

Salt
It was in l830 that Richard Fitzpatrick started the first salt manufacturing business in Key West. He took one of the many low, marshy bays that were

so frequent around the island, and when the tide was high, he would block the entrance from the ocean to the marsh and allow the stagnant water to evaporate under the sun, and the result would be an inch layer of salt from the ocean's water.

Others quickly joined in this occupation because salt was used to ship fish to northern ports. There were also salt ponds ten miles away on Boca Chica and on Duck Key and Knights Key. Some salt businesses used large metal plates on the bottom of the swampy inlets so the salt was easier to harvest. The business survived the great winds of 1846, but the hurricane of 1876 destroyed the salt pens and put an end to the production of natural salt. Enter something called electricity and refrigeration.

There was also a business run by children of eight to 12 years old. If they bought a license by paying a small tax, they were allowed by law to deliver all sorts of things from the boats or from the post to your house on their small carts usually pulled by goats. That was a pretty good business for 20-some kids. There were no child labor laws.(That must have been the start of American Express, UPS, or something like it.)

Like a pattern, the activities of Key West seem marked by the weather, the fear of a hurricane or an actual hurricane. In a way, it was good to imagine that whenever we as people think we are doing well, a natural disaster hits us making us a little more humble, and a little more appreciative. The high tidal waves of the storm of 1846 gave the people of Key West a deeper understanding, appreciation, and respect for the land and the ocean.

The recipe of how to make Key West: Add 20 cups of beautiful island, one cup of Indians, many Bahamian settlers, one cup of Spanish on route to Havana, one cup of pirates, one half cup of land robbers, a bit of politics, some English and American ownership, the fish business, the salt business, and the kids with their goat-drawn carts.

That's why Key West became so popular. We were the open door to South America and close to Havana. They were good workers on the docks. Many of the dark-skinned natives that came from the islands worked on the docks too, and some were owned and worked in the big houses. There were many big houses, and we feared we were going to run out of land.

The young girls wore white cotton dresses that went down to their ankles, and lots of lace for special parties. During the week, most of the girls wore blue smocks when they cleaned the house, polished the silver and worked hand in hand with the hired help, many of whom were free men direct from the Bahamas. A young girl worked learning the kitchen, a separate building at the back of the house with a large fireplace and oven.

In the rear of the large houses were the salt house for keeping the fish fresh, the chicken coup if any coup at all, the cistern to save the rain water, the privy, only a few barns in town, and the one or two bedroom cottages of the help, maybe three or four of them for the servants, dock workers and/or cigar rollers.

In some of the larger houses, after dinner in the dining room of the main house, the head of the house and his wife and children would sit on the front porch, and the dock workers would gather around the kitchen in the back, sometimes gamble or tell stories that children were not allowed to hear. They gossiped on the front porch of what was happening in town, of what party was next, of what they would wear, and who they'd see. Girls usually got married at around 16 or 17, but they started looking at about 13.

A man had to be careful that he could keep the woman that he chose, and many men married women that were so expensive for them, they had to continue working day and night. A girl's family was going to make sure the man she chose could keep her well, so he had to make good money and save. There wasn't much choice. It was better if a man was born into a family with money.   (What's new?)

But, he couldn't loaf. "'Bout only fun a man can have is a couple of beers at the end of the day or sneak down to see some of the sportin' ladies. Can't get caught though. Got to watch your reputation. And you can't marry one of those sportin' ladies." (Prostitutes in Key West; how unusual.)

The young girls were trained to be wives and mothers. They could move easily in society, talk with the other young ladies of their age, entertain, do their chores and, above all, do what every young lady was meant to do; to have and to raise the children. She hoped she would be allowed to select a man who did not drink, was "God fearing", had some money, but, above all, was kind and could support her and the children.

Having children was no problem. That just happened. Every man wanted a boy that could carry on his work. Girls were nice, but every man really wanted a son. The women had their chores to do, but the men had to bring back the money every day. Working on the docks was not easy, but it had to be done. A man didn't have to have a lot of education, but he had to know how to work with other men, and he had to control his family, his wife and kids. He had to build them a house and see they were cared for. There was living and there was death.

The records of death of the first half of the year 1876, by category: From birth to two years old, the first infancy: 68. From two to seven years old, the second infancy:10. From seven to 15 years old, childhood: 8. From 15 to 25 years old, youth: 14. From 25 to 50 , manhood: 24. From 50 to 70, old age: 12. More than 70 years, senility: 10. (There are no figures from youth to senility for gays.)

The shipping industry allowed the wealthy to build houses, great Victorian monuments to their own hard work. Some houses were shipped over from the Bahamas. Others were built by the ship builders under the same rules as building a ship. The houses were put up on blocks to allow the air to flow under them. The board sides were allowed to shift in foul weather without breaking a window. There was often a look-out tower, a widow's walk, aimed toward the reef so that incoming ships that did not know the way could be spotted and looted if they hit a reef.

In the first quarter of the 1800s, salvaging the wreckage became a lucrative business. The wreckers would bring everything portable from the wrecked ships on the reefs; everything from door frames to the ship's siding, from the cargo of fine linens, furniture, sugar and dinnerware. From these findings formal parlors, dining rooms and bedrooms in the main house were built and furnished. The buildings of the kitchen and smaller store rooms were filled. There were the houses for the help, the workers in the master's business regardless if it were shipping, or cigar making, or unloading, or working in the houses.

Cubans in Key West

The mothers would watch their children with a demanding presence even while the children courted. At no time was a young couple to be together without the presence of an adult. But, kids will be kids. They found ways. A popular direction toward marriage would be a pregnant bride, and it was tolerated, but not spoken about. Children just happened, and no respectable young girl would have a child without the benefit of a husband, although she may carry the child only for a few months after she was married.

Many of these marriages worked out well. The bride was sure of her responsibility to the marriage, as was the groom. A hard-working young couple with a few children were a compliment to the entire community, and the children were raised with the blessing, encouragement, and conformity of the Cuban Catholic community.

The man was the head of his house. The woman was there to please the man.

So they thought. The real truth was that a smart woman could get the man to do just about anything she wanted him to do. One trick was to let him think he was superior, but he eventually began to learn.

A Cuban man was head of his household, head of his wife and his children, a challenge to his grandfather for his grandmother's attention. He should be respected in his neighborhood, and he does only so much the women considered wrong. He had the right to drink as he wished, gamble as he wished, and he lived his life pretty much as he wanted. He could go out, because he was a man. Women liked him because he was a man, and all men knew he was a man. He was macho.

There was a respect for the Cuban ways, a respect for the Cuban Spanish language, and a respect for each other. The Cuban people in their jobs as tobacco rollers were not uneducated people. Indeed, they respected education, and they were aware of how education could help them.

Cubans came to the United Sates on the many trips to Havana in the large ships, but especially because of a tax given to the cigar makers of Havana. The cigar industry started in Key West in 1837 by Estava and Williams Seidenburg employing 600 in "La Rosa Espanola" factory. The factories did not use the Virginian tobacco for rolling cigars. A business that made Key West famous was the "Cigar Rollers of the Worlds Most Famous and Popular Cigars". In 1873 over 4,000 Cuban immigrants were brought to Key West to work in the cigar factories, and a continuous flow of ships from Cuba brought tobacco of all grades from the homeland. Mr. Ybor employed 400 in "Principle de Gales". The immigrants left Cuba because of what they felt was an unfair union tax on their labor and their work. Soon, Key West became the capital of the cigar industry.

A reader would sit at a table and read the news of the day or a book or the newspaper to the workers as they rolled the tobacco into thick layers of imported tobacco. Making the cigars was a man's job. In the last 20 years of the late 1800s, Key West turned from a fishing town to share its popularity as a cigar mecca. By 1888, the cigar factories in Key West employed over 6,000 men in more than 200 companies. The unions started to move into the cigar business, and so almost all of the operation, from the small cigar rollers to the large factories, moved to Tampa to avoid the cost and confusion of the newly established and popular unions.

Some of the children of the cigar rollers had married and worked aside from the cigar factories, and they did not follow their parents to the marvels of Tampa, but they were in other jobs and stayed on and worked in Key West. Today, every Key West Cuban family seems to have relatives in Tampa.

Conchs

Somewhere during the middle of the 1800s the people of Key West referred to themselves as "conchs", and the family of these early settlers, those alive today, consider themselves "conchs", a dynasty of special and significant level, a class or family joined through common experiences and family lineage of a very unique order.

A general meaning for the word "bubba" would mean brother or a close friend, but the term means more to the people of Key West. True, a "bubba' is a friend, but he is more than just a casual acquaintance. It is a term of friendship, but combine it with a "conch bubba" and it is similar to a blood brother who has been through the same experiences, one who will never get you involved in any trouble, demands your honesty, respect and alliance.

Key West industry

There was plenty of work on the island. There was constant building of new homes often reflecting the grandeur of the Victorian era. There were schools to be started, a government to organize, graves to be dug, a cemetery to relocate, and the reward of a wreckage every so often, and the wrecker's auction where stolen shipping goods, boat windows, and about everything else imaginable would be thrown on the block for the highest bids.

One of the businesses that sprung up was quite necessary to the shipping community, the making of hemp rope from the sisal hemp plant that originally had been made from the natural product of the Yucatan Peninsula of Mexico. The Key West braiders made a strong rope that was less expensive than other imported ropes. The efficiency of having the hemp rope made on the spot where it would be used helped keep the price low. When the cost of living increased because of the cigar rollers' popularity raising the economy, the hemp braiders moved back to Nassau before 1876.

Fishing in Key West has always been a major industry no matter if fish had to be shipped north in salt or later in refrigerated trucks. With fish, of course, come many other businesses that were nurtured from the bottom of the sea: shrimp, crawfish, which we call Florida lobsters, crabs and sponges.

When fishing was the major commercial industry of Key West, Greek families settled here. They had the special talent of being able to dive for sponges. Key West gained a reputation for the soft camel-colored balls of natural sponges hung in the hot sun to dry. The skill of the Greek fisherman was well known, but his special talent of diving for sponges created a hard-working life for these fun-loving, happy people who easily melded into the other melodies of different kinds of people. "It takes a Greek to find a sponge on the bottom of the ocean." The Greek divers of Key West were commonplace until a bad season of 1939 took all the sponges, thus sending many the next year to Tarpon Springs where they remained.

With the use and skill of the boat fishermen came the desire for the grand Green Turtle, and they would catch the slow-moving old creatures, often by accident, into their nets. The price of the Green Turtle was a reward for the fisherman, and very quickly the area was fished out. The government put a penalty on the farming of the Green Turtles. The land pens had to be destroyed, and the black market for Green Turtles soon was limited, and eventually there was no demand for their meat.

Fish packed in salt to ship north became another industry built from the demands of the day. A ship going north packed with fish would return with the balustrades filled with bricks, some of which were used for streets and others for building the martellos, the protection of the land from the sea, pirates and the invaders of the Civil War. The hurricane of 1876 destroyed the salt business of Key West, and the Civil War aided its death, an attempt to kill the financial profit of this Union town.

18

In l880 a close community, that of Cocoanut Grove five miles south of the wet- lands now known as Miami, was settled and began to grow. Charles Peacock owned the Grove Hotel and hired·Bahamian to run the hotel although the community had long had Bahamian settlers at the mouth of the Miami River. Nineteen years later, in l896, about 3,000 men in Cocoanut Grove voted to see if they should incorporate Miami as another city. Of the 368 men who voted, l62 (43%) were black, either Bahamians or African-Americans. Since the county had already been named Dade in l828, a tribute to a Major Dade who died in a war with Indians around Tampa Bay, the newly incorporated city was to be called Miami, an Indian name.

Nothing seemed worse than the hurricane of l846, a hurricane that even washed the cemetery of Key West into the ocean. What a gruesome sight with the wooden caskets floating on the ocean waves, most never to be found again, a final burial at sea.   In time a new cemetery was created, one that kept the same sense of humor, sarcasm and fun as the blissful attitudes on the island.

Land changes
The washing of the ocean did something even more dramatic. It changed the contour of the land under the sea and the beaches. Many of the swamps were tidal swamps, the water flowing in and out with the contours of the ocean's waves. The hurricane changed some of that, creating swamplands that would receive water from under the land, but it was water that could not run off into the ocean. They became swamp ponds, and they were the breeding grounds of mosquitoes, and mosquitoes brought death. But, many of the people were against filling in any of the submerged land. "Since God wanted a swamp there, He put one there. We should not fool with what He wants."

"No matter what you say, Key West is overcrowded. We already have close to 500 people here, and there's barely room to move around." "Filled-in land would give us the opportunity to build more and to have more businesses, and it's good for everyone. I think we should put the Court House on filled land. It's ours to do with what we want." "If we fill in the swamp, God will punish us by sending another hurricane, worse than the last."

"We voted in l836 on a charter that would not allow us to fill in the wetlands. I think we should stay with that. It has been fine thus far." The arguments had been heard from those that went through the hurricane of l846, and the city authorities took up the subject in l853, only eight years later, to make a ruling that in order to fill wet lands, an owner had to have a permit. Of course, there was a fee for the permit. Politics and taxation never change. In the following years, we have tripled the size of the island in practically all directions. We have filled, and filled, and filled. We have grown, and grown. We still need permits.

The winds of war
In the early 1850s, there was confusion in the newly formed government

of the Revolutionary war, a fight between the industry of the North and the farming of the South, between the Union Army and the Confederacy. The people of Key West were too far away from the daily struggles, six weeks at least on partial news, and never quite sure who was for what. The ships in the harbor were both for the North and the South.

The residents of the South were Anglo Saxon and Celtic and they felt a heritage to both New England and to the South as well as Key West. Some of the Key West of British ancestry simply left for Jamaica, Bahamas, or Bermuda so they could remain under British law of King George III, but when the new country finally won the war, they returned to Key West as loyal Americans, particularly since the taxes of King George were not applied in the United States.

It was not that the people of Key West were not sympathetic to both sides; it was more important to make a politically correct decision. In a large town meeting in 1860, it was decided that Key West supported the South. A U. S. Captain John Brannon brought northern troops into Fort Taylor that night after the town meeting and the next morning Key West supported the North.

Caroline Lowe in 1862 waved a large Confederate flag on the roof of her house. When the Yankees arrived, they could find no flag and she did not admit she was a Confederate sympathizer. They searched her home but could not find the flag, and the Yankees had no proof. Years later, it was exposed that she hid the confederate flag in a hollowed banister post or had it sewn under her hoop skirt

Depending upon who was in town or what ship was at the dock, the flag of the Confederate Army or the flag of the Union Army, and accidentally and embarrassingly sometimes both, were flown. The Southern sympathizers were told to leave, but no one was sure they did.

The next recipe of how to make Key West: Add the shipping business and the salvaging. Add the ship builders. Sprinkle with the Cubans, the cigar businesses, the conch bubbas, the Greek sponge men and the fishermen, and mix with the Civil war. This may come as a shock to some, particularly to New Yorkers who feel they've found Key West.

Flagler's dream
The real drama of Key West did not happen in Key West at all. The competition came from a railroad man, Henry Flagler, whose railroad led to a little trading post up state, a place called Miami in 1896, April 15. The population of Miami was 480. Four years later in 1900 a census counted 1,950: 1,348 white people, 599 black people and three Chinese. By 1910 black Americans made up 40% of Miami's 5,000 people. Fifteen years later in 1925 with a particular property boom, Miami had reached 150,000. Today, the population is over two million, with 45% born in another country, 52% with Latin heritage.

20

It was a Yankee Miami and a Yankee Miami Beach up until the 1920s. The laws of Miami Beach barred Jews and blacks, but they were soon no longer effective. A wealthy New Yorker who was Jewish bought a large piece of property on which to build homes in Miami Beach, and the law was ignored. The island became a Jewish home for retirees as well as working-class Jews to enjoy the warm winter weather.

As long as anyone can remember, there has always been a Cuban settlement along Eighth Street in Miami. The big influx of Cubans came to live in Miami as their permanent home after Fugencio Batista was overthrown by Fidel Castro on New Year's Eve , 1958. Two years later, 135,000 Cuban fled to Miami. Exiles ferried 5,000 more in 1962. Air flights brought 340,000 more in 1973. Between 1977 and 1981, 60,000 Haitians arrived by boat. The Mariel boat lift bought 125,000 more in 1980. In 1988 through 1990 thousands of Nicaraguans fled for Miami; 32,000 Cubans arrived in 1994, and there has been a steady influx of 20,000 a year since. Miami, unlike any other city in the United States, became a capital of South American influences. It was the population explosion of South Americans in Miami that took away the emphasis on Key West.

That was one of the things. It was also the railroad. Then the land boom. Then the hurricane of 1926 and another ten years later. The Depression, and World War I, a whole lot of factors that seemed to be happening in random order, but each one affecting Key West differently. The building of the railroad to Key West seemed to be a dream come true.

To get from Key West to Miami at the turn of the century, a family would have to ferry to various islands, take the small train crossing an island or walk the distance to the next ferry. The trip took three or four days of hard traveling. Going to Miami wasn't very important anyway.

Then Henry Morrison Flagler ran his Florida East Coast Railway (FEC) to Miami in 1896, and he arrived from Jacksonville to Miami in 1901. Flagler was also building luxurious hotels with splendid, professional staff for those who were wealthy enough and would come to the sunshine by train. The train passengers to St. Augustine could stay at the Ponce de Leon Hotel or the exclusive Alcazar. The Royal Poinciana Hotel and the Breakers Hotel were available in Palm Beach. The exclusive Royal Palm Hotel (now the Baptist Hospital on Kendall) was the destination for Miami passengers. Flagler decided to extend his ideas by building a railway to Cuba.

Flagler's plan included a railway which would hop from island to island, a glamorous day venture which would end at the railway station near Key West and the passengers would be taxied to the Casa Marina Hotel, the most elegant of his many hotel adventures, a playground for the rich and comfortable.

There had already been a couple of attempts at moving people on the Keys. By 1895 Key West had mule-drawn streetcars that ran across the island to the La Brisa Hotel on the Atlantic (now "The Reach"), but it was used in getting cigar rollers to work across the island. Flat ferries were available from island to island, and on some islands were large wagons or trains to transport across the land.

Flagler announced his plans to bring the railway to Key West in 1905, but it was not the trudging through the swamps that most people expected, but a series of bridges from one island to the next, finally ending in Key West.

The Overseas Railway was started in 1905 and completed in 1913, but not without critics, obstacles, and deaths. There were constant threats of hurricanes like one in 1906 that destroyed all that had been started, another in 1910 that taught the builders new ideas for safer construction. Land was dredged to create a firmer base for the railroad tracks. Terminal and piers were built in Key West to welcome the train as well as steamships. The railway reached Key West in 1912, costing over $50,000,000 and more than 700 lives. The first train arrived on January 22, the next year, 1913.

Working for the railway were many Chinese workers. Some married the Latin women of Key West, and when the work of the railway was finished, they stayed on with their families, the Asian influence in Key West.

Flagler died in 1913, the year after the completion of his railway, and many people still speculate where he would have tried to connect the line to Havana. Key West had grown to 23,000 people with very little except islands and swampland between Key West and Cocoanut Grove, and the formed city of Miami.

With Flagler's great dream already pouring into the virgin lands of Cocoanut Grove and Miami came a wealthy group of investors not like any others anywhere in the United States, a group of botanical wizards. They realized the potential of the tropical climate of the Keys compared to the semi-tropical climate of Miami. There is still a difference. Some things can be grown in Miami, and not in Key West, and others demand the tropical climate.

Henry Perrine had received a 230,000 acre land grant in 1838 from John Quincy Adams, and he introduced avocados. William Cutler bought 600 acres and introduced pineapple and oranges. In 1899 Solomon Merrick bought 160 acres and planted grapefruit trees on his guava tree lands. Ten years before, Elbridge Gale had grown mangoes in West Palm. William Matheson visited Cocoanut Grove in 1904, held Lignum Vitae Key and Key Biscayne and planted 40,000 cocoanut palms. David Fairchild came in 1898 and Charles Deering who eventually built Viscaya in Miami owned thousands of acres with his brother and they owned International Harvester. They attracted people like John Kunkie Small, botanist for New York Botanical Gardens, and William Krome, Flagler's major engineer, who in 1918 gave property in South Dade for the Florida's Tropical Research and Educational Center.

Thriving Key West

The thriving farming industries at the turn of the century brought new workers, investors, wealthy land owners, businessmen and farmers to that area of the north of Key West that kept getting so much attention, that Miami area. (There must also have been a few florists.)

1913 was also the year when Key West experienced the first international flight to Mariel, Cuba. (It was the start of the "mile high" club.) The flight was supposed to have been flown by Augustin Parla, but he had trouble and landed. A Cuban National, Domingo Rosillo, made the flight in spite of gun shots from the land. Pan American Airlines had their office but only for a few months in a building on Whitehead Street (now "Kelly's Restaurant"). Pan American Airlines moved to Miami. No one realized at the time how important air flights would eventually be to Key West.

Important to Miami, but not very important to Key West except for the many who settled in Miami from other places, was the great land boom. South Florida offered the working classes of the United States an opportunity to take advantage of the dream of Paradise, the sandy beaches, the palm trees, the lazy, hot tropical climate. It offered a plot of land for little down and little a month which added to a mosquito infested lot, if above water, close to nothing. Photographs were often of sandy ocean beaches filmed in the Bahamas. Many Americans bought the dream.

Even the mosquito problem that had made so many people miserable in the building of the railroad, and continued to be a problem for all, was challenged with a new and vital plan. On Sugarloaf Key, 16 miles east of Key West, Clyde Perky had the plan to build a bat building, and everyone knew that bats eat mosquitoes. It was a shingled barn of a tower made of Dade County termite-forbidding pine with criss-crossed beams so the bats would be happy in their new 30 foot tower.

As Cubans, they realized that the bats of Cuba helped control the bat pest situation. They brought over many bats from Cuba and kept them in the bat tower for a couple of days hoping the bats would adjust. When the day came that all the mosquito problems would be over, they opened the shutters for the bats to do their night hunting. The bats flew back to Cuba. The bat tower was useless and a strange monument of a good idea that did not develop according to expectations. It still stands.

Another conflict with Nature came much later, a few years ago on Big Pine Key, when a key deer got a beer can stuck on his nose. A protective neighbor got the deer into a fenced lot and called the Key Deer Protective Society, who immediately assigned a five-foot, 350-pound game warden complete with tranquilizer gun to the rescue of the poor deer. His first shot missed and hit a tree. The neighbors helped him over the crude fence using great strength. His second shot missed the deer, and some believe hit a neighbor. The deer had enough, went to the tree and rubbed his nose, knocking off the beer can, jumped the fence and ran into the swamp. Man again dominates the Keys.

Little towns sprung up along the Atlantic coast as well as the Gulf coast. There was not a land rush in Key West because Key West had little land, much of it made by dredging the ocean, widening the islands for the tracks of the railroad for Flagler, extending the islands for boats and piers, filling in the swamp land, but few were interested in buying the land between the growing city of Miami and the stilted, dwarfed city of Key West. There were few little towns in between. Florida City and Perrine were farm towns. Tavernier was larger than the city of Key Largo. No one cared much for the bug-infested, hot land in between. Marathon was only a village, and the people of Key West still kept livestock on Stock Island.

The big war

World War I, between 1914 and 1918, made Key West revert to its previous role of being in a position that is important to the war movement. There was a pump of new blood to Key West and a reinforcement of the potential for the island and a way to save the island paradise.

The Navy brought the dollars to the community. New shipping lanes were dug; docks and piers were built. There was work for almost everyone. Not only the Navy officers and the crews, but the many people of the military that accompanied their operation, from the doctors and nurses to the barracks builders, moved to the small island. There were always estimates of how many men were here with the military, but that number was a classified secret, and no one knew for sure. (The gays tried to guess.)

The island became a center for Caribbean defenses. The Navy was in town. Destroyers and submarines, the blimps and the Air Force. The Casa Marina Hotel began in 1918 and opened the next year in all of its grandeur.

The values of the people had begun to change. In the generation before, the goals were to be rich, have social position, education and travel. We began to realize that being wealthy did not necessarily bring happiness. We began not to care where the money came from, so long as you had money.

Social position depended upon how much money you had regardless of where it came from. Money bought social position. There were some people who should never be in any high degree of social position. There are some people better than other people, they thought. All men are not equal, or should not be treated equally.

Education was the root to acquire money. Men should be educated, and some people thought women should be educated too. In fact, there were some people who could not tell the difference between men and women, thinking women should be able to vote and take men's jobs. (Get your gun.)

24

The people of the United States began to travel. At first it was the military men and some women of World War I. Then it was an understanding that men should move from their home towns to find jobs and a better lifestyle. The horse turned into the automobile, and the engine produced power boats and aviation. Too soon, anyone in the United States could be relocated, and there was an exchange of people between Europe and the United States; just visitors at first, and eventually between the rest of the World and the United States.

Some attitudes were changing also. We found that Italians are just like we are. We found that all people wanted the same things from life, and those that didn't want the same things could pursue whatever they wanted, and that would be okay with the world. We had a respect for other religions as well as respect for our own. We learned there were many faces of the G I Joe.

The family changed too. No longer would the son of the farmer stay on the farm and take his dad's responsibilities. He could make his own decisions and work where he wanted. The new jobs in the steel mills, the manufacturing companies, the labor camps paid more than the farm jobs, and even the farm jobs became mechanized. "I don't want to stay on the farm and try to squeeze money out of this land. I can go to the steel mills or the coal mines and work for a hell of a lot more. I was in Germany in the war, and I can even get a job overseas. There is a lot I have to learn, and there are a lot of places I want to go. I don't want to be tied down to the farm."

With the birth control pill, we learned to control the size of our families. It was too expensive to have many children, and large families were not needed as labor in the bigger cities like they were needed in farming. Family size was financially affected and forced to no more than two or three children.

With the equality of the American woman, couples could divorce and could even make their own way financially. Women could even have children without having a husband, or people could live alone and be respected. There could be happy single women and happy single men. There were even "gays".

Each of these steps happened independently and step-by-step. It didn't happen overnight, but over a hundred years. The depression of 1893 should have given us some kind of sign, but Key West, unlike most of the United States, was doing well, and we were not a threat to ourselves.

When World War I came in 1914, Key West clung to its history of being a military town, but it still remained the historically richest city in Florida, although Miami was superior in size and wealth. Key West had already realized there was no competition between Key West and Miami. There was a sense of propriety about Key West, a system of superiority depending upon your rank in the military or your job in the city. With the opening of the new railway, the Keys were opened to the curious eyes of the world, not just the men working on the ships and the military. Key West was looking for identity, and we found it.

The roaring twenties

The Casa Marina gave society the opportunity to railway through the new frontier, to maintain the elegance, service, and convenience of having money at the freshly built guest rooms, the grand eating places, the grand balls, the entertainment, and, above all, the wonderful weather when it was winter in the North. Although La Brisa had been built nearly 20 years earlier at the ocean side of Simonton Street (now the Reach Resort), it was mostly for locals to enjoy the swimming, dancing, and entertainment, and a fair consumption of beer and liquor.

Affective January 16, 1920 - Prohibition. Key West ignored the ruling being close to Cuba and having a Latin appetite to eat and drink. Since liquor was legal in the Bahamas as well as Cuba, the people of Key West helped as they could to ease the pain of living alcohol free to some people of the United States. Rum-runners.

With the end of World War I in 1918 and the prohibition adjustment afterwards in 1920, the land rush of Florida was over in 1926. The sudden influx of tourists and the wealthy was over too although it was January 22, 1926, that the La Concha Hotel was opened, the tallest structure on the island at a construction cost of $786,000. It was one of the four major hotels sharing recognition with The Casa Marina, the Jefferson, and the Over Seas Hotel. It sat vacant through the 70's, restored and opened in 1986 by the Holiday Inn.

In the 30s, the States were toning down awaiting what would be known as the Great Depression, the failure of the stock market in 1929 and the long dry days of unemployment in full swing in 1930.

You would think that Key West would be greatly and rapidly affected by the failure of the stock market since there were so many wealthy people still maintaining the island as their permanent or, perhaps, winter home, but the people seemed to ignore the Depression, similar to ignoring Prohibition. There had always been a bull-headedness about local government, a city commission that acted on its own, responsible to no one, and with complete self-interest. Life just seemed to go on.

The Navy reduced the size of the military in Key West, but the town was still not completely dependent upon the military. Food was easy to come by from the ocean. There was a free flow of alcohol. The weather held up.

Eventually in 1934 almost all of the island was on relief. Credit became short. Stores and shops closed. The local government practically stopped functioning. By July 1, 1934, the government and people of Key West realized they could not control the city and offered a "surrender of Key West" in a "state of emergency" to the State of Florida.

The Federal Emergency Relief Administration used the surrender as a publicity stunt, advertised the island and its beauty, and its way of life with reasonable prices, affordable living, wonderful weather and "paradise", and that winter season opened Key West as a vital and live town, one catering to the tourist and his/her every whim.

Key West never had beautiful sandy beaches, but the ocean floors were scraped to create them. (Millions of dollars have been budgeted to repair the beaches by adding more sand, a project to be completed in 2000. We'll see.) Partying events were created to draw the tourists to free concerts or games. Painters with the WPA stayed, and writers such as Hart Crane, S. R. Perelman, Archibald MacLeish, and Ernest Hemingway either owned homes or visited the island. Houses were painted. Some of the large houses were turned into apartments. Some became tea rooms or rooming houses. New restaurants opened. New hotels and motels were built.

Key West recovered in a grand fashion. A year later, September 1936, a hurricane missed Key West but destroyed the railway bridges on the Upper Keys and killed many residents as well as laborers who were working on a road to Key West. The railway bridges were never replaced. Many became roadbeds for the new highway to Key West. The hurricane of 1935-36 was the end of Flagler's reign except for the history. His railway bridges became roadways for trucks and automobiles. The new Overseas Highway was completed in 1938, and again flung open the doors to the new paradise.

World War II years
December 1941 - World War II. Key West tripled in population and tripled in acres as it dredged the shallow beaches to make room for convoy ships, Navy vessels and submarines. Fifteen-hundred acres of ocean bottom were dredged at Boca Chica for the new airport, and Trumbo Point became military housing. Key West had its own International Airport from the early days of aviation. Blimps. Seaplanes. Sonar Submarines. 15,000 service families were assigned to Key West. In 1962 the closed Casa Marina was turned into Army barracks, the Cuban Missile Crisis Center and, later a training center for the Peace Corps.

The bars that had suffered from the Great Depression were repainted. New bars opened daily. The young sailors enjoyed "strip clubs" and the warm evening streets were filled with young sailors and young and not-so-young ladies and locals and out-of-town gays. There must have been 50 strip clubs and bars on Duval south to Truman.

The big word was "sex". The old Freudian theory had captivated the States, particularly the young. The flapper period of the 30s was replaced by the beginnings of a freedom for females with the invention of the pill, a way to heighten the potential of getting pregnant which also helped not to get pregnant. Birth control. The wild women of Key West, with a sailor close behind. The liberal attitude of the people of Key West, who had seen the island through the Depression and many other weaker times. The instant ability to have a party. "Heh schmoo. Want a drink?"

When the small old-town of Duval Street became crowded with hookers and sailors, the military family and many residents wanted a more refined area in which to shop, and the cheaper land was the land fill along Roosevelt Drive, which became gas stations, small shops, grocery stores, catalog stores, repair shops and luncheonettes, and a few bars. The downtown commercial shops moved to the suburbs as down- towns of many American cities did, but Key West's new commercial area was just a couple of miles away. Searstown. Eckerd. There were new buildings, new shops, new equipment, new shopping areas, and everybody had a car. We became used to our cars and going to the stores. The Marketplace. The lesser expensive motels followed with the chain restaurants. Enlisted men's housing. Trailer courts. CBS houses. Conchs called it "new town".

Key West took the end of World War II in their stride because the United States had decided to leave a sizable military, Navy and Air Force in Key West so the country wouldn't be caught off guard. The physical position of the island community to South America and the emerging countries was well realized. It was not the conchs or the tourists that directed the growth of Key West. It was the military, the old fashion American tax dollar that built military bases, roads, and brought in many of the services that aided the military. Key West prospered because the military brought in and reflected the security of the dollar. Land was increased. The island grew in size.

Post-war Key West

When World War II ended in l945 and the men and women came marching home from Europe, there was a different kind of United States before them. They lived as heroes at first. Many were growing families the military men did not know; children to whom they were introduced. The female spouses had changed, willing and able to hold a job in a country fresh with opportunity. There was the G. I. Bill and many soldiers went to college in chosen professions.

Women who had waited for their husbands found their independence interrupted. The golden dream of married, children and happiness did not seem to fit. There was also the social acceptance of divorce and "try-again".

The older men still held the scars of the Depression, wanting to work to have the American dream come true, but a dream that was not real. The new machine industry wanted veterans at first, but often could not understand their hesitation in working. The security of the "God and Mother Boss" was fading. Slowly the soldiers began to realize that life was not fair, that war was a political and economic game that costs lives, that the freedom they were fighting for was not the freedom they got. They had changed, their mates had changed, the world had changed, and their fantasy dreams were just that.

The Miami Cuban Crisis

By 1963 there were 100,000 Cubans in Miami and this influx of people changed the identity of the fast growing tropical city. The Cuban people created their own city on the Eighth Street area of Miami. Few Cubans during fleeing from political injustice joined their relatives living in Key West, but they fled to the large city of Miami, where work was more available and the Cubans had established a large ethnic community. They were hard working and gained direction and in mass they soon established businesses, jobs, and homes, and slowly new ways of living in their new country.

Shocking the world, "The Miami Herald" carried the headline on November 23, 1963, of "Kennedy Dead".

Few Cuban immigrants came to Key West, but the small island had already been established by old Cuban families from the cigar roller's days, and the city was still recovering from the Depression. Work was limited. The city changed. Miami had a larger Cuban community and plenty of work. The city government of Key West was moved from their Greene Street offices to new quarters on Angela Street in 1962, and the old City Hall stood practically vacant for 30 years until 1990 when the City Commission met in the newly restored building on Greene Street.

On September 9 and 10, 1960, Hurricane Donna crossed the mid-and-upper Keys with Key West measuring 70-mph winds. Five years later, a larger storm, Betsy, hit Big Pine Key with 125-140-mph winds and Key West registered 81-mph winds. "The Miami Herald" of September 8, 1965, headlined: "Big Bad Betsy Bears Down on Buttoned-Up Gold Coast". The solution for many in Key West was to head to the nearest bar.

The rock and roll music that matured in the 60s reflected the escape from the harshness of the time: Brook Benton and Dinah Washington with "Baby You Got What It Takes", and the Isley Brothers with "Twist and Shout" in 1963, followed by "It's My Party", "Sugar Shack", "I Get Around", "He's So Fine" and "Rag Doll" in the next few years.

There was also something happening in London in 1963 at the London Palladium, a group called the Beatles with their copyright label of "Please, Please Me". They would later visit the United States and the Ed Sullivan Show.

The love generation

"You just have to love one another. You have to love the flowers. You have to love the animals. You have to love each other." The flower children were young adults with a background of a couple of wars, tons of misunderstanding, miles of discouragement, and a passive answer of "love" to cure all. With the pill, there was a feeling of "free love", a stronger belief in various gods of which we had never heard. There were gurus from the Orient, wise men from the deserts, and local heroes as cult leaders. There was a great desire to follow a direction, but no one knew which direction to take. Experimentation. Love. The early seeds of a drug generation with marijuana leading the escape, alcohol for others, sex for many, male and female.

There was also a great shifting in values from what was previously understood. The war had brought out the independence and productivity of the female. The military provided the open door to black independence, and the blacks had gained some independence and exposure from the war where they served shoulder to shoulder with the white military. There were many attempts at equality for women and blacks. The equality of the individual was the theme. There was even a change in the understanding of homosexuality, a review that decriminalized it as a disease. Being gay was looked upon as a product of either biological or environmental or a combination of both. The gay was able to be a person and he/she also demanded independence. That didn't start until 1973 when gays were "de-classified" as mentally ill.

Somehow into this confusion of directions came another war, a war few knew why we were fighting, what the war was about, what difference the war made to America, where they fit into the war. Some did not participate, many running to Canada. Some participated with hesitancy. Some relived the honor of World War II. Few knew why. The government could not, or would not, give us an adequate answer.

The war with Vietnam was a war apart from the understanding of most Americans. We were not sure who we were fighting or why we were fighting. We were not sure where the country of Vietnam was, and we had little idea of why we should be involved. Why were we losing American lives in Vietnam? The troops returned, but not as heroes as in World War I and World War II. The troops were confused. The country was confused. Why did we fight this war? What did it mean?

Besides, Cuba's Batista had been replaced by Fidel Castro, and we had to protect ourselves with Castro's constant flirting with Russia and the communistic world. The labeling of "communist" was a working man's death sentence. But, the fear left Key West with a community based on the spending of the military and enhanced by the tourists. Sponging was gone. Fishing was becoming more limited. Tobacco was not available for the cigar industries, even for those that had moved to Tampa. Aside from the military dollar, the people of Key West had only the tourist dollar.

We had to realize that on a small island, and Key West was once only one mile by four, everybody seems to know everything about everybody. That's all the news there is. There's not that much excitement. Living close together helps the information. But the people of Key West do not usually misuse the news, but they accept it. You learn to be very tolerant of people who are different from you, people that you see every day, and people that are nice to you and that you depend on to make you happy. The people of Key West are accepting people even though they are knowledgeable. The conchs eagerly accepted the military with dollars. The conchs accepted the gays with their dollars also. Although they had their own values, which were liberal, and their own activities, which were male-dominated, the people of Key West were interested in what was economically good for them.

The working people began to look at big business differently. It was rather like a mother, a protection against being hungry, sick and in danger. The farmers had that. So did the manufacturing mills. The new jobs did not offer the same guarantees. There were strikes and layoffs. There was a death of the unions, and the common people had to fight for themselves against the big boss. It was more a game of how smart you were rather than how hard you worked. No longer was the job protection. Sometimes the job was the enemy. Early retirements. Displacements. Requested retraining. Overqualified. No jobs.

The new industry of Marijuana
Maybe it was the influence from the South American countries, perhaps the Bahamas, Jamaica, or was it just the style of the States at that time. Maybe it was a reaction to the never-answered question of why we were at war in Vietnam. Marijuana became popular, and Key West people did not overlook the craze, but they joined in to make their own money. The trading and selling of marijuana became a second level industry, and the city and the city's politicians accepted it without hesitation. Marijuana was a means of money as well as enjoyment for many. The gays were attracted to the consistent tolerance of drugs, the live-and-let-live attitude and the lifestyle.

There was money in those leaves. The conchs and residents began buying the small house on a canal that led to the ocean. Communities grew up centered around the drug trafficking. It was the untold occupation, the secret that everyone knew, the common lie of denying it existed, and a flip back to the old salvagers days of the island's history.

The effects of marijuana gave the person a sense of freedom that the people of Key West had always known "as a natural high", but it sold to the many tourists and to the new-comers. The conchs understood and accepted the spaced-out waiters and bartenders. The tolerance of drugs congealed nicely with the tourists. Many locals and conchs sold their lifestyle and became wealthier. For the conchs, marijuana was a habit on the same level as drinking alcohol. There was no big fuss, except when the law stepped in.

The value scale of the people of Key West was quite simple. They did not want elaborate homes, big cars, fur coats, beautiful clothes, but they wanted gold necklaces and money to spend on their friends. You could tell how well a person was doing by how many gold necklaces hung around his neck. When there were few, business was bad. When there were many, business was good. There was always a roll of cash.

It was surprising that a father could overlook his 15-year-old son with a neck hanging full of gold necklaces, and the father was making minimum wage at the lumber store. There was no disgrace in dealing in drugs; the only disgrace was getting caught. Some did. Lawyers, policemen, county officials, politicians got caught; some went to jail and others beat the rap.

For some, the added money from drugs gave the opportunity to invest in legal businesses, a flower shop, a gift shop, a restaurant; something that would appeal to the tourists that continued to find Key West. With the newly acquired money, many new businesses were opened, and the thousands of dollars helped local businesses that had already been established.

As law enforcement became strict, as locals began to go to jail, as many families were affected by the use of drugs, and as the price and the profit of marijuana came down, more got out of the business of drug smuggling and the selling of drugs. Some went on to deal in the higher profits of cocaine, heroin and roofies. Some were caught. Many are still working. The use of drugs is still a major problem for the police, and no policeman will tell you that they don't know the local pushers. Residents will tell you that drugs are still a recreational activity for many of all levels and all classes. Check our crime report in the "Key West Citizen".

Ever-changing Key West
Key West had only minor problems of integration of the black Americans into the white culture, because that had been happening since the island was inhabited. The Bahamian were as much a part of Key West as anyone. Integration was a way of life in Key West. After the Civil War, the Bahamian and the African-Americans blended easily, and certainly more comfortably than in Miami. A militant Detroit African-American would find little encouragement for his movement in Key West.

The city moving toward tourism, the building of restaurants and the need for service workers like waiters, bartenders, tour directors and so many more service- oriented jobs, the freedom and obvious tolerance for marijuana, the acceptance of integration and the minority status, and the relatively inexpensive cost of property all added to making Key West an open invitation to the gay movement, the homosexual movement of the middle 60s.

The residents of Bahama Village were particularly vulnerable to the fast dollars of the outsiders, and many sold their Key West family homes for large amounts of money to the shrewd investors who saw the potential of the elegant Victorian homes that had not been architecturally muddled over the years.

Into this hustle of building, rebuilding, repairing, renovating, redoing grew the Old Island Restoration Commission (OIRC) which was to establish guidelines in the Old Town of Key West, guidelines to protect the Victorian elegance of the community and, supposedly, all the area to return to the quaint quiet town that it never was. Most of Key West was interested in renovation, not preservation. We wanted to live in the shells of the old houses of Old Town, convert them to being livable according to our more comfortable standards. We wanted a city with history; not an accurately preserved historic city. The organization's name was changed to the Historical Architectural Review Commission (HARC), but the handling of the home owners by the quazi-jury was hated by practically everyone, yet a necessary step in historical renovation and preservation.

Gay Key West

Many of us were not reared in the tolerant attitude of Key West. We were not reared with knowledge of people who were "different". We were raised in backgrounds of not being able to identify and relate ourselves. If you were gay, there were few people that you could idealize, a role model, someone whom you could pattern your life after, someone homosexual. We invented our own stories, ideals and heroes from the motion pictures where we would escape from the reality of not having a hero identification. We would read. We would see plays. We would pretend. We would dream.

Radclyff Hal was an early novel depicting homosexuality, as was Tales of the City by Armistead Maupin showing the strange life of homosexuality and drugs in San Francisco. The motion picture industry did its best to avoid the gay issues buying a play by Lillian Hellman and calling it "These Three" in 1936 but changing the gay plot to a heterosexual triangle. Not until 1962 did Hellman's play become a motion picture starring Audrey Hepburn and Shirley MacLain titled "The Children's Hour". The film showed a more realistic story of lesbianism. There was the message of a cure for male homosexuals in "Tea and Sympathy" in 1956, among others such as "A Walk on the Wild Side" and "Capucine" with Barbara Stanwyck in 1962. All seemed to be the "greatly confused gay", one without identity, one caught in a web of suspicious intrigue. There were no role models.

As Key West seemed to know everything about everyone, there was always an acceptance of gay behavior by practically every family. It seemed each conch family had a funny brother, a wild sister, a strange uncle who liked to get dressed up, a weird cousin, or a goofy friend, but no one seemed to care. There were always the few local boys who did not marry, the old maid all her life, and there was a morality that made something different, not evil and monstrous, but amusing and fun. Every family had their gay cousin, and everyone in town knew what the gay cousin was doing, and no-one gave a damn. There have always been gays in Key West, but the large gay influx moved into Key West in the middle 70s. They were welcomed, or extremely tolerated for themselves, or for the money they brought with them.

They had the money. They had the talent. There were plenty of big old homes around that needed to be fixed, needed lots of money, and the gays had the taste and the money to do it. So what if they get a little drunk at the "Monster"; so do many straight locals. So what if they party too much at "Delmonico's"? Babe will throw them out. Don't we all get a little too drunk? Who cares? The value of my house keeps going up. Besides, they're fun.

[If you have skipped the the history of Key West wanting to get to the "good stuff" of Cruisin' Duval, and before you have a chance to even look at the history, you'll get a feeling for the city by being in the activity, checking out the bars, restaurants, houses and the people. But you really won't appreciate your experience to the fullest until you know the history of what made the city. Don't forget to complete the story by reading the first pages of the history.]

Because Key West grew from the north down Duval Street, we can organize our trip of the history, the people, the events, the gay bars and restaurants, and hopefully some gossip in a block-by-block identification. Duval Street is only 14 blocks long. Things of specific interest to you may be close by where you are staying. Most of the guesthouses are not on Duval Street, but they can easily be located. There is a list of current gay bars, of suggested restaurants, and places of significant interest such as the bookstore, the Customshouse, or the coffee shop. All are within walking distance of the 14-block strip, a little less than a mile. Take a walk, and take your time. You will not be sorry. You'll see Key West's Old Town like you have experienced no other city.

The old catch of the big cities, exclusively gay bars for homosexuals, never happened in Key West. All places are for everyone, regardless of sexual preference, particularly the bars. As a local said "All money spends the same regardless of where it comes from". Bars that attempted to ban gays were not there for very long. Everyone went to the "Monster," and "Delmonico's". Even Captain Tony attempted to attract a heavier gay crowd, but that lasted only a month with a couple of drag queens.

In the beginning of the heavily gay movement to Key West in the late 60s, all new gays coming into the city seemed to know all the other gays that had established their lives here earlier and had become part of the community. The local gays that had been raised here were not as obvious, and it became a fruitless game of knowing which locals were or were not gay. Then there were those who were not gay, but who slept with the gays, whatever that meant.

There were few lesbians with the early gay movement into Key West. Women were still fighting for equality in the workplace and salaries that would match their positions. The swinging lifestyle of the males in getting out to the bars did not meet the domestic routines of the women. There were gay male couples that did not enjoy the bar scene also. The gay scene seemed to split into groups dependent upon their activities. There were the early afternoon drinkers, the late dance group, the domestic dinner and television group, the supper club group, and so on.

Most couples, both straight and gay, were pleased with the laid-back, easy attitude of the people of Key West. The early morning bicycle rides. An afternoon sunning on Dick Dock by the "Casa Marina". An early afternoon cocktail at "Chi-chi's". Dinner on the patio of the "Sands Restaurant." Early to bed, or early to get home after an evening at the "Monster" or the "Mermaid Room". Some can even remember one of Key West's earliest nightclubs, "The Bamboo Room" with Coffee Butler or the "Roosevelt Longue" with Larry Harvey singing. Early in the morning would come the call of the rooster, always too early for everyone, but necessary.

The trip down the keys

While teaching high school English in Miami, I had heard students and teachers talk about Key West, the wild little fishing village at the end of the islands on the tip of Florida. I was curious. I had read some of this history of the string of islands.

It was late July of 1959 and Big Swede said "I haven't taken that damn Christmas tree down. Got an idea. Let's have Christmas in July in Key West." We agreed to a weekend away from the workplace. I had not started my new teaching job yet. We ran in different directions to rapidly pack and return to Swede's house within the hour.

Big Swede threw the fully decorated but very dry tree into the back seat of his old convertible and another friend had a second car as the two car loads, nine guys in their 20s, were off to see Key West. I was the youngest, undoubtedly naive, but I was sure the world was full of adventure and I had to take advantage of it. I had never been to Key West.

The two-lane road that led away from Miami was lined with banyan trees on both sides. Their long roots were held in limbo until they touched the ground. The roots drilled into the dirt soon to become a trunk. We went through Homestead on Route I from Miami and through the small village of Florida City, which is the land side of the "sea of grass". There was the cutoff to Everglades City, a few buildings in the middle of the swamp before we approached the Florida Everglades. We tunneled the car through the massive overgrowth eventually to find ourselves starting the keys with three-foot sawgrass on both sides of the highway and miles of swamp so still that it looked like solid land unobstructed by buildings.

The original road without using ferries from island to island was completed in 1938 over Flagler's railroad beds and bridges, and the drive from Miami to Key West was mostly mangrove swamps, with the major settlements of a few houses or businesses at Key Largo, Tavernier, Marathon and Big Pine. Travelers feared the narrow bridges and the highway a couple of feet above the gulf or the ocean. The Key West International Airport, termed "International" because of past flights to Cuba, completed the control tower, and it was dedicated March 28, 1974. In 1959, you could either drive, sail or fly, but it was not easy to travel to Key West.

The old road was over Flagler's train beds. The laborers had hand-dug the canals beside the roadbeds for fill to make roads across lowlands. The old railroad bridges were turned into a highway supporting the new road to Key West. The tracks were used as side-rails over the bridges. The railroad bridges became automobile bridges with only a minimum of space to pass. Cars inched by one another.

In 1977 the United States Congress appropriated 109 million dollars for road and bridge construction and, through this fund, the longest bridge, The Seven Mile Bridge, was completed and opened in 1982. The new bridge for Flagler's railroad cost 45 million dollars. The old road built with the train tracks used as safety guards ran beside the newer construction.

We went over the old bridges with breathtaking views from one isolated island to the next. The drivers approached on-coming cars with caution, for someone may have had to pull to the side of the road in order to pass. The view was of the ocean of the Atlantic mixing with the bay waters of the Gulf of Mexico, deep blue to the left and light green and brown to the right.

There was very little between Miami and Key West in the late 50s. A few unpainted fishing shacks. A concrete-block home every so often. Remains of the original old road to Key West where it would have been impossible to pass because the tropical vegetation had regained part of the road that had originally stolen it from the over-growth.

We had a tin washtub full of beer packed in ice. Plenty of beer. Lots of joking. Laughs. Practically no traffic once we left the mainland and got into the Everglades.

The bright sun throwing sparklers onto the water. We stopped to stretch our legs and to take into our lungs the salty sea air. Shirts came off and Big Swede insisted on driving in his Jockey shorts so he could get his legs tanned. One car followed the other, and we looked like nine wild Indians, our bodies starting to tan. The road was straight although sometimes bumpy, or maybe the springs of the cars were not so good. We bridged from island to island.

We saw the white herons, the pelicans scooping around fishermen or boats and dead raccoons hit by cars. The telephone poles lined the way, and a large water line on the ground was on the opposite side from the electric lines.

We passed through the village of Marathon and were eagerly awaiting the Seven Mile Bridge. Built on the railway bed, the road shot into the deep blues and greens of the ocean and gulf. We didn't talk as we drove across the bridge, inspired by the rare beauty of the water and awed by what man had accomplished in building a bridge for cars on top of railroad tracks. Approaching cars, we practically stopped to get by, aiming toward the tight squeeze, sparing only a couple of feet. Once over the Seven Mile Bridge, we pulled over to stretch, but also to relieve the tension that had built as we marveled at the accomplishment of having made it over.

There were people who would not go south beyond the Seven Mile Bridge, particularly those afraid of the tight squeeze of automobiles. The same was true of some people in the lower keys; they had never been to Miami wandering only in the south-western Keyes which included Key West, the largest city of Monroe County. (True today, there are people living in Miami that have never been to Key West but few native Key Westers that have not been to Miami, many "... but only for a visit.")

A few minutes later we came to Bahia Honda Bridge, where the road was built not on the railroad bed but on top of the steel framework over the bridge, and the car puffed its way up the hill to an amazing view of the scattered islands joined only by the roadway, and down the steep incline on the roadway to the next island.

Six hours after leaving Miami, we crossed the Stock Island Bridge at Cow Key Channel and into Key West. The section of more compact, newer homes of Key West built to accommodate the military and a large section of the palm-lined Roosevelt Boulevard had already started commercialization, but none of the restaurants or shop names were familiar to us. The town of 23,000 had moved to the outskirts for more affordable rents and modern accommodations. The Christmas tree sticking from the back seat did draw some attention.

Big Swede, who was by now fully dressed with pants and shirt but without shoes and socks, knew where he was going, and he led us into Old Town and to a Simonton Street motel, a few doors down from "Logan's Fish House" (now "The Edge" restaurant). It was a row of eight double cottages, each with two doors and two windows with a small railed porch, all connected side by side. (Currently owned by "Atlantic Shores".)

"The Sands"

An ocean shanty called "The Sands" was across the street on the Atlantic. It looked like it had been made of driftwood boards, some matching the next and some not. It sat directly on the beach and the sand would crunch underfoot as you ate dinner or as you sat at the piano bar. There was a singer from Miami that would come down on weekends and entertain, a Mister Larry Harvey.

The property had originally been owned by the Catholic Church, but was sold to David Wolkowsky after he sold the "Pier House". He modernized the building practically re-building it, a large dining room with a turret to a never-built second floor that smelled heavily of marijuana. He even built a pier which ran into the ocean, later to realize the land on which he constructed the dock, complete with sewer lines and ready for electricity was on government owned and protected land.

At the top of the gazebo at the end of the pier, properly designed for a bar, was a large metal reindeer looking toward the restaurant. The deer had its antlers broken, and David had them re-attached by a local craftsman, and, logically thinking, put the points of the antlers toward the ocean more like a nice haircut than antlers for protection by stabbing. The distorted symbol remained for years, although Wolkowsky was forbidden to sell anything on the pier.

"Papillon Bar"

There was a little bar seating only a dozen on the same side as "Logan's Fish House" toward the corner. That bar called "Papillon" had only a door and a plate glass window. At the corner of South and Simonton streets was an Italian restaurant and the motel registration desk, and eventually a take-out liquor store.

The little "Papillon Bar" grew to be one of the largest gay bars in Key West. It eventually took over the space of the Italian restaurant. At times it turned into a very comfortable old farts bar that had a good combination of "money boys" or "hookers" who would smile for drinks. There was a regular daily crowd of a couple of dozen people who helped "Papillon" stay open during the summer and it paid the bills. Most of the gay bartenders that have been in Key West over the years started at "Papillon", the "Butterfly".

There was a great difference in being gay in 1959-60 and being gay today. Being gay was against the law, but even if that were not true in some localities, the police, newspaper, and neighbors' attitudes made you feel like being gay was against the law. Even today's young gays can recognize this attitude, particularly in the south and in small towns.

It was felt by many that being gay was a mental disorder, a combination of factors that made the gay guy or lesbian a mix of the sexes, a hermaphrodite, a mentally and emotionally disturbed person that wanted to be the opposite sex. Gays were thought to be child-molesters, sexual deviates, with uncontrollable sexual urges. Gays were portrayed in motion pictures and literature as violent, murderous villains who would sexually devour his/her prey.

Of course, not everyone felt that way. More intelligent, sophisticated, and worldly heterosexuals knew that gays were similar to straights, perhaps more sensitive, creative, and expressive of emotions. There were no heroes for gays to imitate, no images in which to shape their lives. This dreadful image of gays was held until 1973 when the American Psychiatric Board reclassified homosexuality as a life-choice rather than an emotional mental illness. Many still believed that having intercourse with a talented person of the opposite sex could cure any little confusion the gay person may have. Lots of people believed being gay was against God's will or, at least, the church's will.

Being raised under this stigma created different types of gays at this period, and their behavior often hinted of their background confusions.

Practically all of the types of the male gays sat around "Papillon's".

There were very few lesbians in public, usually just the obviously masculine, aggressive "butch" types that characteristically swore, talked dirty, and were vulgarly combative. An exception was a lesbian medical doctor who was quiet and refined, a person that later fascinated me with her experiences of being one of the few women medical students in a world not willing to accept women could be as bright as men. There were a couple of straight women, either mothers of gay sons, or women who liked the witty conversation or protection of being around gay men, drunks or misfits that were often around.

There was a local group of refined older gay men, many of whom had been married, with grown children, now widowed or divorced, many who realized they were gay from childhood, but who had taken a different socially acceptable direction of being married with children. At retirement, they had taken advantage of the opportunity to be themselves, their probably latent gay selves. They were usually well dressed, alert and sharp to comments, often "bitchy" but obviously members of the "in" group. They had their own trite language of "she" and "sister". They were often wealthy and held elegant dinner parties at their private homes. Many had lovers that had died or gone their own way. Many were alone. Most were hoping for a sexual experience with someone.

When there are horney, wealthy older men, there will be the hustlers, those willing to do about anything for the favors or money which was their goal. Many were straight, but some young men started their sexual lives hustling. "Today's trade, tomorrow's competition". In Key West, there was the military too.

There were also the straight conchs that did not mind having sex with the gay men, and there were conchs that were gay, usually with everyone in town knowing it. I later met a grandfather that was gay, and he loved to get powdered and perform in drag. It seems that there has always been a healthy supply of drag queens.

Of course, there were particularly the lesbians that could not afford to be at the bars, and many gay couples that preferred not to associate with many other gays. Their homes were sprinkled throughout the small town, but most locals knew.

And into this whole mess of people was my age group having not much experience in the gay lifestyle, wanting it but not knowing how to gain it, wanting the affection from the sexual responses, fearful of the emotional responses, and just starting to build a life. I had been to the "Blue Feather" in Columbus, Ohio, and had seen the same scene as was at "Papillon". But, I had found some friends.

"Papillon's"

We did not know there was a bar next door that later became a popular attraction to many tourists and nude sunbathers. Had we known, we would have been back there, but it had not yet been built. Later it would become the "Atlantic Shores Pool Bar".

Big Swede and someone else went in to register, and the rest of us hid. Ten minutes later nine guys and a Christmas tree took over the motel room. We were there for a weekend. We staked out our sleeping areas but decided it was a "first one in gets his choice" decision.

Atlantic Shores cottages

The row of joined cottages were used by tourists and locals. The little cottages each contained two identical units. We learned that when the local situations got a little rough, a divorce, a noon-time romance, or just a place to stay, the rented rooms were used by locals. From time to time the owner would clear out the rooms and paint the walls and return the furniture to the room. At one time, they painted number seven.

Ralph Sanchez, a local hairdresser who was a bit tied down in debt, was in room eight with boxes of clothes and his worldly possessions. Ralph had a tendency toward drinking, one that would easily consume half a bottle. Ralph sober felt that no one loved him; Ralph a little drunken felt that everyone did. The evening had been well worn and Ralph had consumed beyond his usual high level. He staggered toward his room and opened the unlocked door.

Ralph made a frantic call to the office. His room had been robbed of all of his things, all of his clothes and boxes. The thief even took the dresser, mattress, springs, the bed frame and headboard. Everything was gone. He insisted the front desk call the police.

The polite desk clerk person knew Ralph and was not quick to respond to his request for the police. "Ralph. Go to the front door and tell me the number on the door." Ralph obeyed and returned to the phone with the information of "seven". "Ralph. We're painting number seven. You're in eight." He was and his room was just as he had left it.

Old Town of Key West was a small, dilapidated village which depended mainly on the ocean for wealth and recreation, but which had seen the grander period of stately homes, a town that had tasted the welcomed money from its physical location as well as fishing, sponging, cigar making, shipping and salt, and was content on its own existence.

The Victorian houses with wrap-around porches were just starting to be turned into guesthouses since many of them had been converted into apartments for the military of WW II. One house in 20 was painted. Some had only the fronts white-washed Many were natural frame beautifully constructed by the ship-builders. Chickens, dogs and cats roamed freely.

The locals were cautious, friendly to tourists, but preferred not being detached from their own special group of local friends. They had been through the Depression, but they were clawing back with the new tourists' dollars. There was still a happy island attitude.

There were no exclusively gay bars in Key West; every bar was everything. Being in a Navy town, the bar owners were used to a pack of men coming in and, as the myths about Hemingway said, the nine of us tried to hit every bar in town, without success. That weekend changed my life because I got "sand in my shoes".

Three of us took off for the local "Papillon's" and walked into a small bar with a dozen people. Since we had been drinking beer coming down the keys, we switched to whiskey and the young bartender seemed glad that we were not having fancy mixed drinks. Most locals drank beer in the afternoon. He asked where we were from and we answered "Miami" which did not impress him.

At the bar were seated two older ladies among the men that we concluded were not lesbians. The clients watched us closely as big Swede talked with a younger Cuban looking man. Swede whispered to me "Let's get out of here" and we left with a new Cuban guide.

Key West seemed to have a lot of loners. Some of those were also loosers. They lacked the energy or have deadened the desire to be agressive, and they prefered to live a live-and-let-live lifestyle of having no obligation upon themselves. We ran into a bunch of them.

I felt that I had been around. Having graduated from college in Columbus, Ohio, and having been to a gay bar and having had an affair - alright, several affrairs - I thought I knew life and sex was all about. Although probably searching for Mr. Wonderful, I was pleased to take advantage of what was available.

We ran into the rest of our traveling group at the next bar which was a strip club. The dancing young lady was not so young nor was she a very successful dancer. However, the bar was filled with sailors in white uniforms, and our little group seemed to splinter talking with people we had never met. Someone was bound to run into someone they knew from high school, but even that did not happen. Rather than traveling in a pact, we decided that we could each go our own way and have just as much fun. Key West was friendly, and we felt not as expensive as Miami. We decided not to have dinner together. Everyone was on his own.

I don't remember much about the weekend moved by alcohol and youth. I missed my first night of sleeping in the rented motel room because I was sleeping somewhere else. The second day was a repetition of the first starting with bloody marys.

My first weekend in Key West was over, squeezing every minute until we left without the Christmas tree about six the second evening, to return to Miami and to my first contracted employment, a high-school teacher.

Background

I had been born, reared, and college educated in Ohio. In my freshman year in college, the Literature teacher suggested I read a California writer named Christopher Isherwood, which I did. After military service in the Army, and severe sinus from the northern weather, I eagerly moved to Miami. I realized in college that I am gay (little suffering; no "big deal"). Alone (by preference). I never came "out of the closet" because I never felt I was in a closet. I behaved as I felt without much sexual anxiety or frustration. Not every gay childhood is one of suffering and pain.

It was difficult for me to get the idea of Key West out of my head. I knew I had a wonderful time with my friends, but it was more than the companionship. It must have included the strange little town although Key West was certainly no thriving city of excitement. It had something to do with the ocean, the fresh smell, the friendliness of the city. Of course, there was the sexual excitement, but I understood that. More than the attitude, it was a calming feeling of being there. It was not understanding as much as allowing me to be myself, a freedom I had never known since I realized I was gay. It also had an energy, a vitality of being alive. I thought I would be useful as a teacher. I looked forward to the new experiences as an innocent child. Key West made me feel at home, and I wanted a home. I was finding myself

From 1934 to 1968 the various motion picture companies had a self-inflicted rule, a production guideline that was a refusal to admit homosexuality existed, either gay males or lesbians. When directors got close to stereotype characteristics, the gays were played with characteristic personality flaws which led them to rape, murder, cannibalism, pedophilia, bestiality, incest, Satanism, or necrophilia. (2) These were all heinous crimes of mad monsters, an impression upon a child that felt he too was "different".

From never being able to establish a role model in the motion pictures or reading about a happy homosexual, Hollywood interest in gays became one of being ashamed of being gay, one which could taint the image of "star" and, concurrently, affect the pocketbooks of the motion picture businessmen.

No one can argue that the studio executives did not know that a gay life existed. A Hollywood star and later interior decorator named William Haines acted in "Brown of Harvard" in 1926, but he would not play the "get married to a real woman" demanded of the heterosexual movie community. He lived openly with his lover, Jimmie Shields, in their plush home at North Stanley Drive, Hollywood. They entertained many of the stars. He openly said that Louis B. Mayer kicked him out of films. Charles Laughton and Elsa Lancaster arrived in Hollywood in 1932 to do "Devil and the Deep", and even Laughton's wife, Elsa, was aware of her husband's passions for men.

Not until the 70s did the motion picture industry produce gay themes, and that was because of the threat of television's popularity. Not until Rock Hudson died of AIDS would the studio bosses show their control of the lives of the stars, and their recognition of the disease. Thank you, Elizabeth Taylor.

Look at the films that were developed. "Frankenstein" and "Dracula" in 1931, "Dr. Jekyll and Mr. Hyde" in 1932, "Island of Lost Souls" in 1933, "Werewolf of London" in 1935, all single men with a lust for the bazaar, often with assistants that were either effeminate or overly masculine and retarded. The horror films repeated these themes of gay distortion with "Bride of Frankenstein" in 1935 and "Dracula's Daughter" in 1936, and changed the background of the movie with swishy partners in "Saboteur" in 1942, "Return of the Vampire" in 1943, and "The Lodger" in 1944. The gay person was depicted as a mad inventor of life, but not by the usual biological way, or the inflicted person who wanted blood. A gay person was the "different" person. The gay kid sitting in the movie audience associated with these villains because he, also, was "different", but hoped he was not crazy.

More obvious in subject matter over the next years, but still containing the suffering, psychopathic homosexual, "The Servant" was released in 1963, James Fox and Dirk Bogarde rushing to become the master. "The Empty Canvas" with Bette Davis followed in 1964.

Once Hollywood found out that money could be made from gay films, they produced a flock of them in the late 1960s, but all with the same type of distorted personalities, either challenging others, fighting for a relationship or self-understanding, or as psychotic killers. "Reflections in a Golden Eye" 1967, "The Sergeant" in 1968, "Midnight Cowboy", "Gay Deceiver", "Staircase", "Women in Love", all in 1969. I could identify with any of these characters because that was my only frame of reference. I realized, however, I was not mad. Well ...

Teaching high school in Miami was interesting, but it was my first career trained job. The salary was $2900 in 1959. I had a Volkswagen and I rented a room close to the high school. Strangely, I seemed to have money during this time, probably because my demands were minimal.

Toward the middle of most work weeks, I would vow not to go to Key West. By the time Friday arrived, I rationalized that I could do my paper grading just as well in Key West as I could in Miami. I'd throw the suitcase in the old Volkswagen and be off.

The Atlantic Ocean
I was smart enough to realize that my affection for Key West was not for the sex. I never really made a great attempt to get sex, rather just allowing myself to be available and allowing it to happen. I was never a hound in heat. Although I have always enjoyed the sexual response, it had never been a conscious, direct motivation for me, or at least for very long. I was more passive than agressive, but I never had frustration with my own sexual responses.

I preferred to be in Key West alone. I'd stay at the Southernmost Motel on South Street because it was inexpensive and clean. It was not because of tricking convenience. It was one block from the beach and many nights I would walk out the wooden pier, strip to nothing, and swim in the sun-heated water. There were few tourists.

The tourists that were in Key West at that time were a strange lot of salesmen from Miami, loners like myself, foreign visitors who wanted to hit each extreme destination of our country, run-aways, couples on honeymoon, or vacationing families looking for an inexpensive run-away. There was little exclusive about Key West.

In the morning, I would go to the same beach where there was a weathered shack that was built from beached boards and leased from the city by a husband and wife who had made it into a shack restaurant. Most important, they had worked with the carnival before coming to the island. (I had worked in the local carnival as a college student in Columbus, Ohio.) She would fix me eggs or French toast and I would spend hours soaking up their memories of the old carnival days.

There has always been a restaurant on the South Beach and,

although owned by the city, somehow they were able to get a beer and wine license as an "exception". The view toward Cuba 90 miles away of flat ocean is outstanding.

Lately, there was even talk of putting the southernmost point monument, probably the ugliest in Key West, at the end of the Duval Street pier, and although not historically accurate, the location could better handle the flow of visitors and would be good for the Southbeach Restaurant. Of course, the southernmost point being a lie would not bother anyone. "What they don't know won't hurt them." And there are many lies within the lore of the city that the locals forget or prefer not to tell the tourist. In theory, never tell a tourist anything that could in some way affect the business dollar. (Some tourist would ask how many bricks were in East Martello Towers, and I told the guides to lie. 26 million, 356 thousand, 829 hundred and 22. Who is going to disagree?

Viola Viet

An unreal person that I had met in Miami had a long romance with Key West and left a lasting impression on the island. With a lady friend named Liz French, who was living in Coconut Grove, I was to meet an old friend of hers named Viola Viet, the rather notorious daughter of a German motion picture actor, Contrad Viet, who usually played a Nazi officer.

Viola's father was dead, and the daughter spent part of her inheritance and rented a house in Miami, but Liz warned me that Viola would attempt to impress me by her Bohemian nature and her foul language, and I assured Liz that I was not ready to allow myself to be startled by someone's behavior. We arrived at Viola's rented house, a once modest, concrete-block, pink house in the Kendall area when it was farmland, but a house that obviously lacked any care or maintenance. There were windows missing, interior doors propped against the wall, dreadful, never-attractive stained wall paper, and dirt throughout from delivery boxes to old newspapers.

Viola was a once attractive blond whose real personality must have been Marlene Dietrich because she spoke in a deeply accented, seemingly sexy voice, much too low to be natural. She asked if we wanted vodka, and she poured us shots into paper cuts. "There you are, darling. Do you fuck?" Even the forward line did not upset me.

When she had lived in Key West, she was slim in figure and wore her clothes well, if not dated, and applied her red lipstick with a heavy hand. She was well liked by some that found her affliction with sailor talk in a deep accent quite appealing, except that too much liquor and too many

Lucky Strikes had stained and rotted her teeth to the point where her mouth and breath were so bad, few could tolerate her aggressive attempts to talk to any military man she could.

A local Key West businessman decided she needed new teeth and the way to acquire them would be a donation from her friends. He went to local merchants and to those who had spending money and requested "ten dollars from her friends to buy her a new set of teeth". Within a few days, he collected $320 from contributors. He went to her apartment, presented the cash, and told her that her friends had donated the money and, afraid of offending, said the money was for "what she personally needed most".

A week passed and she was not seen. Finally, a contributor noticing her still rotting teeth and foul breath asked what she had done with the money. "I spent it all. Two bottles of vodka and the best enlisted man I ever had, darling."

I'm not quite sure what we talked about that day, numb from the introduction. Viola and Liz talked about having once been roommates in Key West after Liz's divorce from a military man. I do remember that somewhere in their conversation, a horse walked in the back door, across where the three of us sat, turned around and exited the same door after Viola said, "Get out of here, darling". I again appeared not to be sho

Viola eventually returned to Key West in the 70's and she had many friends here. She had a short male friend that she would send out to get a bottle of Vodka that she drank while taking a bath.

Traveling south to north

If you are standing on the wooden pier of the Atlantic Ocean on Duval and you look the length of Duval, you would be going from South to North, from the more recently built section to the older section more deeply entrenched in the history of the island. On your right on the beach would be the Southernmost Restaurant. (The same course of Hurricane Georges in 98.)

On your left would be the Southernmost yellow brick house. The first street in front of you would be South Street. (We will follow this same pattern in cruisin' down Duval, going north, the east to your right, the west to your left.) As you step off the Duval Street pier, you are in looking toward a large brick guesthouse on the left.

There are many people who view Key West from the opposite

direction of the way it was built. The city grew from the warfs and docking facilities of the northern part of the island, one least affected by storms. All jobs were related some way to shipping. The city grew to Division Street (Truman) and there was nothing much beyond that point except for a few houses, the Southernmost House being an early one. Trace your way forward in this early picture.

Duval Street, south to north

Notice the amount of vacant land. At the bottom of the picture is South Street with only a gable of the southernmost house showing.

THE 1400 BLOCK
Atlantic Ocean to South St,

Southernmost House

At the end of Duval Street and the ocean is the Southernmost House, a graceful Victorian Queen Ann (style 1876-1910) built in 1899 by Judge Jeptha Vining Harris. It's a yellow brick house that stood isolated from the others costing $90,000. It was south of Division Street (Truman Avenue) and most people felt while the city grew that the main street of Duval ended at Division Street, dividing the people from the swamp. (Picture on front cover, lower right, blue-green trim.)

There is question as to whether the house is really the southernmost, neighbors down the street and a house in Texas claiming the same distinction ... nevertheless. The lot runs hundreds of feet into the ocean, and, although it had been a restaurant and hotel in the past, it had returned to being a private home. It is one of the few brick buildings in Conchtown, and although the builders started with red brick, it was changed to yellow brick.

The house was eventually owned by the Ramos family, an established Cuban Latin resident of Key West for a few generations. Later the house was in the hands of Hilario Ramos, Sr., a prominent Florida legislator. But as with any politician, particularly one from Key West, he was a politician whose desires were both political for the city of Key West and Monroe County, and private. In l940 the house was a gambling club, "Casa Caya Hueso Club". Obviously important, the Ramos family had money.

Hilario Ramos, Sr.'s son was usually referred to as Charlie, and he dominated the beer distribution of Key West, the Budweiser Company, and owned a local gay bar known as "Delmonico's". Eventually Charlie Ramos and his sister, Mathilde, owned the large yellow house.

Young Charlie Ramos was elected to the state legislature in l961 at the age of 24 defeating incumbent Bernie C. Papy, who was called the "boss of Key West". He was charming and well liked.

Charlie Ramos became reclusive for 20 years but ran for Mayor of Key West in l998 on the platform "the bubba system is still alive and well" against an environmentalist named Sheila Mullins with no political background in local politics, and Charlie lost. Many locals were vocal to Sheila Mullins that she won not because of her background, but because the locals voted in fear of having Charlie Ramos in office, another rebirth of the bubba system.

It was during the time of the election that Charlie Ramos started redoing what is called the "Southernmost House" to turn the private home into a guest house and restaurant (although there are no licenses currently available). This was a large financial undertaking for an individual when others businesses were opening with many investors.

Charlie Ramos lived across the street for many years in the large white Victorian house owned by a relative. He was rarely seen outside of his property appearing only a couple of times at City Commission meetings.

When the southernmost house opens to the public either as a restaurant/hotel or a private club, it will be very elegant and very expensive.

Southernmost Beach

Across from the Ramos house is a small beach that has been here since the town started, only half a block long bumping against a motel. It is owned by the city. Some, like the beach along Roosevelt, are owned by the county. Southernmost Beach has had a restaurant on it controlled by the city for at least forty years. The county beach property reaches only to average-tide, the Ramos property extends out many feet into the ocean.

There was once a problem with the Ramos' wanting to extend their property wall toward the southernmost beach into the ocean to hid the pier walkers from looking into the Ramos yard. Since the Ramos familly owns the ground under the tide boundries, the Ramos family won, and they extended the wall. In the reconstrucrtion of the Southernmost House, the Ramos' can probably build a dock although the water is shallow.

Southernmost Beach is surrounded by a large patio and although the inside is air conditioned, it is pleasaant on a nice day to have lunch on a delightful patio a few feet from the ocean. It is moderately priced.

under construction

The first cross street is South Street. To the left (west) one block is the current Southernmost point and monument in a residential district. To the right (east) three or more blocks is Waddell Street and by taking a right on Waddell and to the end of the street is one of the finest restaurants in Key West, "Louie's Backyard", and you'll also see Dog Beach.

Dog Beach

At the very end of Waddell Avenue and the ocean is a small beach no larger than 50 feet across. It is there that locals for years have brought their dogs to swim. Even with the impressive restaurant beside it, dogs of all sizes, usually with their masters on leashes, come to socialize and swim. Many dogs make the trip without their masters, a truly social event. It's fun just to sit and watch the dogs romp and play in the ocean.

The people of Key West have always had a great respect for animals, from dogs and cats through parrots and snakes. One of the city's most attended events is the "La te da" dog show. There are dogs that have learned to stand up in the back of an open truck, and dogs for protection, and dogs for show, but mostly just dogs for companions.

There are probably more cats in Key West than people, a plague of neutering at the Humane Society. Cats own people; people don't own cats. Many houses of full time residents just feed their neighborhood cats, although they may not own them. Part-time residents often do not see their animals are taken care of while they are not in town. Most neighbors will take care of a boa ... unless it is a boa constrictor.

There is a fascination for the tropical parrots, but parrots do not make good neighbors either. Their loud screeches are wild mating calls, but it seems they could wake the dead. Be careful in moving into any apartment, condo, or home that you check the property for neighbors with parrots. They cause lawsuits. They can also tear hell out of an ear. Like many things beautiful, they are dangerous, but they are part of our tropical setting. They don't swim at dog beach.`

"Louie's Backyard", 794 Waddell Avenue
The restaurant is the inside of a private Victorian house, one only a third the size of the present restaurant. New dining rooms and patio areas as well as a converted septic tank have been transformed into restaurant and bar use.

The hut by the side of the ocean is newly created, and on a clear day, if you look out toward the ocean, you will see the old stone house supports from a building that existed there many years ago, another private home. (It was moved by Danny Stirrup on a barge in the early 50s from island to island until its current resting place of a second small island on the left around mile marker 79, halfway to Miami.)

The restaurant is well known for their atmosphere as well as their excellent menu, and it is classified as one of the best restaurants in town. There was a wonderful waiter named Marvin that was there for years. The decor inside is tropical and full of sunlight, but on nice days most people prefer to lunch or dine on the large patio. It is one of our higher priced restaurants but always of excellent qualities. It is one of the few restaurants where reservations may be necessary. However, you won't be disappointed. They are known for their excellent drinks.

Another story that did not make the "Citizen" was about one of our city attorneys. He and his southern wife had been drinking at "Louie's Back Yard", and he decided to drive home, and they were off in his car. He dropped his cigarette, bent down to get it, hit the door handle and fell out of the car. His wife attempted to step on the brakes, hit the gas, and crashed into a wall. He pleaded that he was not driving the car, and the case was dismissed.

The late 50s and early 60s was a time of world confusions, of angry country leaders, of violent actions against the helpless, and of social adjustment. The period was marked by President John Kennedy's ordering a blockade of Cuba because of the appearance of Russian ships being sent to Cuba. There was the constant threat that we were in competition with Russia and that communism was going to take over the world. In the early years many left Cuba, many without money, jobs, and direction.

Over a couple of blocks to the east of "Louie's Backyard" is the large hotel, also on the Atlantic, now owned or leased by the Marriott Hotel chain, who also manage other hotels. It is managed by the Wyndham group.

The Casa Marina
Henry Flagler had inspired the building of the Casa Marina, a hotel built by the Florida East Coast Railroad in 1921, a Mediterranean-looking, huge, red-tiled roof hotel at the end of the Keys, the prosperous Key West. It was Flagler's destination as his railroad snaked down the Keys. The 1935 hurricane canceled the means of a railroad to his large hotel. Large chunks of cement and steel were not replaced in the railroad bridges. The railroad was too expensive and could not be repaired. The demand for the hotel was no longer and the building quickly fell into disrepair. Isolated on a shallow beach, it was alone on the south side of the island. The idea went wrong because of natural circumstances.

The building was used by the military because the location of a military base at the southernmost tip of the United States was a strategic position in protecting the country as well as receiving materials from the islands and South America. The large number of rooms made the huge, white structure desirable for a hospital in the Second World War. It fell to the depth of someone raising chickens in its decline. Later it sat alone for a decade, an unused, white, decaying shell on a lonely beach.

In the 60s, there was only one function from this decaying relic that I can remember. It was a large room at the western end of the building. It opened as a night spot. The room had tall ceilings and large windows looking way out to the vacant, cracked pool, and it had an early art deco feeling, with a staircase that seemed to come from nowhere. Everyone expected Ginger Rogers and Fred Astaire to come dancing down the steps. It was called the "Bird Cage Lounge". Many younger locals went, but the building was beyond the nightlife action of the town, and the bar was too far off the beaten track. Tourists in numbers had yet to flock to the island, and the "Bird Cage Lounge" went under.

Key West has always had a series of "bad boys". These were young men (or women) who were paid by their family or by their inheritance to stay out of the family business, get out of the family home-town, and they end up in Key West. There is a beer heir here, a construction company owner's son, a politician's boy. Why Key West? Firstly, the bad boys have money and they buy houses, party, contribute money to the commuinity, and they are often very social. They entertain. The people that live in Key West like what they offer. "There's good in everybody." Also, the town is liberal enough so the bad boys can do pretty much as they please, and the lawyers love their rewards when the bad boys get caught.

There is also another group of "bad boys" but these, often homeless, live off of Social Security checks or Military Disability checks. They are not social, contributing, or wealthy. But, they are tolerated. They never went to the "bird Cage Lounge" but some slept on the property.

"Bird Cage Lounge" arches

With the Marriott people buying or leasing the building, the bar was either torn down or was incorporated into a new wing of convention and hotel rooms along the western end of the property. Facing the hotel, there is an obvious addition of a large wing of semi-modern rooms added in the early 70s to the western side. In the late 70s another new wing of hotel rooms was added to the left side of the main lobby, one much more compatible with the original architecture, expanding the capacity on the eastern side in the style of the original building.

In the 80s, La Concha Hotel on Duval was leased to the Holiday Inn chain and the Casa Marina to the Marriott group. Both buildings have been expanded, modernized, and renewed. At the Casa Marina, a beachside bar was built. The grounds are well maintained. Casa Marina, with 311 rooms, is one link in the Interstate Hotel chain which also manages the Reach, 150 rooms, and the Santa Marina, with 51 rooms. (There is currently gossip that the Reach, The Casa Marina and the newly acquired Santa Maria will be managed by the Wyndham Corporation.) The Casa remains one of our leading hotels, comparable only to the most elegant that Key West has to offer. It is, however, six or more blocks from Duval Street which may be an advantage to some tourists.

Dick Dock

Next to The Casa Marina, between Reynolds and White streets, was a public beach, Higgs Beach, that was notorious to locals. A wooden pier stretched out in a half-circle several hundreds of feet. The pier became a meeting place for gay people to sun, and this sunning spot became known in the 70s as Dick Dock. Nighttime was a different story at Dick Dock, and soon a law was passsed forbidding anyone on the beach from midnight to dawn. They could be arrested for loitering. The police say the law is because of drug addicts leaving needles on the beach. It's probably because of horny locals and tourists.

Ten years ago a storm blew away more than half of the dock. Several attempts were made mainly by Manford Ible to collect money to repair the dock to its original half-circle shape, but the attempt failed, and the dock is often full to capacity now. It is still a favorite place to sun. Be a little cautious at night although the pier is an excellent spot to view Key West under the sunset. The police patrol after dark, and they are not looking for needles.

The memorial to AIDS victims

If you were to travel up to the next dock (White Street) on the beach, you'll find the remains of the old West Martello, which is now the Key West Garden Club. On the entrance to the pier at ground level is a monument with the names of some of the 725 victims of AIDS Key West etched into black marble. It is a sobering moment of reflection.

Watch the people around the memorial. Some are alert to its significance. Others have put bicycle tire marks across it or footprints which have left their stain. A woman even allowed her dog to do his business on the black marble. A city truck was parked there overnight after a fireworks show on the pier. Some visitors leave flowers or small gifts.

"The Atlantic Shores"

If you were to walk back to Duval from the Casa and "Louie's Backyard", or even from Dick Dock, the same way you came on South Street (east side), you would pass a yellow and bright blue series of buildings running from South Street back to the ocean and containing a liquor store that was "Papillon" on Simonton Street, a small registration desk building with driveways on either side, and a restaurant called "Diner Shores". The restaurant is an excellent meeting place for locals, serving breakfast, lunch and dinners. It's attractive and clean.

The two alleys or driveways on the sides of the office lead toward the ocean to a delightful bar called "Pool Bar and Grill", an oceanside bar with great hamburgs and sandwiches usually filled with bare breasted women and naked men, clothing being optional. The pool-side bar is one of the most popular for out-of-town guests, a guaranteed suntan, all over if you like. Or, just watch. Heavily gay.

The Pool Bar and Grill has always been known for their wonderful hot dogs and hamburgers. The grill used to be inside the bar, and the patrons did not get angry at the mounds of smoke pouring over them and their drinks as they sat at the bar and talked to the many friendly bartenders. Katey Quinn manages the pool bar and grill. Rick Berard is the general manager. It is very popular particularly with the New York crowd.

There used to be a pool attendant named John who wore a loin cloth, and he would lift the deck chair to the place you wanted for a tip. He was not in his early teen years, but he was always on time and did his job with exceptional skill, and everyone liked him, and the fact that he was not a teenager gave a lot of the local guests a sense of security.

The secret of the success of the Atlantic Shores is their concern for the locals as well as the tourists. Many social events are held at the outside bar, namely the Sunday evening tea dance with blasting music and a mob of people, both gay men and lesbians. They dance and drink. Local organizations often hold their social affairs at this bar because of the nearness to the ocean. On Thursday nights the bar staff show a popular film. Locals are amused that they are always fixing the deck, which not only takes a beating from the naked traffic, but it also gets an equal amount of wear from the ocean.

The patrons at the bar are locals as well as guests. The locals complain about the expense of Key West, the high bills for electricity, water, solid waste, and garbage disposal, and there is always the conversation that rents, ownership, and taxes are too high. It is true that Key West is the most expensive place in Florida to live, including Palm Beach. The guests envy the locals living in wonder climate and a relaxed atmosphere with great friends.

Probably the most irritating comment a visitor could make to a local would be "Oh, you bought your house when things were cheap down here". Nothing has ever been cheap in Key West. It is true that twenty years ago one could buy a house for less money than he would now pay, but his wages were also much lower then. Key West has always operated to "market value" and, even during the Depression, the houses of Key West were always at "market value". Incomes have changed. You can get a less expensive house in Kansas, Dorthy, but who wants ... never mind.

Sal Rapisardi owned a part of "Papillon" and acquired the motel next door, the Atlantic Shores. His skill in working with his employees is well known. Straight, married with a son, he has maintained a reputation of sincerity through his association with many of the patrons as well as his employees.

Rapisardi sold the Atlantic Shores property which included "Papillon" and bought "La te da". He also built a straight bar in the bight area called "Brooklin Boys". He sold "La te da" carrying the mortgage, and it has recently been returned to his ownership through a bankruptcy. During the year and a half of not owning "La te da", he built and opened a bar called "Diva's" in the 700 block of Key West, and he rented the space beside for an extention of an English Pub which will is called "Shag". Rapisardi is a most successful businessman, but, more importantly, a friend to many in the gay community.

In crossing South Street, if you look to your left (west), you can see the Southernmost monument one block away. There are small sea shell shops and gift shops surround it. Looking right (east) you can see the signage of "Atlantic Shores" and the Dina Shores Restaurant.

THE 1300 BLOCK
South St. to United St.

Back on Duval Street and across South Street from the Southernmost House and a white frame house is the Southernmost Motel on the odd numbered side of the street. On the west side, across Duval on the even numbered side is a large white once private home, now a guesthouse called Southernmost Point Guest House, at 1327 Duval Street. (I327 is not an even number.) At one time the house used to be across the street where the Southernmost parking lot is now, but the owner did not like the flow of air and had the house moved across the street and turned around. Early pictures do not verify this, however. Some theorize that the house was merely turned in its present location on the same base. It is the only odd-numbered building on the even-numbered side of Duval.

There are several other houses in Key West that have or had the ability to move. Of course, the mobile homes and the motorless trailers can move. The houseboats on Roosevelt Boulevard move, and there has been a group of people who have fought to have them moved. (Hurricane Georges did the job for them.) Tennessee Williams' home on Duncan street was moved there. "Bagatelle Restaurant" in the 100 block of Duval was moved there one summer day. The Gata House one block from White Street used to set in the middle of the park on Truman Avenue. The house that was once on the Atlantic side of "Louie's Backyard" is now around the 79 mile marker. The oldest house in the 300 block of Duval was possibly moved to its present location. Some researchers feel that the house was only added on to, the original being very small. There are also some people that think they see the houses moving.

As the large Southermost Motel property takes up the rest of the right side of the block, there is only one building that blocks their sprawl of motel rooms, the William House The motel has a center pool and bar mostly for clients of the motel, but they will serve a non-resident a drink.

William House

What is now a splendid guesthouse used to be the Casa Blanca, a decadent, falling-down, flophouse run by a woman who would easily throw out the customers who did not pay the evening's rent. Probably more than 20 years ago, it came up for sale, but it obviously was beside the then- front entrance on South Street, and it seemed quite sure that the growing Southernmost Motel would buy the flophouse. They waited for the drop in price, and two guys from Fort Lauderdale bought it instead of the Southermost Motel. These two guys did major renovation. It sold in l997 to new gay-friendly owners, and it was bought a couple of years ago by Tim Ryan.

Across Duval are a couple of the only lots left on Duval that are without buildings. Their neighbor is a combination used car lot and often a taxi stand on the corner at United Street and Duval Street.

Your introduction

One of the first impressions that you will have of Key West is the freshness of the air. There is a constant, soft breeze, and even in the summer when the temperature can get in the middle nineties, the gentle brush of air seems to make the temperature more tolerable.

You will also be aware of the smells of the island. There is no need to hide the smells of the freshly brewed Cuban coffee, the damp, musty smell of an early morning rainfall, and the freshness of the blooming flowers that are all over the island.

The colors of the flowers are in sharp contrast to the sun-bleached, fading colors of the buildings. The salt air, frequent half hour rains in the fall, the breezes take the energy and color from the painted buildings, and many people re-paint every other year.

Particular pride is taken with the remodeling of the older buildings, and the sounds of hammers and saws are frequent. When the old tin rooofs start to show rust, they are quickly re-painted. Larger buildings have been turned into a couple of apartments with stairs running up one outside starting from the front of the street.

It is probably only in our imagination that we feel the people who live in these houses are happy people living in a place heavily without stress, a place many call Paradise. As a gay person, the simplicity of the lifestyle is appealing and desirous. You will also find that you have started to slow down. There's no rush, particularly since you are on vacation. You are starting to un-wind. Now you can enjoy the island.

Living in Paradise

The downtown

In the 60s the downtown section of old town Duval Street became alive at night and was lined with strip bars and peep shows. After dark, the bars were packed with all kinds of people and a lot were military.

The sailors usually wore their uniforms into town, the crisp white sailor hats, and pants with 13 buttons. Before the white wall at St. Paul's church on Duval had a wrought-iron fence, it was lined with posing, bored, broke, and "available" sailors on non-pay weekends. But, the southern end of Duval was very quiet, with practically no businesses south of Petronia Street to the Atlantic.

It may seem that farther downtown, Key West was full of bars. It did have its share, and it had its share of churches, parks, and beaches. For some reason that I have never understood, the town had what seemed to be many shoestores although it was not fashion-minded. There have always been a lot of churches of every denomination.

The south Duval area had a gentler side. There were quiet mornings and peaceful afternoons and soft sunsets. But, the bars were where the action was. The private homes and apartments around the south end of Duval complained of the noise from the motels or flophouses. For most, the guesthouses at the southern end were less expensive, quieter, and simpler. For most, the real action of the town was in the bars downtown, the opposite of the southern end, well within walking distance and full of cats and roosters. (At the least for me, early 20s, adventuresome and horny.)

More and more people poured into town. In the summertime, the town was usually empty as local residents went to North or South Carolina for the cool mountain climate, so dead in October that the locals created "Fantasy Fest" to fill the hotels over the particularly hot Halloween season. As the word spread, and it did spread rapidly with the Tourist Development Council and a one cent per dollar tax on hotel guest rooms to be used for advertising, the summers started to pick up in tourism, particularly with Florida tourists. The Keys drew the active attention of the people of Miami, a way to get out on the ocean, and the Upper Keys became much more alluring to tourists, and eventually to residents.

Another movement was happening. Leaving Miami and driving down the keys was a way of looking at wetlands and wilderness, the Atlantic and the Gulf of Mexico. Settlements of three or five houses were rare at first, and then the attention switched to the many little communities that were opening between Miami and Key West, and although the attention never really left the water, Key Largo, Tavernier, Marathon and many others sprung up into little cities, altogether with a population greater than Key West. Today, some of the upper keys are the homes of people who work and commute to Miami. The upper Keys express a "red-neck attitude" as far south as to Sugarloaf Key.

Where there is business opportunity, there will be business. The downtown section of Key West was plagued by the Depression, stores boarded up and no renters. Shops only ran a couple of blocks up Duval. Thanks to Ed Swift and Chris Belland and a variety of others, that started to change. Buildings were rented by many who closed the businesses half the year, and slowly that began to change too.

THE 1200 BLOCK
United St. to Catherine St.

Across United Street, which is a direct cut to White Street and beyond, are four original, small conch houses on the right (east) side. The first two are one story houses, the third is a double story with the wooden supports substatuted with metal, and a singular one stoy. It is easy to see the additions of a kitchen and a bath with the roof counter to the house's original roof.

They are now small businesses, but the land is probably more costly than the buildings. Some authorities call these sawcut houses, but others feel the basic bedrooms have been built onto adding kitchens and baths. (Notice on this book's cover under the book's name, the sketch shows the shape of an original conch house with additions. New houses are often built using this add-on characteristic.) One was occupied by a fortune teller, another by a scrub club and the third one stoy was a gift shop. The double story remains a private home.

Rainbow House

If you go to your right (east) across United Street half a block you'll see two buildings with pool, a women's guesthouse called "Rainbow House". Men are strictly forbidden in the buildings. It is owned and operated by Marion Serelis, a woman active in the creation of "crime stoppers", and Cheryl Fagan. Does the "one sex only" restriction duplicate the prejudice gays have felt in the past?

There had been previous attempts at creating a woman's guest-house; all have failed. The larger building was the Pines, a predominately male guesthouse owned every few years by a couple of more guys fascinated by the concept of a gay guesthouse, but unaware of the great amount of work involved. Marion and Cheryl bought the Pines and the house on the other side of the pool, joined the two and created a successful lesbian guesthouse.

There is a women's bar, "Club International" on Simonton Street three blocks away, but there is also "La te da" around the corner, a popular hang-out for patrons of Rainbow House, particularly the "Tree Top" bar upstairs, often with a woman bartender. The gay friendly "Grand Vin" north on Duval a couple of buildings is excellent for wine lovers.

"Coffee and Tea House"

Across Duval Street is a coffee shop at 1218 with baked goods and an atmosphere of sit and have a scone or tea, read a book or newspaper and have a chat. It is owned and operated by Mary Vaught and Lynn Banks, who moved the coffee house from 1100 Duval. It is warm and inviting. There is a gift shop with lots of coffee-related items, and very lesbian friendly. The business is new, but the friendly atmosphere will probably be here a long time.

Beside the Coffee and Tea House, according to Rex, who has a tendency to fill me with tales that are questionable in truth, there is the house beside it on the left side (west) of the street set back with a large front yard. It used to be a whore house. What was unique was that the door knobs upstairs were all brown glass, the door knobs downstairs were white, aiming the black patrons upstairs, the white patrons down. I doubt this is true. I think this is Rex's sense of humor.

Often built before the period of strict building rules, many families built houses on what they believed as their property only to find once surveying became necessary for insurance that they were on neighbor's land. The property of Key West has been surveyed a couple of times. However, the surveys do not match. If you own property north of Truman, you were probably the earlier survey; south of Truman was the later survery. A piece of property can be as much as two feet off the survey, usually unimportant to most people, but a real contention to others as well as a joy to lawyers. The white house that sits back on the property really sits on a small lane that runs behind it. The owners had a house and created a street. (Today, we would have a street, buy a lot, and create a house.) It's a value scale misunderstanding.

Up the street on the even-numbered side of the street were what was locally called "the three sisters", three double-storied wooden houses very much alike in floor plan and appearance. The third and a new addition have been joined. Once single family homes, they eventually were converted to duplexes, and as the commercial district grew, the porches were glassed and converted to small shops. This part of town is closely watched by Peter Wagner who has been responsible for some of the major renovation of this area.

Across the street at 1215 is a restaurant called "Karumba!". For many years it was a local's Cuban restaurant with a side window for take-out orders. The little alley running beside it to Simonton Street is packed with conch cottages and small homes, most of which have been redone and preserved in their original design, and there are many Cuban people in the neighborhood. They are friendly, but stick closely to their own local friends and often avoid tourists.

A block over east from "Karumbre!" on the corner of Simonton, visually across from the First State Bank is the "Palm Grill". This popular restaurant block on Simonton Street also contains a half-block north another restaurant called "Cafe Blue". Both are predominately restaurants although both have liquor bars.

"Palm Grill"
Thirty years earlier, a restaurant downtown a couple of doors west of "Captain Tony's Bar" on Greene Street was called "Poor Richard's Buttery" run by Richard Lisher. When there were only a few visitors to Key West and the major hotel accommodations was "The Pier House", the "in" place for a new gay crowd was "The Buttery" for dining. At that time four men could sit at the same table and not be "unusual". There were practically no visiting lesbians in town, although all kinds of couples were welcome. "The Buttery" was an early example of heterosexuals being "gay friendly". We used to call it "understanding".

"The Buttery" on Greene Street was closed, and eventually reopened on Simonton Street in a location of an Italian restaurant. (I remember a bar, and I think it was at the position of "The Buttery", that was shaped like a row boat, but when Richard Lisher bought the restaurant, it was not there.) Lisher sold the bar and restaurant, and it has been bought in the last year by Tim Ryan and redone again. He currently owns "Cafe des Artistes" and "Duffy's Steak and Lobster House". The name of "Palm Grill" was given by a previous owner, and at this time Ryan will not keep the old name on the yellow restaurant, and he will call it "Abbondaza". Ryan will venture into Italian food, but whatever he does, he does well.

"Cafe Blue"

Gail Brockway ran a very popular restaurant in the 900 block of Duval called "Lighthouse Cafe". Probably the most popular and obvious structure was the lighthouse on Whitehead Street, quite visable over the roofs of the one-story buildings across the street from the restaurant's location on Duval. Preparing all kinds of foods, my favorite was always white clam spaghetti with all the shells and unbelievable garlic bread. Gail eventually sold to a French family (and it's currently "Cafe Bianco").

After a couple of years of not running a restaurant, Gail Brockway could not keep away from the kitchen, and in 1997 opened "Cafe Blue" in a restaurant/bar at Catherine and Simonton, previously called the "Full Moon Saloon". Stewart Kempt runs the side bar after 7 pm while happy hour for the gay croud with Travis behind the bar is from 4 pm to 7 pm except Sundays. The schedule will change. (Travis is now at "Chi-chi's", "Donnies's Place" on Truman. Nancy and Lee are behind the bar at "Cafe Blue".)

Many years back, the "Moon" had been "The Italian Gardens", a small restaurant with half being kitchen and some dining under covered roof, the other dining space being open patio with fake vines and grapes, straw and grass covered bottles of red wine.

Most important were the delightful waitresses, most very full-figured pushing carts, but never forgetting you if you ate there more than twice, and never taking orders on a pad, but always remembering exactly what the diner wanted, and never making a mistake. Somehow, all the waitresses were related, or at least the clients felt so because they all looked similar.

You could eat alone and not feel intimidated. Four guys could eat together without a harsh word from another table. Kenneth Williams said in a movie called "Carry on Cleo", "You say to me, 'Caesar, there are ramblings in the Senate.' Well, I say to you 'nonsense, it's just that damn spaghetti they eat.'"

Ater the "Italian Garden" was the "Full Moon Saloon", a group of good buddies that came from a building that was destroyed on United Street to become the parking lot for the Southernmost Hotel addition. When the "Full Moon Saloon" owned the building, they enclosed the patio and walled the open sides and cared for a never-working air-conditioning system. They put in a sunken bar with longue chairs. With Gail Brockway's control, half of the once-patio has been returned to a roofed patio for outside dining. The "Full Moon" bar has been split. The bar pit has been filled. The food is excellent.

A man, not from Key West, had won the lottery of 23 million dollars, and he was telling his story to the bartender. He had to live on $685,000. a year. A drunk from the other side of the bar lifted his head and said "You can't live on that in Key West" and went back to sleep.

"Banana Cafe"
Back on Duval on the other side of the alley is the "Banana Cafe", which has had many different names and renters, but who has always kept a kind of luncheon-deli atmosphere. The porch and side deck are ideal for people watching. Peter Wagner will be too busy working on other projects, but, as owner of the building, he often has lunch there.

Gingerbread Square Gallery
On the same side of the street, north a few doors, is a converted conch house which now serves as the oldest gallery in Key West and currently houses many of the local artists' work. The building itself was once the sewing room of a guy called "Pinky", who made wonderful, zany costumes. Tom Pope designed and had built the unusual brick patio, one of the nicest patios in Key West.

The history of Gingerbread Square Gallery dates back to my history. Richard Heyman and I opened GSG many years ago, but I'll save those stories until the 900 block. Richard eventually owned GSG and had moved from the 900 block to the l200 block and sold the gallery. He sold to one of our earliest artists in GSG, Sal Salinero, and his partner, Jeff Birn.

Valladares and Sons
Across the street a little farther north is the most famous book store in Key West, and it is a real bookstore that sells magazines, paperbacks, and many newspapers. It does not have a back room. It has been there a couple of generations, prominently displayed on the south side of Catherine Street, and it has no hesitation in carrying local writers.

Philip Burton, who had a home on Angela Street, would take his "morning constitutional" walk to Valldares. He was the step-father or adopted father of Richard Burton, the actor.

"El Siboney Restaurant"

If you were to continue walking down Catherine Street five or six quite long blocks, you would find on the southern side of the street in the 900 block of Catherine a restaurant that has served traditional Cuban food, plentiful, rich, inexpensive and tasty. When they were repainting the building in late 1997 and were repairing the sign, only half of it was hanging for a day. It announced "boney Restaurant", but it was soon repaired.

There is usually a line and a short wait, but the restaurant is well worth the walk. The attitude is friendly, but there is no particular attitude against gays, but "no screamers".

The restaurant used to be called "El Cacique", but they moved to Roosevelt and the excellent quality remains the same. Another popular Cuban restaurant within walking distance was on White Street, "The 4th of July", where Cuban men played dominoes at a back table. Fortunately, the White Street area is quite popular to local merchants, and it is going through rapid changes.

Back on Duval Street, there are many small, unique little shops on the west side including a shop that specializes in tribal arts, at one time a fabric weaver, aand a gift/florist called "Baskets". They are unique.

WomenFest and Fantasy Fest

There is something unique that the business community of Key West seems to be able to do, something that I am not aware that any city in the United States can do as effectively. When there is a period that seems to prove over time that business is weak, the constant party energy of the Key West businesses creates a holiday. I guess everyday is a holiday to someone, but Key West businesses make a "special party time" for celebrating some event, maybe not even recognizeable to others.

Our City Commission is resonsible for establishing local variances and creating permission to close streets, allow alcoholic drinks and give permission for police protection. They are a board of seven, one at-large, the others from specific areas of the city. They meet at least monthly. They have been very liberal with our business community often giving permission for a street party under the slightest notion of a possibility. Many local residents object to the City Commission being so libreral because it often disturbs the lives of the local residents. The City Commission is at constant war with our noise ordinance, our short term rental policies, the lack of low income housing, and many other issues. All complaints are directed toward the seven person committee which work for minimal salaries.

Our form of city government places most of the responsibilities upon the City Manager, and the City Commission is responsible to him. His position has often been caught in the bubba war. The position is also responsible for the leadership of the police department. Without a combination of City Manager approval, City Commission approval and police agreement, we would not be allowed to hold the events, and the gay events, we do.

Traditionally September and October are probably the poorest two business months. Aside from Labor Day ending summer, small children are starting back to school and families do not vacation. Key West has it's hotest weather and it's hurricane season.

The first week of September is WomenFest. Jacqueline Harrington has been WomenFest director for two years, and with advertising, the announcement of the candidates for Fantasy Fest King and Queen, a week of cocktail parties, food fests, drag shows, and meetings designed to please the 8,000 expected women, many lesbians attend a variety of other social events. A few thousand people can make a great difference to the Key West economy. This period is really the start of the fund raising season, and the beginning announcements of who will be running for Fantasy Fest king and queen. With this start, the parties do not let up until the final crowning and the parade five or six weeks later.

Fantasy Fest celebrating Holloween, October 3l, is a similar event, purely created to entice business, attended by many thousands for more than a week. The parties are organized and scheduled events in which the whole town participates. These two events keep the account books out of the red ink for these two months, hopefully.

The jobs of fantasy fest king and queen are hardly honorary positions. Their job is to raise money in a town that is drenched in fund raisers. The throne contenders don't have to be of any social position, status, wealth, or even human. We have had animals run, drag queens, bartenders, socially important people, gays and straights. They usually pair off into a king and queen although they can run seperately for either position. There's no gender bias.

Then starts the heavy task of organizing parties of all kinds and fund raising through luncheons, elegant dinners, picnics, square dances, sock-hops, or any other device including begging and re-payment of debts. Few limitations are held. Every vote cost $5.00, and the person with the most votes (collected money) wins, and gets the honor of riding on the Fantasy Fest float with the crowns and announced as Fantasy Fest King and Queen.

There are no loosers. Even those that have not raised enough money to wear the crown have devoted many hours of hard labor to fund raising, and it is appreciated by all. There are only a great bunch of fund raisers to be announced at the last party before the parade, all winners.

Here is where the attitude of the City Commission for requesting permission, the City Manager for allowing it to happen, and the Key West Police Department for protecting it compliments the contestants and the givers to make this fishing village important.

1100 BLOCK
Catherine St. to Virginia St.

The 1100 block is also split by an alley running on the right into a dead end and to the left by the continuation of Amelia Street. Across Catherine Street from Valladarus Bookstore is Kennedy Gallery, one of a few Kennedy galleries in town, and they carry some of the Mario Sanchez prints as well as a large number of other prints. In fact, Mario Sanchez' home and garden where he does his wood cutting and painting are on Catherine Street. Sanches is Key West's most well known and respected artist.

Across the street in Sanchez' neighborhood is a local Cuban fisherman who got caught up in some criminal confusion and he and his wife built a fish sales room called Tomasita's Seafood. She sells his catch from the booth. Grunts are $2.50 a pound. It is the freshest raw seafood in town..

"La te da"
On the east side of the street across from Kennedy Gallery is one of the most interesting old houses converted into business, a place that has easily gained a welcomed reputation by gays.

The classic "snob" story is about Bea Lilly in Chicago at the Dorchester needing her hair done, and the stylist said she would take Bea Lilly before her next client, Mrs. Armour, who was often late. As Lilly was having her hair combed, Mrs. Armour came into the saloon and created a little fuss because she had to wait. As the beautician finished, Lilly said loudly "Tell the butcher's wife that Lady Peal is finished." The building became that type of elegant place.

There was on the non-commercial end of Duval Street a large, fake stone, Charles Adam's-looking, single family house, which was converted into a restaurant; the "Terrace of de Marquis", called by locals as "La te da". A new addition brought a dozen guest rooms and there was an upper-story second bar as well as a bar around the pool on the first floor. It's a 16 room hotel. Small tables encircled the pool, tables set with pink table-cloths, pink napkins, nice glassware and serving pieces. It was elegant, and it was expensive.

The elegant "La te da"

The staff flounced their freedom but the restaurant was enjoyed by all. Chilled strawberry soup, she crab soup, banana pancakes, the elegant dishes that no one fixed at home. Pam has recently been the major manager/waitress. The restaurant and bar became favorite meeting places for all kinds of groups.   Bruce Sagar and Dennis Martin would fly in from Los Angeles for the Christmas season every year. The music was soft and non-intrusive.

But, not always. On Sunday afternoons starting about two o'clock would be the "La te da" tea dance; a hoard of locals and tourists would gather to hear breaking beats of disco and dance sometimes close to nude around the pool. The porches were full of gawkers.

The mob would later find their way down to the Atlantic Shores Motel where by the ocean was a bar and pool, owned by Sal Rapasardi and around the corner from "Papillon Bar". Although the pool bar had a reputation for nude sunbathing, the same disco procedure as at "La te da" would continue until midnight.

In the late 70s, there was the auctioning of party events. At auction, the bidder would pay well for a party hosted by a particular person, an event serviced by prominent people, or at the home of a prominent person. Dinner for eight at "Louie's Back Yard" or the "Buttery". Lunch prepared by a city commissioner. Bobby Nesbitt would play piano at your home for the highest bid. All money would go to charity.

Bill and Sue Sellers

Bill and Sue Sellers bought a chili dinner prepared by and served by City Commissioner Sally Lewis, butlered by the mayor, Richard Heyman, with entertainment by a popular local star, Bobby Nesbitt. Since there was no piano at the Seller's home, they rented a house with a piano for their eight guests for that one evening, but they made the affair black tie with pre-cocktails at "La te da". The women were in dresses of the 40s with small pillbox hats, and the men were formal in black ties, some with shorts and tennis shoes, black tie and no shirt, and tuxedo coats. The party progressed to the scene of the crime, the rented house where the mayor opened the door, the commissioner had made the chili, and it was served at a formal table, and the entertainer was joined by the mayor and commissioner and eventually the eight guests in a sing-along.

a formal affair

Lawrence (never call him Larry) Formica ran "La te da" for many years. He was flamboyant with a pink Cadillac convertible parked in front. The tablecloths were pink. The napkins were pink. Each vase on the tables had pink flowers.

There was an open balcony on the second floor overlooking the

75

pool. At one time Mary Wade cooked "specialties" from a tiny closet kitchen. She later opened her own restaurant, "Wok Around the Clock". The guests would hang on the porch railings looking down at the dancing and swimming gays. A drag here and there.

Chuck Lamb had been the bartender, and Chuck (Sylvia) was never slow on the comments. He had the opportunity to go to England and he was excited about his trip because he had never been out of this country. When he returned, everyone was concerned about his impressions of England.

"Did you have any trouble with customs?" was asked.

"No. I learned to use a knife, spoon and fork before I left" he quickly replied.

A man walked into the bar where Chuck was working and the man was obviously feeling no pain. Chuck refused to serve him. "I want a beer" the man replied, and the bartender said "Not unless you can tell me God's first name." The intoxicated man was stunned, but finally said "Andy". Chuck was surprised and said "Andy. Andy. How did you come up with Andy?" The guy mumbled "Andy walks with me. Andy talks with me." Chuck poured the beer.

"Do you know the graffiti I just copied from the men's room wall?" Chuck asked me. "Little Boy Blue ... for the money."

Humor is the one factor of Key West that is more plentiful than sand. Some people will say it's the "I don't care" attitude, but it's more than that.

One of the events that happened every year around March was the dog show, where pet and owner appeared with something in common, either a look-a-like, matching costume or theme. The owners parade their pets and receive trophies for the participants in a variety of categories, all accurately judged by a jury that listens closely to the crowd of gawkers at the bars.

"La te da" ran for about ten years, but fell into financial debt because of the same reason that so many local bars had closed, and in 1991 closed the patio doors to an era of elegant partying. It went up for auction, and was sold. Resold. Sal Rapisardi, once owner of "Atlantic Shores" and some other bars and including his mother-in-law bought the building and regained some of the elegance that it once had. They particularly rebuilt the upstairs bar by rerouting the staircase to one side of the building creating a large room with stage and massive windows looking onto the middle of an old tree, usually called the "Tree Top Bar". They added rooms on the Catherine Street side, modernized, and had a roof top for sunning deck, which was often nude sunbathing.

Everyone was sure it would someday come back because what can be done with a large house and many private bedrooms with refrigerators, unless a wealthy couple has a very large Catholic family?

Jim Hefferman and Godfrey Thompson took control of "La te da" in 1997. An advertisement for Godfrey's Bar meaning to say "Exotic Drinks in a Tropical Setting ..." slipped by with "Exotic Drunks in a Tropical Setting". He claimed it was not a mistake. Yeah. The manager was Stewart Hair, formerly from "Kelly's". In the summer of l998, they declaired backruptcy, and the restaurant/bar and property went back to Sal Rapisardi who held the mortgage. (Rapisardi re-opened "La te da" October l6, l998.)

Speakeasy Inn
Next to "La te da" is a vacant lot which services their guests' parking, and then a recently renovated building that has been beautifully refinished. Notice the upstairs ballustrade of bottle shapes and diamonds, hearts, spades and clubs. The building was at one time a gambling hall complete with a whorehouse upstairs, and plenty of quiet rooms on Angelia Street behind the Duval Street entrance.

They also sell cigars, but not the Cuban cigars which are illegal to import. Some of their tobacco comes from the Domican Republic, but most is American tobacco. They have a walk-in cedar humidor. Cigars from Key West make excellent gift, by the way.

"Alice's on Duval"
Across the street from "La te da" is a square building that was an ice cream parlor and sold sappodilla plum ice cream. It later became a gourmet food store, the first in Key West.

It was then bought by a guy named John, who had two huge black dogs. John tore out the pained windows and doors and replaced them with steel shutters, loaded the room with good antiques and had a bar painted by a prominent local painter, Van Eno, added a juke box, and never opened to the public.

By accident Sally Lewis, later an influential city commissioner, and I were returning from "Claire Bar" and we heard wonderful dance music coming from John's bar and the shutters were open. He invited us in to dance, which we did. (It seemed that there was some law to keep a restaurant license alive, you had to be opened at least one day a year, and this was the day.) John tried to sell his antiques, sold the building and left town. I've never known anyone who has ever heard from him since.

The space was rented a couple of times. I remember that the kitchen was all new, something unusual in restaurants. It was new because it had never been used. "Alice's on Duval" opened in 1997.

A story circulated that probably had no substantiation in fact, but is thought to be true by the people of Key West, although no one knows who the people were, when or where it happened. Unclear source.

There was a young couple who lived on the second floor of a conch house. One Christmas the husband brought home a large Christmas tree wrapped in brown butcher paper. Since he was covered with needles and perspiration, he undressed and went to the shower and soaped himself. His wife's screams forced him out of the shower, naked, wet, and soaped down. His wife said she saw a snake come from the tree and it went under the sofa. He bent down and put his head under the sofa looking for the snake. Their Doberman Pincer walked by and gave the crouched man a lick. The man lifted his head under the sofa and knocked himself out.

In panic, the wife called the fire department and when they arrived it was decided the man should be taken to the hospital for observation. The firemen picked up the naked, soaped man and started down the steep steps. Somehow, the body slid out of their hands and shot down the stairs.

The husband spent Christmas with a fully decorated tree, a broken wrist and a cast on his leg, and they never found the snake.

Years later Fred Gros was working in his yard on White Street. Since Fred kept the hose under the house, he reached under for it and pulled out what turned out to be a five-foot boa constrictor. His next door neighbor had reported it missing, and it was returned to the neighbor.

It was not uncommon for homes in the South to keep a black snake around the house for the purpose of eating rodents and bugs. As it would sun on the back porch, the family would just push it aside when they wanted to clean.

"The Cuban Club"

You have to be careful when you say "The Cuban Club" because the identification depends upon which structure you mean. There is the shell of "The Cuban Club" on Amelia, complete with turret, which is now residential. There is "The Cuban Club" meaning the San Carlos building in the 500 block of Duval. There is "The Cuban Club" that burned to the ground and has been completely rebuilt with the neighbor next to it, and is now shops below and apartments above in the 1100 block of Duval.

It was the last "Cuban Club" that contained a bar/restaurant called "The Fountains". It was owned by Jay Haskel and Jimmy Hoffa (not that Jimmy Hoffa). Charles Ortel, originally from Cape Cod, managed the restaurant/bar. A beautiful girl named Evelyn, who dated Tim Ryan of "Cafe de Artistes" for eight years, and Lourie McChesney were hostesses. Rusty was the bartender, entertainment, and singer.

A constant patron was Sharon Ganse, who designed clothes and lived across the street with her husband, Tom. Their house, now a real estate agency, had balustrades that once graced the Convent on Truman, and where bought at auction for a dollar apiece.

"La Bistro"

Beside where the Ganse's lived used to be a coffee shop which made the neighborhood reek of freshly ground coffee, and it became a local hangout. It was sold in 1997 and became "La Bistro".

"Mosquito Coast" and "Flamingo Crossing"

At the end of the 1100 block are two buildings owned by one of the nicest couples in town, Dan and Ellie McConnell. The "Mosquito Coast" building contains an apartment upstairs, the office for his kayak tours and a wine bar. They sell sun block, hats, waterproof cameras, and items that one may want in visiting the swampland.

Not enough can be said about the unusual, informative, fun kayak tour. For about 45 dollars, from 8:45 am to 3:00 pm, Dan or his son take out five or six kayaks, two per boat, in parts of the swamps where the fresh water meets the salt water. Each trip holds a new adventure, from seeing alligators, grunt fish, or deer, to feeling the freshness and freedom of the frontier land. A unique experience, and Dan and his son, Sean McConnell, know the swamplands well. It is a trip you will never forget.

For wine drinkers, try "Grand Vin", the wine bar in the large white house. They are welcoming hosts, and often the gay girls meet there. There will be no strain. (The sign for "Grand Vin" is on the back cover, top right.)

There will also be advertised in "Celebrate", a weekly gay newspaper, sailing tours, usually one for lesbians and one for gay men. These often nude tours can be fun and relatively inexpensive. Since boat owners and accommodations change faster than divorces, consult the local paper for those now in business.

"Flamingo Crossing" is basically an ice cream parlor, but with creamy, home-made Italian ice cream. "La te da" used to use their ice cream in bar drinks which made them more tasty. There are coffee and soft drinks. Very habit-forming.

THE 1000 BLOCK
Virginia St. to Truman St.

Fletchers

Across Virginia Street on Duval is a stylish furniture and accessories shop that has a very definite style of heavy metal, natural coral cuts, and thick glass. They ship anything, and you may be able to find that very unusual chair or vase which you have been hunting. Prices may seem a little expensive, but nice things often are.

They don't advertise that Fletchers has a back room, a real sale room for marked-down items. Most of the pieces have just been in the store without much action for too long, or the manager has tired of them. You may be able to get that nice piece at even a less expensive price than you imagined.

Duval Square

Across Duval Street is a large complex of buildings that seems strange at first. There is a block of one-story shops, and on top of the shops is a two story conch city complete with pool. The concept is certainly not new; "to live above the shop", but these are done in a conch manner.

The lot was owned by the Catholic Church on Truman, the most prosperous religion in Key West, services having once been performed in Spanish. They owned not only the church, but also a large convent building which burned in the 30s. The church also owned the property where The Reach is now along with many others.

The lot on Duval contained a wooden hall, once used as a USO by the military and used for the Wreckers' Auction. That building fell to ruin, eventually inhabited only by drifters and, grown over with weeds, half burned, an eyesore. The Catholic Church sold the property.

The starting of the new Duval Square seemed to move through serges of work, down time, and another burst of energy. The builder was using local labor hired by the hour off the streets, not particularly professional, skilled carpenters and builders. Some boards were not straight or not secured properly. They sold the corner piece of property to Circle K. Other pieces were either sold or rented, but the property was still on the less popular side of the island. Eventually two businessmen bought the tumbled building and Lou Petrochelli managed. His partner had been raised in a family that had construction stores, so eventually boards were replaced, brick was laid properly, and the building was repaired to proper demands.

The condominiums on the tops of the stores were sold, but not necessarily to the owners or renters of the stores below. The homes offered an excellent location, a pool, eventually the shops became a work-out studio, dining downstairs, a hair dressing shop, flower shop and is rather one convenient package. The new developers of Duval Square eventually sold everything, and left town.

"Square One"
A restaurant and bar opened in the new Duval Square buildings, "Square One", and it became a place where a specific group of people, the movers and shakers of the charity movements, meet for cocktails and dining. It maintains its popularity.

Michael Stewart is the host and owns the restaurant with Phillip Shahan. Stewart and Shahan came to Key West from Coconut Grove and they ran The Pines, a guesthouse on Eaton now called The Rainbow House. Stewart knows everyone by name.

Patrick (Patty-Cakes) was originally at "Papillon", now the liquor store of Atlantic Shores on South Street, and he has been the main bartender at "Square One" for many years. He has one of the best bar jobs in town. The bar at "Square One" is small, with about 15 seats, and is basically for the service of their dinner customers, although they do have a "happy hour". Sharon works Sundays and Mondays. They are often closed for "special parties".

The gas station on the corner completes that side of this half block although the little shops they built hide even the gas station now. These shops hawk a lot of the reef trips, reservations, and sell the more commercial aspects of the activities of Key West including t-shirts.

To the right and beside the gas station on Truman and running to the corner of Simonton Street is another small mall containing Eckerd

Drug Store and   small businesses. Locals use the video shop or eat lunch at the Sub Shop.

At the south eastern corner of Simonton and Truman are two restaurants with very different fare but both owned by Tim Ryan, who also owns what was once called the "Palm Grill" on Simonton, which has recently been re-done into a yellow Italian restaurant. The older of the two original restaurants specializes in French food which is

"Cafe des Artistes".

The point at which the sleepy, laid-back island changed in the early 80s into large city ways was a $100-a-plate dinner held at "Cafe des Artistes". It was a formal affair for 100 people. Many of the new locals had come to the island to escape the expensive fundraisers, the suits, and gossip was the party would not sell out, but it did. New behavior or old patterns revitalized had been established, and the $10,000 was raised for charity.

"Duffy's Steak and Lobster House"

Specializing in steak and lobster, most of the building is really on Truman Avenue although the front door is on Simonton Street as is the entrance to "Cafe des Artistes". The bar and dining area is more casual in dining at affordable prices, and advertises its roots to be to 1892 although the building addition was done only a couple of years ago.

Deja Vie Resort

Dennis Bitner opened the Key West Club Baths. A steam room, swimming pool, little rooms for rent, and horney gay males was not unlike Jack Cambell's Miami Club Baths. It was a gay sex business on the opposite side of Truman. It was sold and redone into a health club aimed at wealthy heavy customers or alcoholics, and it is currently a mostly straight resort with "clothing optional". Bitner closed the baths because of the lack of business and community threat of AIDS. He died of the disease a year later.

The Caribbean Gallery

Back on Duval Street and across on the left from the little huts that commercialize the island is another art gallery, The Caribbean Art Gallery, which contains some particularly whimsical sculptures of animals.

If you stand at the west corner of Duval and Truman and look left, you can see over five similar tobacco roller's cottages. The lighthouse is above their roof-lines. These little cottages were built by Mr. George Lee, a Chinese worker on the railroad that Flagler built to Key West. He also had a grocery store downtown around the La Concha. (Later becoming "The West Key Bar".) He married a Spanish woman and they had five boys, two of which still live in the keys with their children. Lee's sister was Mary Lee Graham, a city commissioner of Key West in the 1970's. Three houses of the five that Lee, Sr. built have been sold to someone other than in the Lee family.

The present lighthouse was built in 1847 to 1849 to replace the lighthouse which was on Whitehouse Point and destroyed in 1846. It was originally 60 feet tall and increased to 94 feet in the 1890s.

Across Duval Street on the east side are a few old conch cabins to which bathrooms and kitchens have been added. According to our building codes, if you level a conch house you must then adjust to new set-back restrictions which are quite conservative, not allowing the new buildings to be so close. Thus, the old conch houses are redone. One wall is taken out and replaced by a new wall. A second. A third. A fourth. Bathrooms and electrical updated are permitted.

The original conch houses were built for the tobacco rollers, the hired help for the larger houses, or the dock workers. Since a family cooked in a community kitchen, and there were outhouses, the original conch house was usually only two bedrooms, the front room being smaller because of a hall to the back bedroom. The husband and wife usually had the larger back bedroom. The children had the front room. A second type was called the shotgun plan, a straight direction of a hall from the front door to the back door. (See picture, back cover, center.)

Neither type of the original cigar roller's cottage had running water, bath or kitchen attached to the house. When electricity was more available, the kitchens and eventually the baths were connected, what some authorities call the sawtooth house design, but many of the original were simply add-ons with modernizing.

You will notice that the conch houses are usually built in twos or threes. There was always a porch and windows or a door on each wall of the bedroom. The additions of kitchens or bathrooms or combination appear as tack-ons, the roof running in a different direction from the rest of the house. Most people refer to these small cottages as "shot-gun" houses. One authority calls them vernacular architecture (meaning architecture of habit) that he claims derived from Louisiana. (3)

As the cigar rollers became more prosperous, they began to build two-story houses, still without bathrooms or kitchens, and these usually contained a parlor and dining room downstairs, a couple of bedrooms upstairs. A common design was the "eyebrow house", a modification of the Classical Revival style with one and a half stories, the roof lip extended on the top level covering the porch, and creating half windows on the second level. Usually these contained the living room, dining room and eventually the kitchen and bath down, two bedroom up.

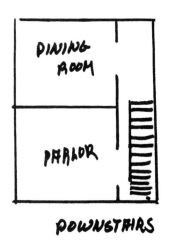

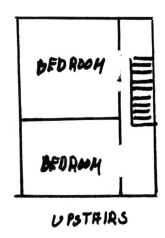

early two-story house floor plan

As the middle class grew in the United States and the prosperity of the middle class grew, more of these two story houses were built containing an individual bath with running water and a kitchen with sewers. During the 60's, 70's and into the turn of the century, most new houses were built in this conch style. They had a center front door with one or two balanced windows on each side. The houses often integrated some of the historical qualities such as a cistern, shutters, or a widow's walk, attempting to give the appearance of being authentically old.

The most tragic effect happened during the interim between the original houses of the 1800s and the attempts to modernize them. The wrong materials were used. What was at that time "in" or "modern" became dated. Wooden pained windows were replaced with jalousie windows. The traditional tin roofs were replaced with shingles. The wooden porch posts were replaced with wrought iron supports in a grape-vine motif or decorative concrete-blocks.

It was decided long ago that the homes of Key West were to be used for living in, not entirely for historical accuracy. The people wanted more modern conveniences and incorporated the more modern features into their old homes. Air conditioners hung out of windows, and the country's fascination with electricity demanded that most of the earlier houses had to be up-dated with current.

As the stove replaced the fireplace, as the refrigerator replaced the salt house, inside water and plumbing replaced the outhouse and the hand pump or the septic tank pump. All of America has had a fascination with the refrigerator wanting one today that has a freezing area, an ice cube maker, push button cold water in addition to a cold area, the bigger the better. For one of the great, bulky furniture pieces of a house, the refrigerator is a status symbol of wealth.

Another demand of our time is for closets. Many people agree that you cannot have enough closet space. Modern blueprints show a fourth of the square footage of a house in closet space.

The conch houses did not have closets; they used an armoire for storage or a dresser. (In the 80s the Pier House built a new series of rooms with baths, but no closets. At the two side walls of each hotel room were armoires, one for clothes storage, the second containing the television and/or bar. People on vacation usually take only a suitcase. There have been no complaints.)

One of the greatest changes in architecture has been the adding of what the British call the "water closet". With electricity, plumbing and water, the Victorians were sensitive to their bathroom habits, and the early bathrooms contained a toilet, a wash bowl, a tub and usually had only one small window. Modern tastes have come a long way and a common practice today is to have a bathroom practically the size of a small bedroom with bidet, shower and tub, well lighted mirrors with an outside view, perhaps even incorporating work-out machines. No wonder the old conch houses have to be rewired and replumbed.

On the outside, so many of the once wooden balustrades have been modernized with decorative concrete-blocks of the 40s and 50s. Brick patios have been torn apart to lay concrete slabs. Decorative bathroom tile has been used on slab-front porches. The ethnic alter has been built over an empty septic tank.

Originally, the outside paint of the house was either whitewash or natural wood showing the boat-builder's carpentry skill. Since the gay movement of the 70s, colors have been added not unlike the Bahama colors of bright blues, yellows, pinks and oranges. In the original color skeme of the natual or whitewashed house, the upstairs porch ceiling was painted light blue, the downstairs porch ceiling was painted a subtle grass green. Locals will tell you the painting skeme was to keep down the mosquito population, the bugs thinking they were in the sky on the second floor and too close to ground on the first level. The theory seems far-fetched today.

The interiors of the early houses were often made of Dade County fir, a wood that had grown to be termite resistant, and the craftmanship of the early boat builders was displayed. Many have been painted and a newer technique used dry-wall for a cleaner and brighter interior.

One of the greatest changes in architecture has come with the windows. In the early conch houses, each exterior wall had a window, and interior walls had at least one door, sometimes a second door in an interior wall into an adjoining bedroom. This allowed for the free ventilation of the natural breezes. Set up on coral blocks, the houses swayed during a tropical storm, the animals safe under the houses. There was never an exterior wall without a window.

With air-conditioning and French doors came solid walls to block unpleasant views or curtail noise. Then came the building of wooden decks. The spaces under the house were blocked to avoid having the animals under the house. (Notice the fancy under-house brick work on the house over the book's binding spine, the patterned brick to allow air under the house, a modern solution, not historical.)

There are many good modern trends. Landscaping has become popular, but not so much with indigenous (native) plants with tropical looking plants which thrive in this weather. The wetlands hold the indigenous plants.

We are still complaining about over-population. There are few vacant lots, and many full-time residents are putting second stories on their once one-story homes. Most new construction is the two-story single house plan, blending nicely with the original 1800 houses. A modern-day trend is the fenced yard with an entrance gatehouse as the front door or door to the yard.

We have managed to keep the many animals that have always distinguished this island. The hundreds of roaming dogs, the territorial cats, the many roosters, the occasional pig, the flying parrots, and the "dirt-baggers".

How do you know if you are in an original conch house? The real estate people have some guidelines: (1) All walls are painted light blue or green. (2) A velvet "Last Supper" is hanging in the living room. (3) There's a flamingo lamp. (4) There's a television light made from shells. (5) The television is in the living room. (6) It's over-crowded with furniture including a Lazy Boy recliner. (7) The carpet is a floral design or laid asbestos blocks, or linoleum. (8) Velvet-draped windows. (9) The front door is open so neighbors can see the many photographs of the grand-children on the television. (10) The satellite dish is at an angle. The truth is in the property deed.

The original name of Truman Avenue was Brannan's Road, named during and after a Civil War Army officer, and renamed Division Street in 1874. When the island was settled it was thought that land south of Division Street was useless swamp. The lighthouse was on the ocean. Everything south of Division Street was filled land. The history of Key West brings out many of the arguments both for and against filling the swampland. We still argue the same contentions. Division Street was renamed Truman Avenue in the 50s.
"Chi chi's" or "Che che's"
    At 1000 Truman on the corner is a back-room bar of maybe 12 seats that has amused many people for years, the old "Chi chi's".

(When someone asked the correct spelling of the bar, the bartender said he didn't know because they never advertised.) It has recently been purchased for over one million dollars, remodeled, and attracting a lot of attention with outside tables and a drive thrugh liquor sales. Father and son, David Jenkins, call it "Donnies' Place" and they promise the water dish for traveling dogs and the ringing bell for the conch train. We'll see.

"Numbers"

At the opposite end of Truman to the right about ten blocks is a bar, "Numbers", two blocks before White Street.   White Street separates the Old Town from the newer section and was the division line of Old Town drawn by the Historical Review Committee of Tallahassee as their first preservation plan. On the south part of Truman was Big Daddy's Liquor Store, and although the Big Daddy chain is not there, a liquor store and an adult strip club for straights called "Teasers" separate a gay bar called "Numbers".

Although "Numbers" is off the beaten tourist track, it seems to get away with naked male dancers who beg for bucks, loud modern music, cheap drinks, a pool table, and is often packed for a sexy, "tacky" night on the town. It is not only dark, but, coming from a brightly lighted parking lot or the sunshine of the afternoon, it take a few minutes for the eyes to adjust to the blackness. That blackness can have its advantage.

Michael (Mable) is often the bartender at "Numbers", and he rules with a firm hand, maybe not as firm as Scotty-Ann or Jerry There are a series of male strippers who perform late in the evening, and these young men are often from Miami or Miami Beach. Not surprisingly not all the strippers are gay or even bi-sexual. Some will tell you they are just down on their luck and nude or partially nude dancing is a means of obtaining money without much effort. The men sitting at the bar stuff dollars into their jock-straps or shorts, and the dancers hustle for drinks, and the drinkers often get a short conversation with the young men. There will be Allen Ferguson, Michael Mortimer, Bill and Ki-ki at the bar in the early evening hours, and maybe "practically everyone" latter on at night.

Almost all of the gay bars have tried the dancers attempting to gather a thirsty group that spends money. The young men usually dance just for the tips. Many are attractive, and there are always some that are less appealing. "Numbers" seems to have attracted more of the entertainment probably because of the windowless bar, the dark lights, and the tackiness of the the performers, not the patrons.

There is a man standing naked who plays the pin-ball machines at the opposite end of the bar. Even with the eyes adjusted, no one seems to mind. Most of the customers are locals since "Numbers" is several blacks off Duval, and it can be quite a walk for tourists.

If you go down one block further to White Street, you are far enough away from the tourists who frequent Duval to see a lot of the local color and excitement of the people who live here. It is a heavily Cuban community with coffee bars, restaurant, art galleries, junk shops, a Fausto's grocery, small conch houses, and the working class at their leisure. There are schools and churches, a gas station that has a deli with the best fried chicken in town, kids playing and animals everywhere. Some people feel it is the heart-beat of Key West, and they predict it will become more popular, and it is certainly less expensive, than Duval Street. We'll wait and see.

In any changing town, and practically all towns are changing, there are always those that speak as a "voice of doom". Key West has its own group. Prices are too high. Electricity is too expensive. There are too many t-shirt shops. Morals are going to hell. It's not like it used bo be. Duval Street is like Disneyland. Getting complaints from locals is not difficult. Many will attack you with our problems before you ask. Yet, the complainer is still here.

White Street gives the visitor the opportunity to see Key West as many of the locals see it. It's a mix of commercial and residential, of businesses and homes. The businesses sell to the locals, a grocery store, a second-hand clothing shop, a paint store, a Cuban coffee window. There are also antique stores, art galleries, insurance companies, real estate offices, and restaurants. Many who live around White Street don't even get downtown to Duval often, simply leaving the commerical tourist for the tourists.

THE 900 BLOCK
Truman St. to Olivia St.

"Cafe Bianco"

After a t-shirt shop is a small French restaurant on the right (east) side of Duval with a very French menu as well as atmosphere, with wicker seated chairs. You can eat either inside or out. The building was once the home of "Lighthouse Cafe" operated by Gail Brockway, who now operates "Cafe Blue".

"Lotza Pasta"

Beside the French restaurant is a house with gingerbread trim, which states something of its history. Around 1899, 100 years ago, there was a shortage of the Victorian trim in Key West. There were houses being built without trim, a special decoration extremely popular with the homeowner, and an indicator of social position. Even houses that were built in the Bahamas and transported by boat to Key West were often without the Victorian trim.

A couple of years went by and finally a boat loaded with the "X"-within-the-circle arrived from Cuba, and the load of gingerbread was quickly sold. The mahogany trim was used as porch trim, but 915 Duval also had a wooden gate with a large "X"-within-the-circle. Several houses with this trim include the Spanish Consulate's House, built in 1890 at 1001 Eaton Street. The house was bought by Alfronso-Carrasco in 1906; it was less than 100 feet from the Gulf. You can assume a house with the large "X"-within-the-circle trim was built somewhere between 1898 to 1903 if it is the original trim. (Notice the top right picture on the front cover.)

A very handsome woman named Mary bought 915 Duval and moved into the building with her Asian boyfriend and one of her two grown sons, where she opened a restaurant downstairs called "White Elephant". She ran it successfully for five or more years while the family lived upstairs. The restaurant was only open for dinner. The waiters, even Mary herself, would cross the street and go to "Claire Restaurant" to carry back alcohol drinks because the "White Elephant" did not have a liquor license.

Another group of people opened "Savanah's" and specialized in Southern American food with tables set in the front yard running to the sidewalk. The smell of Southern cooking including cornbread filled the air. The portions were typically Southern also.

The new owners of "Lotza Pasta" started redoing the building again in 1997, and the restaurant is again open with a different menu.

"Dynasty Chinese Restaurant"
Halfway down the left (west) side of the 900 block across the street is a double-story building containing an excellent Japanese restaurant run by a family that lives above the restaurant. They have always kept to themselves and continue to produce economical and quality oriental food. When they first opened ten years ago, I thought it strange that they served a salad with their specialty dishes like chop suey. Beer/wine, but no liquor.

There's a vacant lot and a few single-story shops and a new two story structure on Walton Lane, an alley to the guesthouse toward the Hemingway House. This cornor property was home to Richard Heyman for many years and contained Gingerbread Square Gallery in a jungle patio setting. The tropical jungle was replaced with a building that ran parallel with Walton Lane, a two-story built in 1996, which now houses Tikal Trading Company.

Great Southern Gallery
Richard Heyman sold the Gingerbread Square Gallery space to Kathleen and Richard Moody, who not only continued their own gallery but also added art supplies. Richard Moody is a talented artist plus he refinished old automobiles. Many charity auctions were held at the Great Southern Gallery. He also plays great jazz saxophone.

The first Gingerbread Square Gallery
Actually, the first gallery was in the 900 building, where the Irish bar is now. It started as a shop with furniture and assessories. Richard Heyman and I had bought the two buildings, and we wanted a small shop although we were aware that we were on the "wrong end" of Duval. We went to New York to shop. Unfortunately both of our tastes seemed to run to more expensive ware than we had intended to handle, but we bought blindly anyway. Mexican straw chairs. A zebra-skin rug. Expensive and fine china. Many ceramic pieces with shells. All with a certain flair. But, the store was not an immediate success. In fact, it was never a success.

The building across the street came up for sale. It was an "L"-shaped property with a house on Olivia Street and a building on Duval at one time The Three Bears Grocery. Richard and I bought it, and we sold off the house on Olivia, which eventually after a fire became part of the Wicker Guesthouse with the backyard an extension of the lot.

Mayor Richard Heyman

I met Rich when we were both freshmen at Ohio State University. We lived in the same dormitory. We were both discovering that we were gay but we didn't have the human anxieties, frustrations, or pains that many gays suffer in "coming out". Specifically, we shared a sense of humor and many secrets. We were never sexually involved. We became friends and were business partners, 50-50 on everything, for 42 years.

I always called him Rich rather than Dick or Richard. I have no idea why.

Rich was from Grand Rapids, Ohio, a farm boy who was tall, handsome, masculine and gay. He was a high school basketball star in a class with a limited number of male students. His mother had children when she was first married; many years later she had Rich, who was raised with nieces and nephews his age. He was the first of the Heymans to go to college.

I had wandered hesitantly into a gay bar in Columbus, Ohio, called "The Blue Feather", and there was this guy who lived on the same floor of the dormitory as I. We eventually shared several apartments but only as friends, not lovers.

I thought I had found the ideal college apartment with two big bedroom, paid the deposit and we moved in the next day. We had been asked to leave the last apartment because I had washed my pants, put pants stretchers in them so they needed no ironing, and hung them above the bathroom heater. They caught on fire and filled the apartment with smoke. I put out the fire, opened the front window to push out the smoke, and Rich was walking home from class. We were politely asked to vacate at the end of the month. My reasoning was that we were above a pizza shop anyway, and the apartment didn't smell very good.. The same night as we had moved into the apartment with large rooms, Rich was in his bedroom and I was in mine, the doors flung open and Rich yelled he was being attacked by bed bugs. We slept on the floor of a friend's apartment that night and got our money back the next morning. We moved into the left side of a duplex apartment above a grocery store, and we took in another roommate. The three of us and the three gay guys in the right side apartment lived in that apartment for our last two years of college, and we became life-long friends.

Rich and I would laugh later at the time the grocer came up and complained that all of his cereal boxes had fallen off the shelf. That was when Randy was teaching us all to Charleston. (One could easily scare Rich.) I climbed on the store shed roof while Rich was taking a bath, went to the bathroom window and yelled. He came down the outside stairs naked and caught me as I exited the roof, hysterical I had scared him. Pure physical abuse, but it was worth it.

When we graduated, we went separately into the Army but kept in contact. I settled in Miami, Florida. He kept to Ohio becoming "Sir Richard" in hair styling, and he would teach school, radio announce and sold shrubbery door to door.

He would visit me in Florida. I had taught a couple of years at Coral Gables High School, and I had an apartment. Rich would come down for a week and always stay longer, and we would laugh and have fun. He was my best friend.

We pooled our money and starting buying properties in Coconut Grove that I would fix to resell. We invested and split 50 - 50. We went through several pieces of property that sold quickly. Coconut Grove was the artsy spot at that time. Eventually, we bought a house on Packer Street in Key West. Rich moved to Key West.

The freedom of Key West, the opportunity to be completely yourself, the acceptance of gays was a quality that we had both not experienced. I remained in Miami teaching college but saying nothing of being gay, and I would visit Key Wet on weekends, having built a studio apartment over 900 Duval. Rich had a greater degree of freedom, and was more comfortable in a small town.

Rich became involved in politics. Since being gay meant little in Key West, he had no reason to hide (or lie) about himself, and the newspaper had to include his sexuality practically every time he hit the paper. He became City Commissioner for four years, Mayor of Key West for two years, did not run for a two-year term, re-ran for Mayor for two more years.

Rich liked the spotlight. He had an unbelieveable ability to remember everyone's name and information about them. He was very likeable. Although I did not agree with all his views, I kept quiet and supported him emotionally and physically. I was still teaching college.

I have never known or been told of anything Rich Heyman did was illegal or corrupt. Immoral, maybe.

Rich had a particular need for recognition, but he did not expect the publicity of his sex life. He hated "... the old gay mayor" label. He would have preferred to be known as the "mayor of Key West and also gay". He bucked the major bubba system of obvious crime and corruption. The crimes and problems of a small fishing town were not solved as it was growing in a different direction, but not in size.

In the late 60s, Richard Heyman and I bought a building at 905 Duval, the one-time Three Bears Grocery Store, which had sold horse meat during the war, was exposed, and went out of business years before we bought it. We had no money to buy merchandise. We decided to paint the interior, take paintings on consignment, and open an art gallery, Gingerbread Square Gallery. Marion Stephens ran the major art gallery at that time.

There was a back freezer room which we turned into an "erotic gallery", not allowing children to roam in. We could place practically anything non-erotic in the Freezer, and it would sell. We expected to sell the whole building hopefully along with the new business.

There was a vacant lot next door owned by a local man, and the owners before us rented the lot for $65 a month. We knew this fee was paying the taxes, and he would never sell. We did not contract to rent the vacant lot but told the owner we wanted to buy the lot. A couple of months later on a Friday evening, he called and said he would take

$5,000 for the lot in nothing larger than a $20 bill. He wanted the money on Sunday but banks were closed on weekends. Rich went one way, and I went the other. From everyone we knew, we borrowed whatever extra money our friends had. It is not easy to borrow $5,000 on a weekend. We bought the lot. On Monday, we revisited our friends paying back the money we had borrowed.

The building did not sell and with more tourists, the business kept improving. Richard and I worked the floor taking in the work of local artists and selling the paintings. We originally took local artist's work on consignment with 25% for the gallery, 75% for the artist. (Today's breakdown is usually 50%-50%, but often 60% for the gallery, 40% for the artist.) I sold my interest in Gingerbread Square Art Gallery to him.

Rich lived in an apartment on the ground floor of 904 Duval, across the street, and he was building and repairing the next three lots across Walton Lane, which we owned. He lived in what used to be the three Walton sisters' home. But across the lane would be the new gallery the southern two lots that contained conch houses, and he was building a new gallery showroom in the jungle garden, which he moved into as a living room. He moved from 904 Duval across the lane to his jungle-like gallery.

The old Three Bears Grocery Store across the street stood vacant for awhile, but a workout studio moved into it somehow erecting a juice bar and building a swimming pool. That was competition to Dennis Bitner's Key West Club Baths on Truman. There were rumblings of an incurable disease among gays, and the new health club's rebuilding of a second story with little rooms that needed no air conditioning because of the large fans on the roof. They were designed by Manford Ible. The desire for natural air conditioning never was realized.

The first gallery location was taken over by a restaurant called "Cocoanuts", which lasted only a season. Another renter was a work-out studio that built a pool and seemed to want to build a place like the gay baths, but that business was declining as physical fitness came into fad. Another chain restaurant, "Viva Zapata", kept it for a few years, but that also failed, and the building stood vacant.

When Rich later sold the Gingerbread Square property to Richard and Kathleen Moody for Great Southern Gallery, Rich moved the business to 901 Duval, the first floor under my new apartment, and reopened Gingerbread Square Gallery. He was there a few years and moved to the gallery's present location in the 1200 block. He sold to Sal Salinaro, a conch artist, and Jeff Birn, a dentist.

Richard Heyman died September 16, 1994.

"Claire Restaurant"

At Olivia and Duval was yet another restaurant/bar that opened in the late 60s on the Walton property, which contained the Walton sister's house and the bakery beside it, 904 and 900 Duval. The restaurant was called "The Affair" and run by Tom Saruta.

There was a young man who played the piano but never sang named Bobbie Nesbitt. He later was a headliner at the Pier House and is currently entertaining in San Francisco at the Fairmont Hotel. "The Affair" was on the less populated and less popular end of town. It closed the next year.

Nesbitt at "The Affair"

Marvin and Claire Paige, he from New York and she from New Orleans to New York, leased the property in the middle 70s and turned the space into "Claire Restaurant/Bar". Marvin knew the restaurant business well and his wife knew the theatre and entertaining as well as being a successful artist. Rich and I maintained the rentals of the upstairs apartments. "Claire Restaurant" became the most popular night spot for interesting dining and a wild, social bar, the most "in" spot since the "Monster".

The atmosphere was charming with inside and outside patio dining and the tourist's favorite game of people watching. A customer could draw and color on the butcher block paper table cloths, drink and get drunk without any interference. The bar had stiff drinks for a little more than average prices. The food was different for Key West, but the restaurant kept many of the local favorite foods. Good food, good waiters, good times for all. Jason Robards said in "A Thousand Clowns", "With all these successful people around, where are all of our young failures going to come from?"

There was one young, attractive, successful writer from New York who had an "unusual" warning sign. When she was sober, she had quite beautiful eyes. The more she drank, and she would usually drink sitting across from her now estranged husband, the more each eye had a tendency to move toward her nose. She often drank until her eyes were close to her nose, cross-eyed, and at that point, you knew she was drunk.

Since her, I have met an older woman from whom you can get an indication of how drunk/sober she is by where her arms are. If her arms are at her sides, she's sober. The more she drinks, the more her arms start upward. At waist level of gesturing, she's tolerable. She's impossible when her arms get above her head.

Most important were at the people at "Claire". Everyone was there. Writers. Painters. Business people. The rich and the poor. Tennessee Williams held court. Bobby Nesbitt was one of the first entertainers at "Claire'" and although he rarely sang at the time, the piano bar would be the center of attention as people drank and dined. "I never dreamed any mere physical experience could be so stimulating ..." Katherine Hepburn in "The African Queen".

As five people, four tourists and a local, were sitting close to the raised-level outside patio closest to Duval enjoying dinner, Paul Ware knew the person walking up the street. The walker put his opened palm through the white fence and begged "Do you have $25 for a chateaubriand for two?" to Paul's horrified guests. "Go, and never darken my towels again!" Groucho Marx's line in "Duck Soup".

Eddie, a local customer of "Claire", was probably born into too much money, Chicago beer money, and most people assumed that he received monthly checks to keep him away from the beer business. As a man in his early 50s, he continued to become more strange as the years went by.

He lived in a very large Spanish-style house, drove an old Rolls convertible without a cloth top but with a lawnmower in the back seat. He insisted on doing most of the work on the house himself. Wires sticking out would be simply wrapped, shoved back into the wall, and plastered over. It was said that when he flushed the upstairs john, the garage door would go up.

At one point in his building, he invited a dozen people for dinner. The dining room was very enchanting with beautiful silver and dinnerware, a table set for royalty in a room with red velvet draperies and crystal chandelier. The problem was that he had not completed the roof, and a dozen people ate and drank to cross beams open to the sky. Another beautiful night. Elizabeth Perkins said, "Maybe we should just grow peckers and join up" in "Sweet-hearts Dance".

The politicians would come to "Claire" after their meetings. Jimmy Mira, Joel Kofort, City Manager, and Jody, and others including June, Rich's secretary, Peter Ilchuk, Virginia Panico. If you wanted a few words, you would know where Rich was.

Eddie went to "Claire Restaurant" barefooted in his bib-overalls and carried a bushel basket. He ordered a martini and asked to see a menu. Eating at the bar was not unusual at "Claire". He ordered. From the basket he pulled a doily, all eight pieces of a silver place setting, a lace napkin, a wine glass and a silver candelabra with candles that he lit. As each course was served, he put the food on his place setting and continued to have dinner. When dinner was finished, he put his goods back into the bushel basket, paid the bill and tipped generously, and left. Money was no object.

He had a lady friend called Liz, (Betty French). They would argue over stupid things, and she would sometimes stay in a small apartment off his large kitchen. She awoke one morning to find Eddie laying concrete blocks across her doorway from the kitchen, so she packed her clothes, crawled out a window, and left. "When my mother took me to see 'Snow White', everyone fell in love with Snow White. I immediately fell for the wicked queen." Woody Allen in the film "Annie Hall".

As the members of Eddie's family died, he became wealthier and wealthier. A childless aunt left him one fortune. Another came from a cousin. He would parade around his house naked, which was not a pretty sight, or in an old fur coat. Had he not been so wealthy, he would have been institutionalized. Toward the later years of his life, his only friend was Liz, for only she would tolerate his behavior. She died before Eddie, and he continued to wander the world, throwing money in all directions, a pathetic sort of soul.

There were only two lesbians that I knew at this period, a heavy-set woman named Tiny, who supposedly killed her baby by accidentally rolling over on her, and a little girl from West Virginia that could pick up an iron four-legged bath tub and throw it on her truck.

"Claire Restaurant" introduced the first girls' gay bar on the island by having a weekly "girls' night" on Thursday evening. Some called it a meeting of the local construction company, jokingly, the "Tongue-in-Groove Society", but the house would pick up more and more members each week it was open. Seldom-seen girls began to appear. Key West got its first guesthouse exclusively for women.

Most of these girls were not the stereotype rough and tumble expected in a semi-gay bar. Many were professional business women, and dressed it. Many held responsible jobs. Some were wealthy. Others met the stereotype. The greatest difference was that these women had jobs, responsibility, and independence, and the freedom to choose their own life styles, and they had the money to back their decisions. Lesbians were here to stay.

One Thursday evening, I was sitting at "Claire" beside a blind girl, and she asked me if I would help her to the ladies' room. She stretched out the wand she was holding, which became a walking stick. I helped her down the stairs, and across the patio into the dining room, and waited outside the bathroom door. We returned and were seated at the bar. She was pleasant, and we had a couple of drinks. She said, "I'm going; got to drive home. It's getting late." She got up and walked out the door, and I sat there stunned.

The waiters at "Claire" were fun, many having worked at Province Town or New York. The restaurant would book parties. At first, two parties were especially threatening to the waiters, a Saturday night party of lawyers and their wives followed the next Saturday night by a motorcycle group from Miami.

A few dozen lawyers and their wives would surround the bar, the men in dark suits and paisley ties, the women with hair groomed exactly alike, neat, conservative dresses with strings of pearls. They ordered beer or a simple mixed drink and were aggressive to the bartender, and loud. They tipped poorly if at all. They all ate chicken and had no wine.

The next Saturday, the waiters and waitresses were afraid at the thought of the motorcyclists coming from Miami and, perhaps, not understanding the waiters' outfits of Harley-Davidson t-shirts. The few dozen Levi-clad men, unshaved or bearded, in leather jackets with chains, and boots with their tattooed girl friends in short denim skirts and halter-tops surrounded the bar.

They were polite and ordered pinacoladas, martinis, and fancy drinks, and were friendly to the bartender. They had many drinks, but the bar was quiet and civilized. The motorcycle group tipped well and had dinners of roast beef or steak or seafood with an appropriate wine. The leader of the pack made arrangements with Claire for the group to return the next day for lunch. Marie Dressler said in "Dinner at Eight", "If there's one thing I know, it's men. I ought to. It's been my life's work."

Something must be said to how the waiters were able to identify the big tippers of an evening. If the waiter did not know them or had not heard of them from another waiter, he had few clues. Ther was a difference between the out-of-town visitors and the locals. Where the out-of-town guests may have dressed differently, they were at least dressed in somewhat proper clothing. The locals with money did not have to dress if they did not care to. The locals did not have BMW's and Mercedes', nor did the men wear jewelry except for a few golden chains around their necks. There was not proper place in Key West for the wealthy to live, and you could rarely tell the price of the house by the address. A house on White street may be large or small, expensive or inexpensive. The person fast in paying the bill may be rich or pretending. Manners could give the person away. The really rich never talked about money; they didn't have to, and they had learned not to be rude. Somehow, the waiters knew. The domineering, agressive snob who disliked everything, had nothing. Beware of a man too well dressed.

As the 70s approached and developed, "Claire Restaurant" went through many transitions, but it never lost its popularity or spark. Restaurants were opening and closing all over town. Marvin and Claire opened a "Claire Restaurant" in New York City and took many of the staff. Rusty was one of the few regular staff that did not go to New York with many of the other bar people and waiters. He stayed back to tease Gregory George, who is now a well known photographer but was a waiter at "Clair", by calling him "poodle breath". Eventually the ten-year lease on the Duval property ran out.

Marvin and Claire were divorced after this, Claire headed for Mexico and eventually settled in her home territory of New Orleans. Marvin ran the New York restaurant, eventually remarried, spent some winter days in Key West. He changed the New York restaurant's name to "Chelsea Lobster Company", which he still runs.

"Bogarts" and the Casablanca

When Rich and I sold 904 and 900, the building was in a sad state of repair, and it did not sell as rapidly as we had hoped.The building went through a year of remodeling and opened within a year, which was the legal time limitation, as "My Funny Brother". Rich was too involved with politics and had could not be of help and support getting the property to a place whee it could be sold. It was sold to Louise Cutterback of Palm Beach and the Kehoe brothers, originally from Ireland. (It is now "Bogart's", a tropical Irish pub, and "Casablanca," a guesthouse with a cocktail bar at the top of the front steps.)

If you were standing on the left (west) corner of Olivia Street and Duval, to your right (east) one block would be "Club International", to the left (west) would be the Hemingway House.
"Club International"
Newer places were constantly trying to cash in on the market, but the success of a place is based on how long it lasts, and many were short lived. One business that lasted was in the "Simonton Street Station" building where the Holt brothers, two popular musicians, and their wives entertained many straight audiences.

The building was rented to several different groups, some trying to make it into a gay club for men. The experience of Thursday night girls' night at "Claire Restaurant" should have hinted that the times were moving so there would eventually be a bar for lesbians. The bar was leased by Donnie, and it rather grew into a girls' bar without much preplanning or analyzing.

At one time Travis, who lived across the street, used to work at the bar. (His old house is pictured in the lower-center, front cover, the typical two-story conch house.) Travis moved to 832 Olivia, but he still stops in at "Club I" which is about one-third gay men. Donnie, the owner, wants even a higher percentage of gay men, better profit.

Eventually as more lesbians arrived in town, females dominated the bar, but lesbians do not seem to roam as much as gay males. "Club International" remains the major lesbian bar in Key West. "It has that new car smell. Finest smell in the world ... except maybe pussy." Keith Gordon in "Christine".

Rick Worth painted the large mural on the Olivia Street side of the building showing the Seven Mile Bridge and distorting a little history in a comical way. (A piece of the mural on back cover, upper-left.)

Dyke Island

Much later, two ladies, Lynn Parker and Linda Shearer, gained control of a 120 acre isolated island 27 mile from Key West and they tried to sell T.H.E. (Total Homosexual Environment) Island of the Keys, a plotted development of more than 300 lots called Buccaneer Beach Estates in 1989. Lots sold for $5,000. and many were sold to both gay men and lesbians as campsites. A few trailers were moved onto the island. Weekends were spent completely isolated from Key West.

County politics and the environmentalists strongly objected and soon made the ladies remove the footbridge that ran from the mainland to the island, and the idea failed. Calculated political confusion made the girls replant mangrove plants, repair roads, pay fines, and challenge ownership. Lynn is still in town and publishes "What's Happening".

Hemingway House

Aside from the weather, one of the earliest tourists attractions was the home of one of the greatest American writers, Ernest Hemingway. It is a block to the left on the corner of Whitehead and Olivia Streets. His writings continue to capture the imagination and interest of school children and adults alike.

In 1931 Ernest Hemingway and his wife, Pauline, bought the house at 907 Whitehead Street for $8,000 at a tax sale on the courthouse steps. The property was in desperate need of repair, but it seemed to be a fair price for the property at that time, even though the Depression was starting. The strange house made of limestone had been built by Asa Tift (some say William Kerr), who brought the ironwork for the house's construction from New Orleans. The style of the house was not unlike many found in New Orleans. Double porches were added, and a walkway was created from the upstairs to his backyard studio over the garage where Hemingway did his writing.

Although some say he converted a cistern, Pauline built the first swimming pool at a cost of $20,000; it ran 65 feet and was fed by two salt water wells. When Ernest Hemingway returned from Europe on a writing assignment, the extravagant cost of the swimming pool infuriated him and, so the story goes, he threw his last penny into the pool.

Fame came to Hemingway early in his life, and he demanded privacy for his career, but his home became a show place. He built around the property a brick wall, the bricks being paving bricks from some destroyed city street.

Much is made of Hemingway's reputation as a heavy drinker. Many bars of Key West would like to have the publicity that Hemingway drank mainly at that bar, but the truth is that Hemingway probably drank at practically every bar on the small island. A small brass sign on the "80l Bar" says "Hemingway never drank here". It is true that he would gather with his friends, sometimes on a couple of days' spree, and get drunk.

What is not often emphasized is that he was a very disciplined writer, not drinking while writing. He would awaken in the early morning, cross the bridge to his studio, and often not return until the late afternoon. He would then, sometimes but usually often, go for drinks. We only have to look at the amount of work he produced while living on the island to realize that he could not have produced at the quantity or quality of writing under a drunken stupor.

He was also "on assignment" often in Europe. He was in Paris in 1940 working with a fellow writer who eventually published 13 books, Martha Gellhorn, who became the next Mrs. Hemingway. They moved to Cuba and were divorced in 1946. Martha Gellhorn was Ernest Hemingway's third wife and she died February 18, 1998, in London.

Another myth is that Hemingway had many cats in Key West. The famed six-toed cat was owned by a neighbor and is called a polydactl (more toes). It can be traced from England to Boston by the Puritans and probably once freed in Key West. While Hemingway lived in Key West, he had only two cats. After moving to Cuba with Martha Gellhorn, they had over 50 cats, but that did not happen in Key West.

His home with Pauline in Key West continues to be a tourist attraction, one of the most successful, privately-owned attractions in town. Larry Harvey sells tickets at the front gate by the brick wall.

In 1998 a local painter named Loren was trimming a window in the Hemingway house, and a tourist asked, "Do you live here?" probably meaning Key West rather than in the Hemingway house. Loren answered "Yes". The tourist continued, "Can you tell me where on the island is the ocean?" She caught herself in the ridiculous question and stated, "Oh, I know that's a dumb question. It is where the sun sets." Loren went for a drink.

Larry Harvey

Dr. Lawrence Nelson Harvey is from Virginia, graduating from Dickinson College and eventually getting his Doctorate from Porcia Law School. While teaching at Porcia, he purchased the Louisa Mae Alcott home on Pickney Street and later found it had been a brothel, to his delight.

As a teacher and administrator as headmaster, he was working for a private school in Coconut Grove when he found Key West around 1966. He would travel by bus to Key West to sing at the Ambassador Hotel and the Sands. He was a favorite of many people with a strong voice and could often be heard at the "Pigeon House", delighting the guests.

Larry became a guide at the Hemingway House using his entertaining skills, his delightful sense of humor, and his outrageous laugh to amuse the many people who tour the famous private home. He sat first under an umbrella and eventually his own sales house to sell tickets, and he tells marvelous stories of the tourists' strange questions concerning the Hemingway cats. He adds his own spice.

Larry was a friend of Jerry Herman and introduced "Hello Dolly" to Keys' audiences. He has been a welcomed surprise to his yearly participation in the "Key West Classics" and when he is matched with Denys Fitzpatrick in a number, well, that's the tall and short of it. Allen Ferguson is Larry Harvey's companion.

At a Christmas party many years ago held by Sally Lewis, Larry was to perform as Santa Clause. Sally's father was a tall, stately, large framed man. Larry was much shorter and thinner. Sally's father's Santa Clause costume was not an "ideal fit", but with the addition of many pillows, Larry became a fat, jolly Santa Clause. He dressed upstairs in Sally's house, and he was suppose to enter the backyard by going down the outside wooden staircase. At the top landing, Larry started his "ho-ho-hos", his belt broke, and through his laughter was a new meaning to Christmas.

THE 800 BLOCK
Olivia St. to Petronia St.

The 800 and 700 blocks of Duval are heavily shopping blocks and there is a great deal of variety of small, independent merchants that have something unique to sell.   There are art galleries, towel shops, gift shops, clothing shops and many more. There are also places to eat from juice stands to restaurants. To many, the two block area with the entrance to Bahama Village is typical of a small town shopping area with everything, shops, restaurants, bars, and art galleries, within walking distance. The pace is leisurely, and the merchants and owners are often the salespeople.   It is an area well protected by walking police, often an area of husbands and wives shopping together. There is a constant blend of tourists and locals, and few street hawkers. There are your local homeless, a never resolved problem.

"Croissants de France"

In the 800 block on the eastern side of Duval is a bakery which makes much of the bread and pastries used by various restaurants in the neighborhood, and equal to those of Paris. Although the service counters are often crowded, the quality is well worth the wait and locals use it constantly.   Try a delightful coffee and croissant for breakfast, a croissant with crab meat and chicken for lunch.

A bakery truck loads early in the morning the fresh pasteries and breads to be delivered to many stops prior to breakfast, the bakery staff starting at four in the morning. (Even in a small tourist city, there are night workers such as guards, reservation desks attendants, bookkeepers, newspaper men, telephone operators, etc. They sleep while the tourist town parties in the daytime.)

Cuba, Cuba

On the same side of the street, beside the bakery, is a shop/gallery that carries unique merchandis by Cuban artists from paintings to strange little Spanish-flavored houses in miniature. Obviously important to the Latins, the merchandise is very exciting and implies a quality of production that can be expected when Cuba is lead toware democracy. It is owned by Larry Winters.

Tropical House

Dennis Beaver had a guesthouse in the middle of the 900 block, sold it and re-bought another in the middle of the 800 block where he lived for many years with his friendly grandmother. The small guesthouse is very intimate and charming and is in an excellent location. Very active in the Key West Business Men's Guild, he is a leader of the gay community and respected in local activities. It is not unusual to see Beaver riding down the street on his bicycle with a wicker chair held in one hand, a find or a repair job.

Duval House

Two double-storied, grand old houses have been joined with a backyard pool and apartment into a charming guesthouse called Duval House across the street from Tropical House. It was one of the first guesthouses in the early 60's. Two men, Billl and Bob, came from California, saw the potential of Key West, sold out in California and built one of the most outstanding guesthouses in town which was immediately gay friendly. When Bill died, Ben sold the guesthouse. By that time the property had extended to Center Street, a little-known street running parallel between Simonton and Duval.

There are many little back streets like Center Street that are seldom traveled by the tourists. The streets may only be eight feet wide, and in many cities they serve the same function as alleys, but because a street was often made in front of a row of cigar rollers' cottages, and stayed there because of use, they are popular for housing usually being less traveled than the main streets.

There are shops, churches, apartment houses, private homes both large and small on these little streets. One advanatage to Key West is that you cannot tell wealth by home address. Someone may live on Poorhouse Lane in a mansion. The street name is not an indicator of wealth nor is the section of town (with the possible exception of Truman Annex, which also has some "affordable", modest homes.)

The tourists

The travelers come to Key West feeling that the shop owners are really small town people with little sophistication. The tourist often try to use the techniques used in larger cities on the small shop merchants. "Can I get a 20% discount?" "I saw it cheaper up the street." "Can you forget about the tax?" "I wish you had it in blue." The merchant soon learn many of the tricks, and most are not willing to meet the tourist's demands. There are also some tourists who never bargain, never quibble, never downgrade and look at the products at asking price. Both types become the discussion of the salespeople at lunch or over a cup of coffee.

There is a misconception by the tourists that many of the salespeople and merchants of this tourist city are simply "left-overs", unable or unwilling to hold a respectable job in the larger cities. With few exceptions, nothing is further from the truth. Many of the merchants have had the technical experience of the larger businesses, and have chosen not to be a part. Generally, the merchants are well educated, but have bored playing the large city games.

The small shop merchants have had enough so they are willing to take a chance on their own abilities, and risk the possibility of insulting speculation from the tourists. Granted, some salespeople are dull, uninterested, cheap labor, but the owner being closer to his employees than in a large corporation can easily spot this attitude, and he /she is not often willing to pay the price. Yes, merchants can be arrogant. So can the shoppers.

"The 801 Bourbon Street Bar"

The names of the bars and often the ownerships change over 40-some years. As an example, the "Jungle Club" was a strip joint and eventually became "Big Daddy's" and when the Big Daddy's Liquor Group registered the name in Florida, "Big Daddy's" at 801 Duval became "Big Mama's". A fire gutted the building on the first morning of the new year at two o'clock. The second floor was completely destroyed but, as so often happens in Key West, it was repairable.

Nick Ryder bought the building and the liquor license and opened it as a kind of sailing sports bar. Nick Ryder sold to Peter Ryder (no relation) and it became "The 801 Bar". (Back cover, bottom left.)

Peter Ryder had run a large gay bar in the northeast, and had sold out. He also ran the "801" for many years as an openly gay bar. The bar against the back wall was eventually moved to a center bar. The opened upstairs was closed to make another bar upstairs. A small building beside was converted into a back-room bar on the first floor. According to Gary Young in "Point Break", "you're a real blue-flame special: young, dumb, and full of cum." (In 1998 Peter Ryder sold the bar and license to a new group, which had opened "The Bourbon Street" across the street, and the bar was later referred to as "801 Bourbon Street".)

One interesting aspect of "The 801 Bar" was that it was at the entrance to Bahama Village at Petronia Street, with a large metal and concrete entrance donated by Ed and Joan Knight. Bahama Village was predominantly black, but never exclusively so. When the later restoration of houses started in the early 70s, many of the significant homes in Bahama Village had not been previously modernised in bad taste.

Although there was little direct racial prejudice, there was some confusion. The city commission did not allow the blacks of Key West to have much of a voice in the government. Charles Major, Sr., was the head of the National Association for the Advancement of Colored People for years, and well respected in both the white and the black communities. His son, Emory Major, Jr., tried to lead in his father's footsteps, but presented few new directions except for the militant themes. His major idea was to get blacks into city government. He backed a program of redistricting the city into six districts, one commissioner elected from each district with an additional elected mayor from any district to replace the five-member at large commission that had controlled the local government. One of the districts was predominantly black and Emory was elected from that district by running against his father as the district's representative. The son lasted only a few months. The bribery charge against him cost him the seat on the commission, but the Governor of Florida appointed another black for his position, Carmen Turner, and Emory accomplished what he had planned, even if he did not share the spotlight.

The 22-block enclave was named Bahama Village in 1988, with special emphasis upon the black heritage and the black settlers and conchs of the community. In 1998, the conch train promoter, Ed Swift, designed a new train stop in redoing a grand house on Whitehead and Petronia attempting to attract tourists to Bahama Village. Currently the mix is about 60% black and 40% white, but the blacks can live anywhere in town they desire and can afford. The lack of affordable housing for all has attracted many whites into a lesser expensive section of Key West.

Unfortunately, the original owners of the conch train station on Petronia made significant profit from the sale of their house, but not close to what the prices would eventually be. Todays black owners of property in Bahama Village are alert to the constant increase in real estate prices. The property is now, as always, not inexpensive, but at "market value", and that market is high all over Key West.

There was a $8,340 grant given to the Bahama Conch Community Land Trust to record eight interviews of the people and their memories of the early developments in what is now called Bahama Village. It includes a charming interview by Idalene Van Dyke, a conch who lived most of her life at 412 Division Street (now Truman Avenue). Even some land funds are being used to build additional housing in the community.

"The 801 Bar" is an important piece of property, not because of any event that happened there but because it was an integrated bar most of its life. The Petronia entrance to Bahama Village was a barrier to some tourists, but locals did not feel a threat. Key West took easily to mandated integration because the island had always been integrated. Blacks and whites drank together at "Big Mama's" as they do now at "801 Bourbon Street".

Uncle Bill

Uncle Bill had been in the Marines, stationed in Key West in 1944. Originally from Michigan, he came back in the early 60s to Key West and bought a house.

Bill had been reared in a financially successful family, and he was an alert businessman. Uncle Bill had a passion for yard sales, junk sales, and building materials. He often had his parrot on his shoulder, sitting on a stained towel. Bill would wander from yard sale to yard sale.

His house on Von Phister became a mecca for stained glass windows, sliding glass doors, glass blocks, concrete blocks. He would combine his materials into a wonderfully whimsical house containing many rooms of all different types of materials. He would take in boarders to help him with his projects. A half coral wall would turn to brick, to concrete blocks, to an altar niche, to a bird cage. The bathrooms and kitchen were done in pieces of tile he would find or people would give him. If you were finished tiling your bath and had some tiles left, you would call Uncle Bill.

You would think the neighbors would be horrified, but the very opposite was true. When neighbors found a good buy or leftover building supplies, they would take their find to Uncle Bill. Every so often, Bill would throw a party for neighbors and friends to show off his new addition. He yearly gave a party called "George Workington's Wash Day". Bill was fond of the earlier actors and actresses and had good humor. "I never see pictures where the man's tits are bigger than the woman's." Groucho Marx referring to Victor Mature in "Samson and Delilah". Not to like Uncle Bill was not to like Key West.

A society leader

"She only said 'no' once --- and then she couldn't hear the question." George E. Stone in "43nd Street". Another local character was a prominent older local lady who wore two hearing aids that were only mildly successful. She also liked the younger sailors, and she would tell this tale on herself.

While she was in the ecstasy of love making with a young sailor, one of the hearing aids had been bumped aside. The passion rose and soon the other was useless. Having finished this late afternoon affair, the young sailor, getting out of bed and walking toward the bathroom said, "Where's a towel?" She politely responded, "And I love you too, darling."

But characters were not only a few people; they were many of the people in town. Someone commented, "It's the only island insane asylum."

THE 700 BLOCK
Petronia St. to Angela St.

Somewhere in the 50s or 60s, probably in the 700 block of Duval Street, was a nightclub called "The Tomato Patch", and in those early days of integration, the bar was patronized by both blacks and whites without much difficulty. The vacant lot beside it was a burned out building and had a black and white slab flooring and the front wall still standing. It looked more like a movie set than the remains of a building.

"Bourbon Street"

Over the years, a bicycle shop gave way to a spa and hot tub business on this property. An Italian restaurateur called Twigs (Anita Branchu) rented the building beside the open courtyard, added French doors to it, and had a delightful patio. The Boston northsider, Twigs, eventually had enough of the business, closed shop, and left town, but she returned. (She now does an impersonation of Frank Sinatra, who died in May of 98, at local clubs.) The same space eventually became the Duval Deli.

In 1991 the building and patio space were rebuilt into a two-story, conch-style structure which contains the Duval Deli and Yo Sake. The upstairs was to be a restaurant, but plans sometimes do not come true. It is now occupied as the New Orleans Hotel.

Jimmy Gillian, maried with two children, and Joey Schroeder rented the space for the "Bourbon Street Bar" and eventually bought the building, added a back area with apartments, and a lot large enough for a pool, and they eventually bought the "801" from Peter Ryder and changed the name to "801 Bourbon".

Bill Divins once owned La Bodega on the corner of Olivia and Simonton with his wife, Jay, and their two kids. It was really the first take-out sandwich place in town in the 60s. Jay and Bill had met in San Francisco, married, and returned to Key West. La Bodega was not only a corner deli, it was also a little grocery store.

It also became a place where people met and shared a cup of coffee, the really first of the coffee houses in Key West. You could sit either inside the restaurant-deli or on the benches of Simonton and

Olivia and watch the world walk by. I've seen people hired for small labor jobs, also a kind of employment office. A couple of people could run the whole operation; make a sandwich, pour coffee, sell bread or canned fruit, greet the neighbors, give direction, sell a pint of baked-beans, all within a few minutes. The restaurant is now the Siam House, a Thai restaurant.

Bill told me of another bar, but I have never been able to confirm its existence or location. (Bill knew not only the history of Key West but he knew a lot of the in-gossip of the island; an excellent source. What he didn't know, he made up.) Bill's description of the place was that it was a series of tin-roofed conch fronts with front porches circling a planted open area that was free to the sky. A piped grillwork contained water lines and electric fans; every 15 minutes the large fans would start and the water would pour down like a hurricane on the tin roofs. Bill said he opened and worked the bar, but within a year it was torched by locals.

Chittum's
Practically across Duval Street at the northeast corner of Petronia stood a large concrete one-story building that at one time was the Margaret Ann Grocery, and it grew to be the social center of the walking locals. Although not singularly important, turning grocery shopping into a social affair makes a statement about the people.
The idea of a grocery store as a social center has not been strange to the people. The same amusement is enjoyed today by Fausto's Food Palace. The Fausto family bought a grocery called The Gulf Stream on White Street as a second store around l996. The Margaret Ann Grocery went out of business and the building stood vacant in the 60s.

It was a warehouse of furniture when during the 60s there were few shops on the southern part of Duval, and the warehouse burned down. The lot remained vacant for years and a nephew or son inherited the lot and sold it.

A new building was started in 1990 and opened the next year as Chittum's. It has delightful clothes and yachting equipment and is definitely "up scale". The building and business again went up for sale in l998, and was sold, but the merchandise remains high quality.

"Club 2l", Petronia

Across Petronia Street from Chittum's in the 700 block is currently the "801 Bourbon". Thirty years earlier, it was called the "Jungle Bar", complete with bare-breasted dancing girls against the back wall. It was at the "Jungle Bar" that I met Cecil Baines. I was 23 and he must have been at least 40. He was a black bar owner of a late place on Petronia Street called "Club 21". It was a very comfortable bar that picked up more white customers in the summer when the predominately white bars closed early. You could hardly get in at midnight because of the crowd drinking inside and outside of the bar. When Cecil owned the bar, I am not sure he had a license, but he was one of the most influential people in town.

Cecil Baines taught me to play nickel-dime poker in the back room of his "Club 21". When I was contemplating a bad card choice, he'd wander behind me and give me a thump on the back of my head, and the three other black men seemed to know I was in training.

A wealthy woman staying at the Pier House had been robbed of her jewelry, some pieces which were family heirlooms. The woman's husband went to Cecil Baines knowing Cecil's knowledge of the community. Cecil called the husband on the phone an hour later and told him to go to the hotel room's door. There was the stolen property. Cecil knew everything that was happening in Key West.

I loved Cecil Baines, and he was protective of me probably because I did not hide my stupidity. That was obvious. He grew old and his son and beautiful daughter-in-law took over the bar, but they eventually got out of the business.

Although integration was in the 60s, I don't remember much black and white friction in Key West. The blacks of Key West have been here as long as the whites. Many of the families had come from the Bahamas and it is still not unusual to see a blue-eyed black. The demand for slaves brought the brown-eyed African blacks to America. Others came and settled on the island from the building of Flagler's railroad, as did some Oriental families who settled on the island generations earlier.

Gambling was a way of life in Key West. The island had roots in the pirate days when it was first discovered by Spaniards. It also had the Caribbean influences of dominoes, cards, dice, and cockfighting. The salvagers would bet on the possibility of a ship hitting the reef. There was always a card game going on somewhere. In the 1960's, everyone including the police knew about Cecil's back room, and you either went to it or turned your head. Into the 90s cockfighting was eliminated, but only to be replaced by a gambling ship. Betting on sports, the lotto games, and bridge are still standard forms of gambling here.

Along with gambling comes crime, and although there were few serious crimes, the small town had its share of burglaries, but little more. When tourism became popular there were hotel, motel thefts and thefts from automobiles, bicycle and mopeds, but few more serious crimes. Most crimes of burglary were linked to the need for money to buy drugs, or the more severe case of "a drug sale that went bad."

In the 60s when everyone seemed to know everyone else in their section of Key West, locals knew every step of criminals or slippery-fingered people, and their actions were easy to trace, identified by how much money they had to spend in the bars. Since marijuana has consistently been against the law, and there are many gays in their younger years, there is a different value related to the activity of smoking marijuana on the island. Pia Zadora suggested in "Hairspray", "Let's get naked ... and smoke!"

The Key West Police Department
In a City Manager form of government like Key West, the Chief of Police is responsible to the City Manager and the Key West City Commission. However, the City Manager can be fired by the City Commission. It is not very complex, but it opens the door to a great deal of political manipulation.

Over the years, we have had many city managers, conflict coming when the manager does something, or does not do somethng, to please outstanding political forces of the city. We are not divided by Republicans and Democrates, but we seem to be divided by political forces of (1) old time conchs, (2) newcomers, (3) hotel and motel people, (4) non conchs or newcomers, but those tht have been here, (5) old conch families with money and investments here, and (6) gays. Of course, someone could fit into a couple of categories. The Chief of Police must also contend with the police's union. Add all these factors, and the Chief of Police's position in Key West is like walking on and balancing eggs.

Remember the job that must be done. In a party city that loves their drugs, a tourist city that requires drugs, a city whose outstanding leaders have made money from drugs, drugs are against the law. In a town where favoritism has always been primary, bubbaism, the law must treat all equally. In a prejudical society, the law must have no prejudice. The Chief of Police's position comes with tenured officers, internal power playing, political favorites, and blackmail. Can the Chief of Police create a police force without stepping on toes?

(I lived on a Duval Street second floor apartment for more than 18 years, and although drugs are not my lifestyle, I could see and knew local drug dealers, pimps, whores, male and female prostitutes, thieves, beggers, and the drug salesmen and women. You can't live in a town of 23,000 and not know what is going on particularly when it is so obvious. At that time, we had police that rode by in cars, seldom stopping.)

Our situation has gotten a lot better particularly concerning the police who now walk or ride bikes, and are obious. We now have men, women, and gay cops.

We refuse the term "drug infested city" but look at what cannot be kept out of the newspaper, although they try, our police and jury dockets are full of drug cases. (If I know who is dealing, why don't the police?) As if we do not have enough trouble locally, Miami joins in. (I can still get any kind of drug in Key West within a few minutes.)

To our visitors, don't even try. We have undercover police that would rather throw a tourist in jail than a local who may be related to someone. If you are offered drugs for sale, the salesman could be a police officer also. Check the number of out-of-town drug arrests, and you should hesitate. If you must get high, get at least a legal high. (I even fear in writing this knowing of some actions on previous writers that have questioned our police's action.)

The Alligator Bookstore

On the left side of the street beside what is now the New Orleans Hotel was an alley and a square building with the neon sign of "Heartbreak Hotel", the once notorious Alligator Bookstore, a hangout for hungry gays with racks of dirty books, magazines and eventually videos. In the back were little rooms with projection equipment, and for a quarter for a couple of minutes, you could watch the dirty, gay films.

Paul Stewart said in "Champion", "This is the only sport in the world where two guys get paid for doing something they'd be arrested for if they got drunk and did it for nothing."

There is the story of a local man, when getting away from his lover, went to the Alligator, took a booth, watched some movies, fell in love with whomever was on the other side of the adjoing hole, waited outside the booth and watched his lover exit the adjoining booth. I hope it wasn't a true story.

All the gays would joke about the Alligator Book Store, but many locals were going in or coming out, and no one seemed to mind. "I like your movies, man. You've got a great penis." Val Kilmer in "The Doors".

"The Key West Citizen" reported that while one guy was in a private booth with his pants down, someone else in his private room stole his wallet, and he called the police. Patrons would listen to "Let's hear those quarters drop" from the lone attendant. No one cared what you did. The ending of the Alligator Bookstore came when the shop employee and a friend hit a drunk over the head with a ball bat to rob him of less than a couple of dollars, and they murdered him.

If you went down the alley to the left of the front door of the Alligator Book Store, you would find a small compound of what looked to be two or three private conch houses. It was a private club for a season in the 60s, called "The Mangrove Guest House" and it was supposed to be competition for the Club Baths on Truman. Membership was one dollar and you were given a locker in which you could put your clothes or your bottle, but most people undressed and took their bottle to the bar. You had to bring your own liquor, but you could buy setups. There was a dark room, a plastic small pool, and many bunk beds. No local would ever admit that he went there, but you would see them coming out of the alley. It was not particularly exclusive. Mae West put it exactly in the movie "Myra Breckenridge": "We've got a big mob here, and I'm a little tired today. One of these guys will have to go."

There was a vacant lot beside the Alligator Book Store on the north side of Duval that was used for years by the Five Sixes Cab

Company. (When you used the telephone in the 60s, you had to dial only the last five numbers. Five Sixes Cab Company's number was 6 6666. Now you must dial 305 296 6666.)

"Crabby Dicks'"

Burt Lancaster said in "The Rainmaker", "It's gonna be a hot night tonight and the world goes crazy on a hot night and maybe that's what a hot night is for."

On this piece of property in the 90's, someone built a large building whose front-porch upstairs overlaps the sidewalk. It remained vacant for a long time. The shops downstairs were rented, one to Regie and Bill for the moving of their clothing and shoestore called "The Island Shoe Box". There were attempts by various restaurants, but no one seemed to be able to make a go of the upstairs restaurant until in l997 "Crabby Dick's" laid out the floor plan that made it popular, and it is still there. It was a gamble.

Fritz

Fritz was a local dog groomer who had his shop on Flagler Street. He still liked to gamble, but his passion for dog racing is now tamed. Besides, the city got rid of the dog track on Stock Island years ago.

He had watched one racing greyhound for months, and the dog was to run in an upcoming race. He waited to place his bet directly at the track because he did not want to pay the bookie fee.

He had a woman client who had an apricot poodle and he cut and trimmed the dog weekly, although he did not really like the dog because the dog was always humping. The woman would comment to Fritz that he had to find her dog a girl friend, and Fritz did not want to because he didn't like the dog. She brought the dog in one Saturday for its weekly due. "Hope you found him a girl friend." He avoided the comment in a rush to get to the track and to bet on his favorite greyhound. The apricot poodle was particularly frisky and not behaving, and Fritz missed going to the track.

His bookie called around four o'clock and told Fritz that his favorite greyhound had won and paid 172 dollars, but Fritz had not bought a ticket.

The woman came to the shop about five o'clock, and Fritz explained to her the difficulty of cutting the poodle. She said "the vet says maybe you will have to masturbate him. Do you do that?" (Fritz admits that she probably meant "castrate".) Fritz flew into a frenzy. Not only was the dog difficult to cut, but the apricot poodle had cost him winning at the track. He blurted out "Hell no. I don't even have time to take care of myself let alone your dog." She never returned with the apricot poodle.

"Mango's"

Walking on the same side of the street as "Crabby Dicks'" toward the Gulf is a large restaurant and bar on the very corner. As the town was growing away from the Gulf, this restaurant seemed to change hands several times, never really being able to get that combination of crowd, waiters, and atmosphere. At times it was gay. At another time it would try to attract the straight group.

In the next block down, there is a very successful restaurant called "Antonio's", and this restaurant took over the management of "Mango's" and made it successful. You can sit outside among the trees and do our favorite game of people watching. "Look, he probably gets more ass than a toilet seat." Bill Rusconi in "Out of the Dark". Under a small awning is a staircase upstairs for an evening gay bar called "Limbo".

There was no anti-gay attitude in Key West at any time. The locals took it in their stride and paid little attention. Years later that did not change, and as late as l998, the City Commission passed a ruling that of the city's 435 employees, 29 were eligible in a domestic relationship for partner benefits including insurance for spouses and children. Amusingly, the people of Key West do know what is going on. "Forty-two percent of all liberals are queer. That's a fact. George Wallace's people took a poll." Peter Boyle in "Joe".

Even the hurricane of 1965, Inez, with 85 mph winds in Key West seemed not to discourage the growth of the city. It was a heavy rain that cleaned out older limbs of trees.

The violence and the progress of the late 60s was captured in two headlines from "The Miami Herald". On Friday, April 5, 1968, the newsboys shouted "Martin Luther King Is Slain" and on Monday, July 21, 1969, the "Herald" capitalized the headline "MAN WALKS ON THE MOON". Both headlines challenged the world, and both previewed the coming events of our country.

"Diva's" and "Shag"

Not exactly across the street from "Mango's" but back a few buildings is the flashy "Diva's", a new drag bar owned by Sal Rapisardi, who also had the "Atlantic Shores" and once "La te da" and who opened a very successful restaurant on the Bight called "Brooklyn Boys", a basically straight bar with an excellent kitchen, but open and friendly to gays. (Diva's is pictured on the lower right of the back cover with the red doors.) "Diva's" opens into "Slag" inside as well as a door on Duval.

"You can always put that award where your heart ought to be." Bette Davis in "All About Eve". Outstanding at "Diva's" is the handsome bar, shipped at great expense from California. The shows are usually drag queens. "I haven't seen a body put together like that since I solved the case of the girl with the murdered legs." Steve Martin, "Dead Men Don't Wear Plaid".

Merry was usually behind the bar during the day, but she has returned to the "Atlantic Shores", and Chuck Lamb comes in for a few hours around 4:00 pm. Chuck has worked for Sal through many of Sal's bar ventures. When Sal was putting the bar together in 1997, he considered hiring Chuck (Sylvia) and J. R., another smiling bartender. Both pour excellent drinks and are entertaining. Sal got the two together and told them "There's only one thing that you two have to remember. There are more than four drinks to a quart."

There are some gay people who do not like the connotation of drags in a community. Of course, there are all kinds of gay people, from masculine mechanics to hair dressers. Some people's impression that "gay men are sissies and want to be women" is not an accurate labeling, and it is not. "Fallen Women? You mean women who've tripped!" Maggie Smith in "The Missionary".

However, there are some gay men that, for whatever reason, want to appear in drag. "Oh, that. That's just part of my clothes. I hardly ever shoot anybody with it." Dick Powell in "Murder, My Sweet".

"Diva's" and "La te da's" upstairs bar, "Treetop", have new stages for entertainment. "The 801" used to have drag shows upstairs, and the "Epoch" had drag shows and the largest stage. Some people get amusement and entertainment from the witty drags, and that's the game of a tourist city. "Oh, my God! Someone's been sleeping in my dress." Bea Arthur in "Mame". The number of drags at Fantasy Fest is anyone's guess. Tsai Chin in "The Virgin Soldiers" said, "OK, Johnny, you give me 15 dollars, you get nice filthy time."

Many of the more popular drag queens have been here for some years and may participate in drag only to their amusement. Others keep the employment as a full-time job. Names that we all remember are "Parky", "Ma Evans", "La La Bell", and "Hell-n-Bed". Miss Emma Royd and Alesha Smellgood left town. Some gay men do drag just for their own amusement.

When the younger college kids are here for spring break and there is the difficulty of checking for legal drinking age, rowdiness, etc., one local bar terminated all verbal contracts with locally employed drag queens to gain more profit. (Gays are easy to forgive insults. There are still bars that say they give a percentage of the house income to AIDS projects, but fail to reveal what that percentage is. Some big Hollywood entertainers are known to eat most of the profit in "expenses" from a benefit. The gays do not push the point.)

There are many charitable causes that happen at "Diva's" usually in the evening. There is a fraternity-like relationship amoung the employees of the bars. Since many of the employees of a gay bar may be straight, the understanding reaches beyond gender limitations. Should one bar and the employees face a problem, the other bars join in. When the "Copa" on Duval had a fire, a few days later the other bars were holding parties asking for donations for the employees. When "La te da" went into backrupcy, "801 Bourbon" held a donation fundraiser for the employees. When an individual runs into a serious problem, the community is often there to help. Key West in many ways is still a very small town.

Chuck Lamb (Sylvia) works the upper level bar after 4 pm during happy hour, and he has a stream of customers who came in specifically to see and hear him. Fortunately, he has changed little since "Papillon" days. He maintains his hearty laugh. Bill and Sue sellers are frequent patrons. Claire, a retired schoolteacher, and Hal leave their Harley-Davidson at home, and they visit Chuck. Claire and Hall have been together for more than twenty years, and someday they may get married. Maybe not.

Chuck usually entertains with his quick wit, but a few years ago, he started singing country music, and he was very good. Complete with cowboy boots and red shirt, he became a favorite at the gay clubs. He often sang with Trish, the bartender of "801 Bourbon" and they charmed many with their country music. Trish was also "Queen of Fantasy Fest".

Chuck and three of his friends went to Amsterdam a few years ago, rented a houseboat, and managed to hit every spot in town within a few minutes. When you can get him remembering the funny things that happened during that trip, you've had your evening's entertainment.

Chuck told us that a couple of weeks ago a certain horse came into the bar about every night evening about six. The horse would order a drink, drink it, and he would not laugh or cry. Even Chuck's humor did not work on the horse. One afternoon Chuck was talking with Hal who offered $100 to anyone who could get the horse to laugh and cry. A well known drunk overheard the conversation and decided to take a shot at it. When the horse came in that evening, the drunk went over to the horse and whispered something in the horse's ear, and the horse broke out laughing. Another whisper from the drunk and the horse started to cry. Hal gave the drunk $100.

After the incident, Hal asked the drunk what he said to the horse to get such emotion. The drunk told Hal that he first whispered to the horse that his peter was larger than the horse's, and the horse laughed. In the second whisper, the drunk told the horse he would prove it and showed the horse his peter was larger. The horse cried.

One of the favorite games they used to play was for one bartender to call the second bartender at another bar and buy him/her a complimentary drink over the phone. Management put a quick halt to that game.

However, if you are looking for an apartment, a job, your lost dog, or your lover has strayed, always ask the bartenders. They know the hour by hour action of the town.

It is difficult for many of the waiters and bartenders to work in the same bar or restaurant for a long period of time. The purpose of entertainment is to satisfy the customers. If you have to listen to the same stories, hear the same music, watch the same drag shows night after night, it becomes routine to the employees. The tourists love it, but the employees and the locals may become bored. Attractive at "Diva's" is a constantly changing show.

Rapisardi has also taken control of the shop to the left facing "Diva's", an attached room in which he opened an English pub type of bar called "Shag". Supposedly, it is a more conservative drinking establishment. His plans for the attached bar come at particularly confusing time since he held the mortgage on "La te da", and they have gone into bankruptcy. He'll work it out.

The 700 block of Duval contains three or four major gay bars, "The 801 Bourbon Pub", "Bourbon Street", and "Diva", and "Shag" but once you cross over Southard Street, you're into a commercial shopping area. There is another cluster of predominantly gay bars down two blocks.

THE 600 BLOCK
Angela St. to Southard St.

How did this clustering start? When eyes started to turn to the small island in the sun, there were accepting attitudes in order to make a profit. The vacant downtown stores. The trolley. Hemingway's house. Tennessee Williams' presence. Gore Vidal. Although the Little White House at the Truman Annex was converted from a double house in 1946, it was used by President Truman 11 times, the last being in March of 1969. Publicity. Word of mouth in the gay community. Please do not consider that opening gay bars has much to do with advancing the gay movement to a better understanding of gay men and lesbians. Not at all. Operating a gay bar is strictly for profit.

There was little prejudice, but the major prejudice of the 60s seemed to be of the difference between the "outsiders", meaning those not born conchs, and those born on the island, conchs. It was not that the conchs did not like many of the outsiders. It was more that many of the conchs did not approve of the changes that outsiders thought would improve living on the island. The conchs were not against the outsiders as much as they were against the outsiders' ideas of change. If you are conditioned only to a corrupt government, you accept a corrupt government. After the Depression, the conchs were eager to sell their properties to make a profit. They would sell to anyone at prices that, to them, seemed extraordinary.

Local government positions, most of the commercial shops and businesses, home ownership, and the city's decisions were made by the long-established residents. It was called the "bubba" system. Challenges to these decisions were awkward, to say the least.

As the locals watched the city changing, some did not like the changes, and they decided to leave Key West. Most just stayed and accepted the changes, many unwilling to do much more than complain about how Key West used to be, but not willing to leave and, obviously, still liking many of the qualities of the town. Not unlike the cigar rollers, some moved from Key West to Tampa, another large Latin community. Some threatened to move, but didn't. The bubba system was no longer working as it had in the past.

Logic and change had moved in. Sometimes the locals' own children liked the more positive, less political, decisions, and this presented a family barrier where Cuban families always stood up for Cuban families regardless. The bubba system began to fail. Corruption was discovered, and even some of the old families were against corruption and questioned their Cuban associates. The days of fast money and big spending were coming to a close.

The major argument was that so much was changing on the island, and the next 30 or more years would prove that to be true. Good or bad, better or worse, bubbaism was threatened, and many resisted the change. Some of the conchs offered no resistance, and a few welcomed the changes. Many conchs had made a great deal of money. Aside from the weakening of the bubba system, few prejudices were rarely radical. There would always be that West Virginia visitor who had never seen a drag queen, and a gay guy who would proposition him. Angela Lansbury said in "The Company of Wolves" "Beware of men who are hairy on the inside, too."

The newcomers to the island brought a new respect of not being ashamed of being gay, a freedom for women, a change of values to living one day at a time and appreciation of that day, a philosophic look toward tomorrow, and included an influx of dollars. Many had their Key West homes for the winter. Some retired or lived on modest incomes and made Key West their year-round home.

With the influx of so many new people, Key West developed many different social and business groups. New groups formed because of interests or social habits. There was little division between the activities of the conchs and the newcomers. The invitation from the conchs was economic, political and social. There were environmentalists, politicians, the fund raisers, the hotel and motel group, the business guild, and more. The gay people of Key West fit into all of the activities quite well, and they were accepted by almost all social and business groups.

Even in the gay community, there were different types of gays based upon their activities. There was the breakfast club, early afternoon drinkers, the cocktail-hour set, dinner group, a bookstore group, the Copa late people, the beachside group, and about any number of people would gather for any common reason. There was even an unrecognized group that preferred to associate only with the wealthy gays. There was a kind of social order recognized by only a few gays, a pecking order that no one seemed to want but that some held for their own social stability. We have to admit that there are some people, and some gays, that do not like anything. The various interests mixed to a degree, but there was conflict.

With emphasis upon drugs and the relationship of drugs to the social structures and to finances of the individual, a double value grew. Most waiters were against drugs if asked, except what they may do on Saturday night. The waiters liked the high rollers who brought out a wad of big bills and did not question where he obtained the money. The older new locals were not tolerant of drugs; the younger new locals were more tolerant. Some gays came to Key West to enjoy the drugs, and they stayed. The laws were against drugs; enforcement of the law was a problem. People went to jail; both locals and tourists as well as new people of the island, including conchs. The fountain of drugs and drug-related money slowed but did not dry.

Some will disagree and say I have put too much emphasis upon the use of drugs in Key West. I question that I have. I cannot understand a waiter who has to hold down two jobs, lives in an apartment with three roommates, has little spare time and little social activity, who would abide by this description if it were for some reason not related to his freedom as an individual. Many locals take drugs. Many tourists take drugs.

Coconut Grove, Florida
I did not go to Key West every weekend because I got involved in buying my first house in Coconut Grove. Living in Miami in the 60s was interesting and threatening. I made friends at work and broadened out to friends in the community. Few knew of my passion for Key West. Few knew I was gay. "Insanity doesn't run in my family. It practically gallops!" Cary Grant in "Arsenic and Old Lace".

Erna and Garland Faulkner
The Southbeach of Duval Street was the same beach of which I had heard wild stories of a New York woman named Erna Stow. She was the first woman to have bought a seat on the New York Stock Exchange, and she had become quite wealthy, had the diamonds and

furs, and she would come to Key West in the winter and display them. She would go to the Duval Street Pier, throw her mink coat on the beach or give it to one of the gays to watch, and as he preened, she would go into the water, diamond rings and bracelets held above her head.

Erna also liked her sailors; many of them. The police asked Erna to calm down and when she wouldn't or couldn't, the police made an active attempt to get rid of Erna by stopping her car for every minor infraction or suspicion of an infraction. She left Key West, married, and moved to Coconut Grove. (I bought my first house in Coconut Grove. Erna and her husband were my next-door neighbors, and we spent hours talking about the old events of the island.)

Erna Stow married Garland Falkner, a slim, athletic, much younger Texan and, although they would come to Key West on weekends, their permanent residence was Coconut Grove.

A couple of years after Erna's death, Garland married Polly Davis, an older, very wealthy woman of Miami society who had made her money from vast landholdings in Kansas, the growing of wheat. She died and he remembered that her desires were to be cremated and have her ashes thrown over the wheat fields of Kansas. The body was cremated in Miami and returned to Garland in a suitable canister.

Garland called the Kansas city in which Polly had been raised and made arrangements for a small service of her friends, after which the group would go to the local wheat fields, and he would throw her ashes over the waving stalks. It would be the following Thursday at five o'clock in the afternoon, and he made reservation for the hotel as well as for his plane reservations to Kansas.

Thursday, he went to the airport, checked his bag, and arrived in the small Kansas town at two o'clock in the afternoon. The hotel room for the gathering was fine. The proper people had been notified. His room was adequate. The only problem was that the airline had misplaced his bag, and the canister with her ashes was in his bag.

Three o'clock; no bag. Four o'clock; no bag. He walked down the street and into a tobacco store and bought three of the largest Cuban cigars, although he did not smoke.

At the five o'clock service, which was attended by 20 or more people, her friends remarked that Polly's husband did not look so well, but all knew the strain of death. They drove to the wheat fields in eight cars and, after a few words, he scattered his wife's ashes onto the wheat fields of Kansas. When he returned to his hotel, his bag had arrived. He revisited the wheat fields the next morning ... alone.

Coconut Grove, Florida

Most young people started out with the same program: a shared apartment, an apartment alone, collecting the furniture from junk stores, redoing tables and chairs, saving money for a big adventure. Everyone seemed to want the same thing: a home that he/she owned.

I found my security in a two-bedroom, one-and-a-half baths, white-tiled-roof structure on Douglas Road, Coconut Grove. It probably wasn't the best neighborhood, being only a few blocks from Grand Avenue, but that did not bother me. The lot was large and had several full grown trees, including an oak and a large avocado tree in the backyard.

Since I had not as yet saved all the money for a down payment, I offered $2,000 down on a land contract to rent the house until I had paid enough rent to equal the 15% down payment. The owner agreed. I called the Teacher's Credit Union to borrow some money. After all, I owned my car and I had a job. It was a $20,000 house, $2,000 down, and three years of paying rent until I could actually go to the bank for a mortgage.

I painted the house inside and out, scrubbed to the raw wood, tore out walls, painted my own wallpaper with sponges dipped in paint, and converted the garage into a rental apartment. My building experience was the "about" system; about level, about straight. Imperfections were covered by paint and paintings on the inside and vegetation on the outside. Vines eventually covered a lot of the poor building practices and gave it some old-world charm. The house was rather Spanish, rather old looking. Quaint.

Working on the house became a strong motivation for me.

Obtaining a home that I felt I hadn't had, working to make it look better was a welcomed relief from grading papers. I didn't date girls or guys much and had a limited number of friends. I was always scraping together money, and redoing the house became my lust. I loved it. Buying, fixing, and selling real estate would later make me financially independent, but I did not know this when I bought my first house.

This was the period when the "Hamlet" was the popular bar of the village of Coconut Grove, a hamlet of Miami. (The spelling had been changed from "Cocoanut Grove" to "Coconut Grove" years before.) It had a beer-and-wine, long, narrow pub-kind-of atmosphere with terrific sliced beef sandwiches. All kinds of people would stop in: workers from the docks, boaters, local residents, women shopping, University of Miami students, and kids. It was not a gay bar, but there were gays at the bar. There was a woods across the street and some people were known to enter that woods at night after a few drinks at the "Hamlet", and that could be exciting.

"The Candlelight Inn"

The other downtown Coconut Grove spot was the "Candlelight Inn" on Commodore Plaza, a dinner place with a cocktail bar. Max used to be behind the bar, a stocky, friendly old bartender who would limit your drinking to what he knew about you. He would pour me a very heavy first drink and cut back the second. There was shrimp scampi on the menu for $2.95. Husbands and wives, dating couples, singles and anyone else made up the evening crowd. I talked with Arthur Godfrey one afternoon for a couple of hours as he was waiting for rehearsals at the nearby Coconut Grove Theatre.

My friends used to say that if you got a job as an attractive waiter, or even as an unattractive waiter at the Candlelight Inn, you were guaranteed a trip to Europe within two weeks, if you played your cards right.

"The Candlelight" name moved to 27th Avenue under the direction of Robert Stickney, who had attended the University of Miami. Stickney had been the college roommate of Charlie Ramos, Jr. of Key West. "The Candelight" was a predominantly gay bar and restaurant, and Bob went on to open other gay bars in New York, and most recently the "Mecca" in San Francisco.

Actually, San Francisco was the place that really was in full swing during the starting of the gay movement that I recall. After the Second World War, there was a club called "Finnochio's" in San Francisco that became popular because of female impersonators, today called drag. A greater sense of individuality and freedom allowed many straights to admit they were amused by these illusionists. Newspapers and magazines carried stories about the entertainers and compared the freedom of the drags to the sophistication of the gay movement in San Francisco.

After the war, Miami had the Jewel Box Review, located where the Miami Herald now has a parking lot on Biscayne Boulevard. It reached popularity with female impersonators doing a Las Vegas-type nightclub act, entertaining for straight audiences, and it was often mentioned by local writers. Gay men and lesbians crowded into a bar to the side of the large nightclub, most not wanting to be seen by the straight audience.

Moving to Coconut Grove in the late 50s, I came to my own realization of being gay in Miami. I had been to a bar on Miami Beach called the "Shellborn" owned or maybe just operated by Martha Ray. It was a backroom bar, so you had to walk through a front bar with five to ten people sitting and drinking, to open a back door to where the music was blasting, packed with people, and a party.

It was quite similar to another Beach bar called "The Red Carpet", a notorious gay bar with drag shows. A friend from Ohio where I had worked at a carnival told me of a date he had with a performer and a snake. After the show, the two guys threw the snake into the car and took off on foot for another bar. It was one of those chilly nights and the boa wrapped himself around the warm engine. They had to take a cab home.

There were a couple of bars in downtown Miami, namely "The Carnival" by the bus station, but it often got raided. Gay bars were against the law. "Vic's" was a piano bar with a back room called the "Mermaid". Most downtown bars lasted only a year. There was the "Roman Room" on the second floor of a Second Street building. Even the bar at the bus station, the "Zomba", turned gay for a while.

Many years later "Fusions" opened to hillbilly music and a second floor rooftop that caught many a drunken eye. A couple of years later Bob Sloat opened "Uncle Charles" close to the community college, but that was closed. Later he tried the "2 by 2" near the courthouse, and left downtown for "Charlie's" on Bird Road.. In the Taj Hotel was a service elevator which took you to a second floor which contained a public bath which was notorious in the gay community. However, over these 15 years, the police had made it very obvious that they did not want gay bars at a time when the gays were starting to gain respectability.

So gays took their bar business away from downtown. One section of bars including the "Foxhole", "Red Rooster", and the "Red Pig Pub" opened several blocks from downtown on Second Avenue, north. Michael Straight closed his gay bar in the Dallas Park hotel to open his "Ramrod" club in a similar area.

There was "Googies" out Le Jeune Road toward the airport that always had cars around it and beer bottles on the bar, but rarely was anyone in the bar. Everyone was outside in the dark back under a large tree or in the underbrush.

In 1966 Channel 4 of Miami presented a program called "The Homosexual", spotlighting Richard Inman, who was outspoken concerning gay rights. He was probably the first person in the Miami area to publically come out of the closet. (4)

One of the oldest running bars was the "Warehouse" on Eighth Street, but it was constantly searched by the police. Later the "13 Buttons" opened in a warehouse district, and the "Hole" got a lot of the alcoholic group. "Klingers" was opened in the old "Monk's Inn" but only lasted a year.

The oldest lasting bar was probably the El Carol close to Eighth Street which closed a couple of years back. The "Cactus" on Biscayne Boulevard has had its good and bad times over the last 43 years, but is now going through an expensive renovation. "Cheers" became "Splash" in South Miami and remains popular. Gone are the "meat racks".

The true story is that Miami, being only a little more than 100 years old, has never wanted the influx of the gay movement. The population is heavily Latin and Catholic, and not liberal. Even Coconut Grove with its reputation of being "artsy" does not have a gay bar.

A second factor is that many of the gays moved from Miami to Fort Lauderdale or Miami Beach, two very heavily gay communities. Some came to Key West. No one can even count the number of gay bars in Lauderdale. There are more gay bars and within walking distance from each other in Key West than there are in Miami proper.

The John's Committee

The old Grove bars, the "Candlelight" on Commodore Plaza and the "Hamlet", were safe places for a schoolteacher to be. There was the John's Committee, a state group of headhunters whose purpose was to search out communists, but communists were difficult to identify. The group's purpose became to hunt out "undesirables", which meant gays. The "Miami Herald" published license plate numbers, names, addresses, and employer names of the owner of any car found parked at night around a two-block area of any gay bar. Miami had always had one or more gay bars, but during this period it was suicide to go to any bar with a reputation.

The viciousness of the John's Committee was so challenging that many gay teachers left the state. Anyone could be accused and, without a trial, found guilty. The John's Committee published a blue booklet that the Florida State government ruled contained pornography because of the photographs in bathrooms their investigators had taken. Files were sealed, not to be opened until 1993, and no one would admit he was a member of the John's Committee when the files were finally released.

The early 60s was a time to find an excuse to stay in the house at night, or to get out of town. "Hey, don't knock masturbation. It's sex with someone you love." Woody Allen in "Annie Hall".

It was a time of individual freedom. Gays established a gay church. Many articles were published concerning homosexuality not being a choice of the individual, but implied heredity. The blacks wanted freedom. The handicapped wanted their rights. Women wanted to be recognized as individuals with equal rights to men.

Gays began fighting for their own rights in Miami and Miami

Beach. When the police first stood against the gays, the police won by pure force. As the issues restricting freedom were raised, the police departments became less belligerent. In 1972 when the city government attempted to ban cross-dressing in Miami Beach, the demonstration was one of walking down Lincoln Road protesting in what became Gay Pride Week. The cross-dressing law was struck down two weeks later.

At the 1972 Republican Convention in Miami Beach, hundreds of gays and straights demonstrated for individual freedom. The press put forth articles demanding equal representation and the lack of discrimination against gays. It took five years more. In 1973 the American Psychological Association publicly stated that homosexuality was not a disease. It was simply a "lifestyle". In 1977 the city commission approved a human rights ordinance banning discrimination in employment and housing based upon sexual orientation.

Anita Bryant was an entertainer and the Citrus Commission Spokesperson. She wanted the rights ordinance repealed by referendum and she won in a practically two-for-one victory. Although she lost her job as spokesperson, a chance to reinstate was repealed a second year. But the people of Dade County and Monroe County were aware of the bigotry of their voters.

Miami bars were raided. The police roughed up gays. The University of Miami made special concerns for their bathrooms on the second floor of a specific classroom building on campus, and a university-owned building of The Alhambra Apartments in another part of Coral Gables closed their men's room often.

Cruising was dangerous. If a gay person were not in the closet, it was time to find one. Scared of the bars, bored at seemingly intellectual teachers' cocktail parties, always on guard as to associations, finished with the Douglas Road house project, and bored with having to stay home and not having the freedom to go out and socialize with gays, it was time for me to find an excuse for a more exciting place, and that was Key West.

Back home in Key West
The sounds of Key West would linger through the streets at night,

slowly fading except for an occasional car or a noisy bike rider. Then silence.

Nothing is more appealing than the predawn hour into the rising sun of dawn on a morning on any street in Old Town. The black canvas starts the silhouettes of trees. The last few lights of night begin to fade or shut off as the morning approaches. The roosters can be heard in the background. A drunken young couple stagger home toward bed. The guys on bikes finish their night of selling drugs. Bathroom lights start to turn on. The sky lightens. A cat hurries across an empty street. A taxi lumbers. The rooster sounds are drowned by people starting to move. The naked, sleeping girl across the street pulls her draperies closed. Another day.

Then starts the beginning of activity in the commercial section. Those curious who are awake earlier start to meld in the streets. The smell of Cuban coffee, con leche Different kinds of noises. The mix of conversations. Around ten o'clock, the shops start to open, and before noon there are many in and out of the shops doing their daily routines.

Around noon, lunch-time, the streets are worn with locals meeting people to enjoy the lunch period of an hour or longer, and the talk and the gossip. Conch fritters. Shrimp in their pink shells. In the summer the streets are quiet after lunch except for a frequent beer delivery. In the winter the streets lose half their bustle in the early afternoon, and the beach is inviting. It's just too warm, and the action of the streets dulls until four to six.

In the afternoon, some shops close and employees race to neighborhood bars and coffee shops, and the conversations begin of rude customers or bad sales day. As it gets close to six, the streets clear, but there is the noise of those who stayed too long in the bars, and those getting ready for the evening's action.

Henry Faulkner
Henry Faulkner was a wiry little artist from Lexington, Kentucky, who was a friend of Tennessee Williams. He would peddle his bicycle up and down Duval Street singing Bessie Smith's songs in a falsetto voice at the top of his lungs. He would spend the winter months in Key West.

At one time, Henry had a pet goat named Alice, and Alice would follow him around town, as true as a dog. The bartenders would put out a bowl of water for Alice (a custom still done at the "801 Bourbon Bar" for traveling dogs.) The goat would wait patiently as Henry would consume his afternoon cocktails.

Above all, Henry was an excellent artist. His paintings were crisp, original, colorful, and appealing, and many of the residents of Key West as well as of Lexington collected his work. Often, Alice would appear in his paintings.

For years Henry had been saving in a barn in Lexington pieces of architecture and treasure that were to be used for a home he would someday build for himself and his friend, Tennessee. Columns from Rome, windows from a Spanish church, wall hangings, chandeliers. After Henry's death, all would be sold at auction, and the house was never built.

Tennessee Williams

The literary genius of Tennessee Williams can not be disputed, and he was closely tied to the artistic temperament and tolerance of Key West. He came to Key West in 1941 on a visit and he stayed at the Tradewinds, a once grand boarding house and bar under the watchful eye of Mrs. Black.

In 1949, Tennessee bought a house on Bahama Street and had it moved to a lot on the edge of the mangroves, Duncan Street. It was a typical conch-style shot-gun house that he added to as his popularity and wallet could afford. He added a working studio, a covered patio, and a swimming pool. Danny Stirrup, a local conch architect and a conch who would someday be my next-door neighbor in Key West, designed a large kitchen, and Frank Fontis built a gazebo in the front yard complete with a picket fence. In 1955, Williams won the Pulitzer Prize for "The Rose Tattoo", but the house was better known for the variety of Williams' friends that frequently visited and the new friends he would bring back home from the city's bars.

Tennessee Williams must have been aware of Faulkner's talent, for he had several Faulkner paintings in his home. When Williams was coming into his own and becoming nationally known, Faulkner was working on a painting, and Williams signed "T.W." to a canvas.

(No one ever accused Williams of being a good or even average painter.)

The painting was donated to a local charity auction, and the auctioneer got top dollar for the painting, $750 by the successful playwright, "T.W.", impling Tennessee Williams. Three days later the truth came out. Williams demanded the falsely signed painting be returned to him. The gallery had to buy the painting from the new owners and give it to Williams, at the gallery's expense. Many felt Williams had known all along of the forged painting with the author's signature. (Strangely, the Faulkner painting would have been worth much more on the market in the following years than any with Williams' signature.)

In the early 60s, Tennessee was good friends with a very wealthy older woman. Marion Viccaro and her brother, George Black, lived a couple of doors down from Viscaya, the 70-room James Deering castle near Coconut Grove, in a large mansion on the bay. They were far from my class as a young English teacher. Marion Viccaro and Williams would travel to Cuba in wild drinking sprees. George Black lived alone in the big house after his sister died. (Now the street is filled with famous people like Madonna and Sylvester Stallone.)

I knew a young man, Black Irish, who rented the gatehouse of Marion Viccaro's palatial home, a gatehouse larger than most homes, and we had many parties there. Later, Black Irish was killed as his Cadillac was smashed on a Dixie Highway accident late at night.

I used to go to Studio M. in Coral Gables, a theatre production company, and watch rehearsals. Williams would sit in the back row of the theatre, script in hand, making rewrites on a story that he seemed to want at that time to be an incestuous mother and son plot, but that developed as "Orpheus Descending". He would rip off the sheets of new lines and give them to the actors to be memorized by the next rehearsal.

I first met Tennessee Williams around 1960 when I was in my mid-20s at the home of South Miami architect Henry Spitzer. I was too old or too educated or maybe unappealing for him to chase around a coffee table, and I considered him to be "with such an ego". I knew his plays, but I particularly liked his short stories.

During the next years, I visited the house on Duncan Street in Key West many times, usually with Viola Viet, Betty French, Danny Stirrup or Frank Fontis. When Williams was not in town, we would use the pool anyway.

Some years later after his friend, Frankie (Frank Philip Merlo), died, I would see Willisms at "Claire Bar", but he would be surrounded by fans and talking about his new play or about himself. He was completely self involved.

I was walking behind him and, I believe, Henry Faulkner when they approached three young boys sitting on the wall a block north from "Claire Bar". Drunk, Williams went over to the kids and asked them to sing a hymn with him. One of the boys said "Go away, faggot," and slightly, if at all, touched Williams, the boy probably thinking "just another drunk", and the drunk did fall. Falling was not unusual for Williams. When the press got the story, Williams played it off in his usual grand style by saying that it was just an accident caused by literary critics.

All people around the author knew without question who he was, for he was not hesitant to talk about his accomplishments. Many of those that hung around him were aware of collecting anything that he touched. During his lifetime, half-completed paintings that he would discard were stolen. He would give paintings to Viola Viet and she would sell them. His garbage can would be raided and particularly letters signed "Mother God-damn", a campy pseudonym, were collected by Frank Fontis.

I was working at Gingerbread Square Gallery when we got the news that Williams had died. A telephone call from Texas Kate asked me to go over to the Duncan Street house to be sure the doors were secured. I walked over, checked the house, returned to the gallery and called her to satisfy that all was secure. Two hours later, she called back and asked me to go over to the house and wait for a security company from Miami that had been contracted to come down and guard the house. It was a hot day and a ten-block walk. I was working, and I refused. To my knowledge, nothing was stolen from the house after his death.

The house on Duncan Street was sold to a young couple with the understanding they would never profit from the fact that Tennessee Williams had lived there.

Stell Adams, Williams' cousin, read palms and had been a stewardess on one of the early airlines, and she had taken care of Tennessee's sister, Rose. She scraped together a living from palmreading. She lived on giving advice to those that felt she had some kind of psychic power, or wanted just to play the game. She was rarely without "Sugar", a mutt of a dog whose tongue was always half out of her mouth. Williams did not leave her a penny.

Another association with the writer came a couple of years after his death. As Director of The Key West Art and Historical Society, I wanted to put together an art show of paintings by Tennessee Williams. I called the people I knew that had his paintings and we gave a show of 40 paintings at the East Martello gallery. My comment: "He was an excellent writer".

The 60s was a period of fantasies being fulfilled at the movie houses. The movie stars were our idols, our dream, our reaffirming of the American way and the American dream. There were three movie houses in town: the Monroe, the Palace at the San Carlos, and the Strand.

"The Epoch"

The Monroe Theater was built in 1912, and it lasted through the many years of Key West usually as a sorted motion picture house. In the 70s, it was sold or leased to the "Copa" group of Fort Lauderdale. During the seeds of the sexual revolution of the late 60s, and the new, loud music, new dances, abundance of gay men, the Lauderdale "Copa" was very popular and successful, and the businessmen brought their ideas of a similar type of watering hole to Key West. What had happened in Miami was a large influx of Cuban immigrates and a nasty police department philosophy against gays. Non-Latin gays exited to Fort Lauderdale in mass, others going to Miami Beach, some coming to Key West.

The island offered a different kind of audience than the Fort Lauderdale "Copa" had expected. The Lauderdale "Copa" drew from a much larger audience and was mostly gay men, but the lack of anything happening and the constant mingling of gays and straights gave the Key West "Copa" instant success. Opening past dark and running until early in the morning gave tourists and locals a new form of entertainment and a latenight life-style mixing straights and gays.

A second bar at the "Copa" was the "Garden Bar" and opened around three o'clock in the afternoon in the back half of the property and could be separately entered through the back parking lot, which overlooked the police station and fire departments. Starting earlier and eventually melding into the "Copa", there was always a crowd around the bar that was open on all sides to a garden, but roofed for the protection from the sun. The bar itself was unusual in that the bartender would have to crawl over the bar, for there was no bar gate. This said something about the age of the bartenders they wanted, and got. The Key West "Copa" and the "Garden Bar" continued to do well. One of the bartenders at the back bar was fired for improperly stirring a drink with something personal.

There was also an upstairs bar sometimes with entertainment. An insulting and clever comedian would tear you apart before you climbed the stairs. Many found him cutting and amusing.

Fom late-night fire, lightning or whatever, the Key West "Copa", owned by Joel Weinstein, burned down in 1995. The fire department bragged they had made it to the fire within five minutes of being called. (The firehouse abuts the "Copa's" property.) Collections were started for the bar people out of work, and plans were set for the rebuilding.

An 8,000-square foot-building opened in 1996 as "The Epoch" owned by Joel Weinstein. The upstairs bar overlooking Duval Street is called the "Cloud Room". The downstairs is the main disco room, and in the back looking across is the police and fire department next door to "The Terrace". The building has been for sale since 1996.

The San Carlos
The original San Carlos was a Cuban immigrant group who met to continue educational and social directions. A wooden building was built in 1871, but it burned down 15 years later, 1886. It was rebuilt and was destroyed by the hurricane of 1919. In 1924 the San Carlos was again rebuilt of concrete in its present location.

The San Carlos was a concert hall and school earlier in the century, but in the 50's it had fallen into a desperate state of lack of repair. Above the theatre lobby on the second floor was a school for Cuban children, but these rooms were vacant and junk-filled and not accessible.

There was a balcony in the concert hall and in the middle of the balcony someone had built a crude projection room, turning the concert hall into a motion picture theater. As a concert hall, there was no wing space, fly space or dressing rooms, not even a bathroom behind the curtain line, but the acoustics were excellent, and the building made an easy transition into a motion picture house, the Palace. Little if any money was spent on repair, and the building fell deeper into shambles, and finally the San Carlos Institute again held the lease.

Efforts were made to revitalize and redo the building back to the concert hall and school it had once been. There were several fund-raising events, but somehow the donations seemed to disappear. Glue was pumped into the cracks of the building supposedly to hold it together. Various officials of the organization accused others of not holding the group together.

There was a major hitch in the organization. The building was still owned by the Cuban government and with the population of Cuban refugees in Miami and the constant flow of Cubans coming to the United States, both good and bad, fund-raisers were held, but often failed. The U. S. government was not about to fund a building for remodeling which belonged to the Cuban government.

In the 80s, the Cuban government attempted to clarify the ownership of the San Carlos to the Cuban people of Key West, through the State of Florida. The Governor of Florida gave control of the San Carlos to Raphael A. Penalver, Jr., a Miami lawyer, as President of the San Carlos Institute. The San Carlos Board of Directors signed a lease with the State of Florida through the Historical Florida Keys Preservation Board. This caused confusion between the Miami Cubans and the Key West Cubans, and they were at odds. More fund-raising and grants. After years of hiding behind plywood boards, the San Carlos reopened to the public in early 1992 with all of its once-grandeur and splendor.

Attempts to reorganize the school at the San Carlos had generally failed. Attempts by other local theatre groups to utilize the building met with opposition from the Hispanic organization. Although it is currently available, it is rarely used.

The Strand Theatre

Perhaps the most modern of the movie theaters was the Strand Theatre with 20's ceramic walls and the heavy, castle-like decor like the old Lowes Theatre chain. In the late 60s, one film played for years: "Deep Throat", and it was rare that any other film would be offered, with the exception of "The Devil in Miss Jones". Locals lost interest after a couple of viewings; and the movie became dated and the building was sold.

Ripley's "Believe it or not"

The 500 BLOCK
Southard St. to Fleming St.

When you cross Southard Street, what will immediately catch your attention is the re-vitalized Strand Motion Picture building, now housing "Ripley's Believe It or Not". It is one of the most photographed buildings in town.

Look to your left on Southard and down a block is the "Green Parrot", one of the oldest and most distinctive bars in town. It will be full of every type of person from shrimpers to lawyers. The courthouse across Whitehead Street also houses the jail beside it. The "Green Parrot" was once called the "Brown Derby". If you were to continue down Southard Street another block, you would be at the Navy gate.

The "Gate Bar"

Locals play the bar names as a game. Remember the "Gate Bar", the entrance to the Navy yard on Thomas Street? The name had changed many times and the type of bar had changed with the name. The "Gate Bar" was the first or last place a Navy man could get a drink off base, a rowdy, pool-table, military bar where you could always see a fight. It later became "No Name Bar", later a gay bar, a disco bar, "Old Plantation", a topless girlie bar called "Peek-A-Boo Lounge, which shared the building by filling in the walls of the covered patio to create another room, a girls' gay bar. The gate to the Navy yard was rarely guarded during peacetime and the neighborhood changed. It is now the "Peek-A-Boo Lounge".

Back on Duval, across the street from "Ripley's Believe It or Not", is a small street or alley called Applerouth Lane, earlier called Smith Lane. About two blocks long, but because of its location across the street from the decorated and painted Strand Theatre on Duval, it has been the scene of much activity of Conchtown. It is another hub of the gay scene and only a couple of blocks away from the activity of the 700 block of Duval.

"Bamboo Room" became "Donnie's 422"

Walking toward the courthouse on the left (west) side of Applerouth, 422, is the Bamboo Room, which was started around 1950 and was one of the earliest night clubs in Key West. It was only a single room with a raised platform and chairs to the left, a long bar to the right, and a small stage behind the bar. Coffee Butler used to entertain there. Wilhelmina Harvey was also a regular. The small room would be packed after dark, often with the sound of Dixieland music. "Big Daddy! Now what makes him so big? His big heart? His big belly? Or, his big money?" Paul Newman in 1958 production of "Cat on a Hot Tin Roof".

Wilhelmina Harvey was raised in Key West, met her husband-to-be in her father's drugstore, had a son, and later got very involved in local politics. Ida Baron had come to town playing saxophone with an all-girl's band. Larry Harvey and Bobby McKinsey would be sitting at the bar. John Brown would stop by. It seemed always busy, and the music would fill the street.

The Holt Brothers bought the license and they and their two pretty wives entertained to the pleasure of the audience. Over the years, there were several others who tried the location; the "Jungle Club", "Angelina's", "George's", and a motorcycle bar called "Nasty Nancy"s". A young lady named Leslie bought the bar July 5, 1991, remodeled and added a garden section, and returned the beer and wine bar to its original name of the "Bamboo Room". (Back cover, left, half door, walls painted green.)

"416 Bar"
On the same side of the street was the "416 Bar", a ladies bar that was operated by Stretch and served beer, wine and food. The bar struggled through a few years, and it seemed the city was not yet ready for an exclusively lesbian bar.

Big Ruby's Guesthouse
Across the street is Big Ruby's, a popular gay guesthouse. The owners have continued to build additional rooms on to what once was an old house, and most of the construction of the building is new. Although caught in the middle of a very busy community, the street is quiet at night, and the rooms hold away loud noises. It is a very popular guesthouse, and in the middle of all the evening's gay activity.

"Saloon One"
Beside "Big Ruby's" on the right (north) side of Applerouth Lane is "Saloon One", one of the few "leather" bars, but the weather has been very warm. "My what unusual leather pants. They look like cowboy chaps. Oh, they are cowboy chaps. Well ... I was just thinking... they look like cowboy chaps." Jack Weston in "The Ritz". There were some gays who wanted to give the appearance of being tough. Some wanted to pose. Key West is very warm for too much leather. "I didn't stuff my pants. God did that." David Keith's line from "Heartbreak Hotel". (Spine cover top, just bikes.)

"Saloon One" happening
Someone we all knew, a man in his 30s with enough money to make Key West his winter home, took a little too much of the spirits one night and

staggered from the "Saloon One" to go home. He had a vicious hunger for pizza, bought one, got home, turned on his oven to high, and fell across his bed fully dressed, soon into a sound sleep.

He awakened to firemen running through his bedroom, the house filled with black smoke, a broken-down door, and an awful smell like burning rubber. The firemen were laughing at him saying they had put out the kitchen fire of the stove, and he could not imagine why the accident seemed so humorous to them. He stumbled his way into the kitchen to find his stove soaked in a puddle of water, black smoke still pouring from the drawer under the stove. He could see the stove drawer pulled out and his collection of neatly arranged but mostly melted rubber dildos. No wonder the firemen were laughing. Nothing is sacred.

The "Saloon One" had a disco room in front toward Duval, a disk jockey, a small bar, and it was dark and the noise was very loud. The patrons loved the atmosphere, and the dark. "Baby, you got me hotter 'n Georgia asphalt." Laura Dern's line in "Wild at Heart". Enough said.

The main bar of "Saloon One" was started in 1982 and went through many changes including a patio entrance, a shed for preparing meals, a dark side room. Dancing gave way to pinball machines. It is still very active and shares one liquor license with "La Tratoria", which used to be a side room to "Saloon One", but a main Duval address to "La Tratoria".

Jimmy Buffett's "Margaritaville"

Although Key West had the reputation of being a kind of place that the famous personalities visited, it also had the reputation of being a favorite place for the rather eccentric film makers and stars. When Jimmy Buffett bought "Tux's" restaurant and bar, Buffett did not demand to be recognized. He was famous and wealthy from the musicland of a different type of stardom, one self-assured, solid, and understated. As his "Margaritaville" in New Orleans was easily accepted by the people, he seemed more like the conchs of Key West, and he was eagerly welcomed. He converted the black and white of "Tux's" to a warm, friendly restaurant and bar, and he immediately had a following that has remained faithful. In September of l998, he sold his Key West house for $1,050,000 and was looking for a smaller house.

Fast Buck Freddies

The same building in front of the Saloon One on the north corner of Duval and Applerouth Lane was the original home and shop of Tony and Bill, the founders of Fast Buck Freddies. They had their shop in front and lived in the back room, showered in the back yard, and scrimped on food. As their history shows, they were very wise in their business dealings.

They had many bolts of wildly colored and patterned fabrics with very large tropical designs, and they would center and staple the cloth to painting stretchers, and sell the prints. The cost was minimal; the quality was excellent. Every motel and many homes had one of their fabrics hanging on a wall.

Key West's first nickel and dime store, The Kress Building, was built in 1920. Fast Buck Freddies went to the Kress Building on Duval in 1978 with much more space, and they eventually bought the building over the next 15 years from David Wolkowsky, who lived in the penthouse apartment on the roof. Locals say that Fast Buck Freddies is the only department store in Key West.

Fausto's Food Palace

If you would have taken a right (east) on Eaton Street, just a block away is a social center called "Fausto's", a grocery store that proclaims "You Can't Beat Our Meat."

A woman was doing her shopping, and she went to the checkout counter with cabbage, black-eyed beans, and collard greens. The clerk checked the items and put them into a brown paper bag as the woman paid for her goods, and she received her change. As the woman bent to pick up the bag, a seven pound ham rolled from under her dress onto the floor. Without a second's hesitation she yelled "Who threw that?" and by the time the clerk had looked around for the guilty person, the woman was gone, but without the ham.

Danny Stirrup

I had met Danny Stirrup in Key West. He was a draftsman, older than I, sometimes an architect with the right signature, who knew more about the conch architecture of the island than anyone else. He was born and raised in Key West. He designed the conch train station at the 100 block of Duval, the Polynesian House at 1415 Alberta Avenue and many other private homes. He knew all the local conchs and his best buddy was Clayton Papy.

I expressed to Danny that someday I would like to buy a small conch house in Key West. He called me in Miami to say that he was thinking of buying a large house and that on the property was a small conch cottage. He queried if I were interested. It would be expensive: $4,500. (This amount was Danny's down payment on the whole property.) I drove to Key West that Friday with dreams that could have filled volumes. (I could borrow the money from the Teacher's Credit Union.)

Danny had a tendency to want to be important and at one time he told me that he was "in constant contact with the White House". We all had a tendency to drink a little too much. I had been to bed with someone who worked for a Kentucky governor, and this trick gave me an ashtray with the Kentucky seal on it. Danny, in seeing the ashtray, asked "Where did you get that?" I answered "I'm in constant contact with the White House in Kentucky".

Home in Key West

The cemetery

If you were to have turned right (east) on Angela Street between the 700 and 600 blocks and walked three blocks through the residential district, you would have hit the cemetery, newly fenced. During the same storm that ruined Flagler's railroad, the hurricane washed many of the caskets south into the Atlantic Ocean. Many bodies were never recovered. "I feel like we've died and gone to heaven - only we had to climb up." Mildred Natwick in "Barefoot in the Park".

There was one problem, when I found out about the conch house and property. It was one house away from the Key West Cemetery. "How dare you say 'penis' to a dead person!" Lily Tomlin in "All of Me". That in itself would not have spooked me, but I also had heard the story of Elena, and that made me concerned.

There was a horror story elaborated upon by the conchs of a beautiful, dark-haired Cuban girl named Elena Hoyos Mesa. She had been married but her husband deserted her and her family had the marriage annulled, and she returned to live in her parent's home. She was sickly.

A German x-ray technician named Karl von Cosel came to town and fell in love with the frail girl. He was in his middle 60s and she was

147

23. She wanted to go to a Halloween parade but was too ill and stayed only a few minutes. She had to go back to her family's home where she died of tuberculosis a few days later.

She was buried in the Key West Cemetery, but Karl von Cosel abhorred her being in the cold ground, and the parents allowed him to build a crypt for their daughter's body. Two years later her body was dug up and put into the vault, and the body disappeared.

Von Cosel was arrested in 1940 for "illegally exhuming a body" and although a few years had passed, the embalmed corpse was found fully dressed in white satin and amazingly preserved, and there were tales of his sexual assaults upon the dead body, a sexual pervert. "You're dead. I killed you. Care for a little necrophilia?" Jonathan Pryce in "Brazil".

The statute of limitations had run out and prevented prosecution of Karl von Cosel. He moved to Zepherhills, Florida, and would sell picture postcards of the once beautiful girl to interested tourists. The corpse was reburied for the third time by her family in a grave without a headstone. The family feared the return of Karl von Cosel.

Although I could not get the story of the beautiful Elena from my head, Danny showed me the cottage anyway. It was not impressive from the outside; a falling-down front porch, a window to the left and the door straight ahead from the steps. Unpainted. He unlocked the front door. I walked into a long hall and put my foot through the flooring onto the ground a foot and a half below. Rotting floors.

Once I bought the house, I never thought about the story of Elena. I found great amusement in walking through the cemetery and reading some of the mostly forgotten cemetery stones that marked the graves of some strange and interesting people.

Some of my favorites, aside from B. P. Roberts epitaph of "I told you I was sick", was that of Thomas Romer, who was born in Nassau, Bahamas, in 1783. He "Died Key West 1891. Good Citizen for 65 yrs. Lived to be 108. Unaccountable for 43 yrs."

Another was the burial ground of "General" Abe Sawyer, who was a midget but insisted on being buried in a full-sized coffin.

A third was the ultimate paperboy of "The Miami Herald", Joaquin Godinet, "Bolo", who delivered the newspaper for 65 years, from 7/1/01 to 5/21/72 starting when he was seven.

When I would leave the house and go for a drink to "Chi-Chi's" to return toward dusk, many times I would help a young couple over the chain-linked fence, and their bottle of wine or beer, so they could be alone in the cemetery, a reasonable request since the gates were locked at sundown. There were few places to be completely alone, but the cemetery was one.

For the next six months, I worked on the house at 809 Packer Street by coming down to Key West on Fridays and not returning until Monday early morning. I bricked the back yard, and the left space to the house was an outside shower without consideration for Danny's bedroom window. We joined the houses with an eight-foot wall running from my house to his, a wall with a gate to get to the back yards.

Having already found out it would cost $600 to move the house from encroaching on my neighbor, Edith Kidd, I went to her to report the infraction. Her response? "I've lived in this house too long to worry about that." The encroachment was never resolved.

When I was working on the house, the neighbor would stand on a box and look through my second-room window, just out of curiosity. "Can I help you with something, Edith?" "Just Looking." Finally, this action became irritating, so when she looked into the room a few days later I had just taken a shower and I was standing naked. She never looked again.

Dirty Rose

Dirty Rose, a lady of the streets, liked her shrimpers and vice-versa. She was not the typical street person. Large bosomed, maybe a little oily, long, black hair with a defined gray streak, over 40 or 45, Dirty Rose would stay with her selected seedy boyfriend, but she did not consider herself a prostitute because she would not take money in exchange for her services. She would, however, take shrimp. Two large freezers were inside her kitchen.

When Dirty Rose found herself in need of money to pay the rent, she would wander by my house and ask if I wanted to buy some shrimp, and we would set up an arranged time for later that day. I would go to her apartment and she would fill my shrimp order for the guessed amount into a brown paper bag. I would pay her the price for shrimp and be on my way. Dirty Rose was not a bad girl; she was just more skilled in the shrimp business.

The smell of water boiling into which a can of beer had been poured, the dropping in of medium-sized shrimp for three minutes, the plate with crackers and breaking open the shells and eating while reading an evening paper became tranquility; my own home in Key West, and my own entertainment.

"The Key West Citizen"

One delight has been the evening mullet wrapper, "The Key West Citizen". It was aimed at the town's actions, social and anti-social. What a way to start an evening. Now the paper comes in the mornings, excluding Saturday.

Everyone read the paper exactly the same way, reading the headlines on the front page and turning directly to the crime report on the second page. The crime report was the most popular not because of any bazaar reasons but because it was often the source of laughter. You could get a full description of one of your friends' awful conduct of urinating in public and a report of the $27.50 fine.

There were very few serious crimes, few murders and no mass murders. Somewhere on the pages of the newspaper was an article concerning a local person who had his sewer concreted by the city because he hadn't paid his sewer bill in five years. He thought he would run up a bill and then go in and renegotiate the bill with the city for a reduced fee. A special section announced those people who had not paid their real estate taxes. It was wise to wait if your money were getting good interest in the bank over the interest of the fine. The social page always included one or more of the local politicians. There were highrise crypts for sale at the cemetery. And, the sports page.

For years "The Key West Citizen" was under the control of Margaret Foresman, the only woman editor south of Atlanta. Later, Jim Tucci became editor. Under anyone's control, mistakes and misunderstandings do appear.

This approach to life, the style of humor, is played in every aspect of life in the keys. Even our newspaper, "The Key West Citizen", uses the form of humor in reporting the crimes and in many articles. It was innocent imagination. "Now, I'll be the innocent milkmaid, and you'll be the naughty stable boy." Estelle Winwood in "The Producers".

Headline: "Alleged robber armed with bananas" was the crime report story of a young man who "... allegedly tried to rob a convenience store armed with nothing but two bananas and a frozen pizza".

In the sports section was the picture of a young fisherman from England and his 33 pound fish, and under the picture it stated he "... got his rocks off ..." by catching the fish.

A caption at the bottom of a page stated "Even flowers need a hard blow to pollinate the world".

Headline: "Pig's head missile hits business". The man ... alleged tossed the pig "... because the business had refused to rent a trailer to him."

In a crime report titled "Unexpected viewing", the article stated that "Only a day after police retrieved two nude men from atop a restaurant table there, they received word Wednesday afternoon that a man was standing fully exposed ...".

Headline: "Man forced to wear dress". A man "... said he was robbed at knife-point and he was forced to put on the dress and walk to his uncle's house six blocks away."

An article titled "Couple find intruder": "A couple who investigated a strange noise in their home Saturday ended up finding a woman wearing a polka-dot dress sleeping in their closet."

Headline: "Soldier charged for pinching officer". This was the story of a hotel employee who found a police officer attractive, pinched him on the butt, called him "baby, baby" and was sent to jail.

A woman waiting in line at a drive-in reported to police that two men "... wearing only what they were born with" walked to the drive-in window. A similar incident of "two stark-naked men standing on a porch ..." was reported. "One of the men ... put on a pair of shorts. The other man pedaled away on a bicycle."

Headline: "The woman suspect wasn't". A vending machine robber at a local motel attempted to hide his identity by wearing "... skirt, blouse, bra, wig, panties, fake breasts and brand new pair of red high heel pumps, size 10, police said."

Sometimes the newspaper would get a small touch of class like the woman who found her boyfriend in bed with another woman "... in flagrante delicto. The woman with the knife allegedly entered the room yelling 'get out of that mother----ing bed'" and the man ran naked to the county jail for protection.

In "Hot beans battery", a man was arrested during a domestic argument when he tossed the mixture on his woman. In a local grocery store, a man was "... arrested after a sausage fell out of his pants ..."

"A Key West woman was arrested for allegedly grabbing men's crotches on Duval Street early Monday."

A woman was arrested for eating and grooming herself in a convenience store without paying. Notice the crime report's detail which was apparently from the police report: "The officer allegedly observed her eating potato chips inside the store, then met with a witness, the store employee. He said the suspect first served herself a glass of soda and drank it, then opened a can of tuna with a can opener, which was also for sale. She also allegedly helped herself to Vlasic dill pickles, Perrier cherry-flavored water, potato chips and liquid Tylenol (cherry flavor). After the subject finished eating, she proceeded to open a box of Tartar Control Crest, apply Hair Control (Aqua Net) to her hair, then opened a package which contained a hairbrush and combed her hair. (She) then opened a jar of Vapor Rub and applied a finger-full to her nostrils. The subject then proceeded to open a package of Carmey (lip enrichment) and applied some (to) her lips ..." She was arrested.

An ad appeared in the 80s when Jim Tucci was editor from a woman wanting to rent a clean, efficiency apartment "with a very large dick". Misprint. The typesetter meant "deck". We argued if it were true, that the apartment owner died of a heart attack having answered the phone 350 times in a half hour.

In 1998 the "Citizen" tried to recreate these stories by elaborating on them, taking away the most treasured quality, that of spontaneity. The stories just happened from the police report, and they were funny because of the incident, the police report, or the description. There is no need to announce something funny. It just naturally happens.

One article that seemed to go on and on was the story of a young military man that was accused of sexually molesting a Doberman Pincer at eight o'clock in the morning under a trailer parked on Stock Island. It was probably the most speedy release from the military that the armed forces had ever known. We speculated that the young man was out of the service by noon. There were no dog interviews.

In the 80s, Richard Fowler had a fund-raiser to become a judge. Having known him, I had little to ask him, so I stated "How do you feel about bestiality"? He indicated that it was strange that I should ask because his current wife, Sandi, as a public defender had this wild Doberman Pincer case.

Many people would wrap their fish or fish bait in "The Key West Citizen". That was not quite the same thing as wrapping your grouper in the mullet wrapper. Since the local newspaper reported on local crimes and events of fishing, the grouper gained special attention. The grouper is a species of fish which is very tasty and very popular. The local fishermen catch grouper and will sell the fish for profit. It is legal.

A square grouper is a bundle of marijuana often wrapped in burlap and hidden in newspaper which can, to a certain number of people, be very popular and enjoyable, and the square grouper also can be sold for profit. It is illegal, however.

In the 60s and 70s, square grouper was quite common, and the result of selling square grouper was very profitable. It was not uncommon to see wads of bills thrown on a bar. Houses, boats, and beachside property were bought, cars were new, and an unbelievable number of gold chains and rings adorned young local's necks and wrists. Since Key West had been a smugglers' island where men looked for ships that ran aground and looted them earlier in its history, the illegal contraband didn't bother the morals of the people. Getting caught did.

Many had come to Key West for the open freedom and the relaxation and marijuana provided the means. Generally, many police knew who were selling while others turned their heads. Drugs were common and drug arrests were rare.

As the street price for marijuana increased, there was more obvious use of coke and heroin. The police began to tighten the availability, and more arrests were made. Prominent citizens were also taken to jail.

By the 80s, the hope for a person finding a square grouper washed ashore became risky. There was no hiding the fact of dealing in drugs; everyone could tell by the cash flow of the individuals. Several of the big distributors were caught; most just gave up the business for other legal business opportunities. Then Miami got into the open drug business in Key West.

With the heavy use of coke, crack, and heroin in the 80s, practically anything could still be bought on the streets. One explanation for going out of business is that "it went up his nose", snorting drugs. Businesses still close for the same reason. Miami drug dealers in Key West are common today and businesses, often restaurants and bars, are giving the same excuse of "... up the nose" where their casual use has become a habit that dominates their lives. Recently, we have found many younger drug infested dirt baggers, a profession now. Unfortunately, the new drug is roofies.

Through these years the effects of some of the drug users still remain. Because of the availability of drugs on the island, it is not unusual to find a person who is "burned out" as well as many who are working jobs beneath their capacities. As the conch train pulls tourists through our streets, many tourists complain of the number of dirt bags, the homeless, some strung out on drugs.

During the early 70s, Key West still seemed very far from the mainland and improvements and changes came slowly. The military bases quickened these changes. Money changed Key West.

Although Old Town Key West was the largest and wealthiest city in Florida in 1895, it changed. The exceptions were the influences brought by the military and the building between Key West and Miami. With a black population of ten percent and a strong Cuban heritage of the natives, the population between the two cities changed dramatically. The keys had a building boom from Stock Island to Key Largo. Many "second home" people from New Jersey, Michigan and Pennsylvania bought property here to avoid the bad northern winters.

Stock Island was so named because that is where, years ago, the people of Key West kept the livestock. Homes, trailers, shops and businesses had moved onto the key and, aside from the bend in the road for the Cow Key Bridge, it's difficult to know where Key West ends and Stock Island begins. Many consider Stock Island to be the future homes of those who will service the hospitality industry in the future because of increasing prices of Key West real estate and the inability to solve the low-income housing problems.

Clusters of houses reach all the way up the Keys with all financial levels of houses. Sugarloaf has become a town centered around the Sugarloaf Lodge, and the people from Marathon are so self-sufficient they rarely come to Key West. Key Colony Beach, Layton and Marathon are considered the Middle Keys while Plantation, Tavernier, and Key Largo are the Upper Keys and are much closer to Miami than to Key West. Some of these communities are fighting for independence from the county government. The improved highway system has allowed someone to live in the Upper Keys and work in Miami, and Key Largo is a close distance for a second home for Miami people.

Housing has always been a problem in Key West. Someone felt his city taxes were too high, and he called to have his house inspected and reevaluated. The city condemned the property. The same person decided to paint his house in a camouflage pattern, bought the paint, outlined the design, and threw a painting party for his friends. Only hours later the Old Island Restoration Commission was at his door, and he would be fined by the day if the house were not repainted.

Key West had its own electric company, but blackouts were common. The bars would be fully lighted by candlelight. There were no television sets, or air conditioners, or ice machines and the radio could pick up

Cuban stations. The City of Key West still owns the City Electric System.

Electricity controlled the water pressure to the homes and apartments, and the faucets often dribbled. A pressure pump to get the water to a second floor was illegal, but almost all two-story buildings had their own pressure pumps in the 60s.

Before the water pipeline from Florida City to Key West in 1941, the quality of water caught in the cisterns was questionable. Ice was scarce. The ice man used to deliver chunks of ice to homes and the bars, but it was expensive. With refrigeration, newer ice-making machines were welcomed, but the bar patrons continued to take the left-over ice of the first drink and pour it into the second, a savings to the management.

Sidewalks were always in need of repair with little money to repair them. Dogs roamed freely and the person walking would have to look down to see where he stepped. It was not uncommon to see a cat chase a dog. Chickens scratched the yards and pet pigs would be on dining room tables.

One bar owner claimed to the Board of Alcohol and Cigarettes that his cash registers would not work on his beach side bar because of the salt water. It would be necessary for him to work out of a cigar box, which he did with their permission.

Fresh vegetables were either grown in the warm island climate or shipped in from Florida City. There was plenty of fish, conch, shrimp and crawfish, called Florida lobster. Cuban coffee, particularly in the morning, would lead many of the group gathered around the coffee shop to the morning's gossip or work schedule.

Except for the northern end of Duval, the "Sloppy Joe's" and "Captain Tony" areas, the town was quiet and at rest. Even for late drinkers, the streets were usually empty by one or two o'clock in the morning. And the quiet of the night. The sound of rain on the tin roofs. The first rooster.

With the introduction and long stay of the military, time and the government's money soon mended some of the small inconveniences of Key West. Water flowed and pumps were no longer needed. Electricity was more constant, although there were still blackouts. Air conditioning was introduced. Sidewalks were starting to be repaired, but to many the "improvements" were an unfair balance to the loss of the slow, easy pace of Paradise.

The national news of the 70s was depressing, again with politics dominating the events of the day. "The Miami Herald" reflected this skepticism in its headlines of May 5, 1970, in reporting that four students at Kent State University were slain by our National Guard. A repeat of tragedy in September 6, 1972, with "Olympic Shoot-Out With Arabs", again capitalizing "NIXON RESIGNS" in August of 1974, to the August 17, 1977, and "Elvis Is Dead".

The two major hurricanes of the 70s seemed to support the people of Key West. The Governor of Florida ordered the evacuation of the keys for Hurricane David on September 2, 1979, and the sun was shining in Key West. A second hurricane, Frederick, was due in October of the same year, and it hit northern Florida. We rushed to the bars.

Toward the end of the 70s, Key West was no longer identified as a sleepy village. It had grown away from the military town it had been. The locals started to loosen control of the city because of constant infiltration of outsiders. The scars of the Depression had healed with the new found money. The Anita Bryant influence on Miami rejecting discrimination in housing and employment in 1977 made even more gays leave Miami for Key West. A new-found freedom was escaping the "rat race of business" often accompanied by drugs.

The conch train
The years had brought popularity to the local conch trains, a series of open cars pulled by motorized engines with a live driver, a practically memorized manuscript and the driver's own personal flair for telling stories of the island in his own fashion. The trolleys were open buses with the same drivers' vitas. The drivers take the same route day after day. If you are one of the people that live on the street route, you've heard the driver telling the same story, using the same lines, day after day, seven days a week.

There was a man on Simonton Street with a wide porch running across the second floor of a Victorian house. He would put on his bathrobe, pour his coffee or hot water, wrap a doll in a baby blanket, and when the conch train would start up his street, he would walk onto the porch with the baby in one arm, the coffee cup in the other hand, and just when he would get the attention of the tourists gawking at everything, he would pretend to trip, dumping the coffee and baby from the second floor onto the ground. The passengers would gasp, the driver's speech would be interrupted, and the man got his revenge on the conch train enterprise.

156

Rex Brumgart

Rex was one of the most popular drivers of the conch train because he was completely unpredictable. A very masculine man was caught walking in the middle of a block on Duval without a storefront or alley in which to hide. Rex announced over his microphone, "Key West is known for its many transsexuals. What may look like a man to you, the guy on the other side of the street, is really Miss Betty Jones. Good morning, Betty Jones." What else could the guy who was being gawked at by a train load of people do, except wave? His wife did not accept the news kindly. (How long have we been influenced by men playing women? Charlie Chaplin in "A Woman", 1915. Jack Benny in "Charley's Aunt", 1941. Red Skelton in "Bathing Beauties", 1944. Ray Bolger in "Where's Charlie", 1952. Tony Curtis in "Some Like It Hot", in 1959. And on and on.)

One summer afternoon around four, two guys decided to invite 20 men over for an impromptu cocktail party in their home. Rex was not invited because the hosts knew he was working. Rex pulled a full train load of tourists to the front of the house and announced "Ladies and gentlemen. We are going to see a typical Key West party. We'll walk through the house. Please do not order a drink, eat the hors d'oeuvres, or talk to the guests." 30 strangers walked through the house as the astonished guests froze, and they went out the back door onto the conch train and continued their trip. The hosts could only laugh once the invasion was finished.

The conch train would turn on Atlantic Boulevard to Bertha Street and ahead was the county beach. Rex would announce to his passengers, "The Island is well known for its flora and fauna. Many people put their plants in hanging baskets", and just as he would turn his train onto the beach area, he would comment, "Look at the basket on that one", purposefully embarrassing some sun worshiper in swimming trunks.

A very elegant, older man who had retired and lived in a large house across from the library was throwing a party for a mix of the locals. Every light in the house was on and paper bags with candles lined the walkways, yard, and pool. He was on the porch welcoming his guests. As a conch train loaded with tourists was passing, the driver said over his microphone "Hey, what's going on?" and the host responded "My husband just had a baby," and the train quickly traveled down the street.

Another conch train driver noticed as he started his drive there were two young men on the train, cameras hung around their shoulders, and he was quite sure the two young men were gay. As he started off in his half-filled train, he was aware they needed information on where to go in town. Into his spiel, he inserted comments that he thought would help the young men on their vacation. "Over on your right is one of the largest gay bars in town. Mostly men. It opens at three." "Behind that blue building on the right is usually full of gay girls." He could tell by their reactions that he was giving them the needed information.

A woman and her husband sitting directly behind the driver looked from side to side. Finally, the woman said "That's awful. Awful." The driver said "Pardon me?" She was quick to reply: "All these gay bars and things. They should all be shipped off to an island". He responded with "Exactly."

Not all days are suitable for the conch train. If it is only misty or in the fall when it rains about two o'clock in the afternoon for a half hour and then dries the ground during the next half hour, the passengers are given plastic slipcovers, and the train continues. You knew it was a bad day when the conch train did not run.

Rex's best friend was Richard Perkins whom he had known for years. Rex met Perkins the first day Perkins was in town, and they remained close friends over years. Although Rex would come to Key West only in the winter with bad weather in New England, Perkins saw the advantages of Key West, and with his eastern restaurant closed in the winter, he opened another in Key West, a duplication of the "right and social set". The restaurant was later sold to Joe and Beth Pizzo, but they ran it for only a year, and it was again sold.

"Dickies"

"Dickies" was a restaurant and bar on the opposite corner from the electric company off the beaten track to the east of Duval. It became very popular in the late 80s not so much for the food as for the customers, mostly locals and some winter people who would gather around the piano in the evening. Bobby Nesbitt, who started at "The Affair", went eventually to "Dickies", played and sang at the piano. The restaurant was filled with diners enjoying everything from meatloaf to lobster. It was a place to see and be seen, and it lasted a few years. Richard Perkins owned "Dickies". The weather drove him south in the winter when his New England restaurant was not as busy.

Richard Perkins arrived in Key West in a Mercury convertible, and during his first day he drove down Duval Street, past the Women's Club. Rex was standing on the porch of the Women's Club, and yelled to the stranger "Do you know eleven inches?" The car came to a stop, and Rex walked over to the car and said "If you do, have him call me." A chat between the two men, and Rex motioned for Richard to move over from the driver's seat. Rex gave Richard Perkins his tour of all the interesting places in the city while driving the new Mercury"

Richard Perkings and Rex were having dinner at the "Monster" months later and they were seated across from one another at a small table off B.J. Flats. Two ladies were eventually seated at a table across from them. Rex asked one of the ladies, "Do you have a wet pussy?" The astonished lady answered "What?" and placed the menu over her mouth to hide her laughter. "So do I" said Rex. "It must be the humidity." The two tables were joined for dinner.

A couple from New York married 20 years came to the island, an attempt to solve the marital problems that had festered for many years. Both had not been to Key West before. He loved the swimming, boating and fishing, and she hated the heat, what the humidity did to her hair, and the people they met.

They had reservations for an early dinner at "Dickies". She was late, but finally arrived, and they ordered lobster. Both dinners came and she excused herself to go to the ladies' room, and did not return. He waited, eating at his lobster and proceeded to eat the lobster that was intended for her. He paid the bill, never to return to New York again.

She had gone to an awaiting cab that had her luggage, to the airport, all prearranged. Moral: "When dinner comes, eat it."

The t-shirt shops

We had a particularly bad rainy day. In fact, it rained and blew all day, a total of 23 inches of rain. The streets were flooded. The electricity went out. People were water skiing in the streets and a row boat was in front of "Sloppy Joe's". Plastic garbage bags and rain coats came out. Nothing was dry.

An industrious t-shirt shop printed a dozen t-shirts with "I SURVIVED TWENTY-THREE INCHES" across the chest and on the left hand tail of the shirt, in small letters, was "of rain". The demand was so great for this t-shirt that the store printed three dozen shirts the next day and continued printing throughout the week. A collector's item.

Another collector's item was the t-shirt that grew from another local happening. It seemed the fire chief was caught selling marijuana in front of a school, arrested, convicted, and disappeared. A local t-shirt shop's big sale item stated: "WHERE IS BUM FARTO?" It was honestly his name.

During the rainstorm a story went around that had no relationship to fact. In a low spot on the island, the water had risen to the porch level and a man standing on the porch was approached by a small boat. "Get in" said the boatman. "God will save me", said the man on the porch. The water continued to rise and the man climbed to the roof. A second boatman came by and told the man "Get in". "God will save me" the man replied, and he climbed to the peak of the roof. A helicopter flew over and the pilot yelled "We'll throw you a rope." "God will save me" and the man refused the helicopter pilot's offer. The man drowned.

In heaven, the man met God and asked "Why didn't you save me?" God replied "What are you talking about? I sent two boats and a helicopter."

There were some things that were true about Key West, and some facts that have been stretched to be more enticing. It was difficult to tell truth from fantasy.

The conchs

Fantasy was often displayed in the ethnic humor, but the joking was about the original settlers of the town, the conchs. Granted, a conch is a muscle in a shell. However, using the term in a Key West manner, a conch is a person born and raised in the Keys, but this has been distorted to a "fresh water conch", a person not born in the Keys but one who has lived here seven years, and an "honorary conch", a political appointment for any imaginable reason complete with certificate. All other people are either "locals" for longevity or "outsiders" who may not be particularly liked by locals because they changed the ways of the town.

The older conchs do not find humor in this kidding. The younger conchs probably abuse this ethnic joking, particularly among themselves, more than locals or outsiders, but they feel they have the right. The young conchs rarely joke in this manner with the old conchs.

"What are the three happiest years of a young conch's life?"

"The third grade."

No non-conch would ever repeat the story, particularly to a conch. The humor is in bad taste as is all ethnic humor. Birth rights have responsibilities and liberties. Conchs can tell stories about conchs. Jews can make fun of Jews. Blacks can tell black stories. But, don't cross the line.

The compound

In the early 70s Danny Stirrup, my next-door neighbor at the Packer Street house, came up with an interesting idea during one of our Bloody Mary sessions. He had found a piece of property that had a total of 12 houses on it. There were six two- bedroom houses on Catherine Street and two more around the corner on Watson Street and four little cigar makers' cottages with a dirt road leading to them at the far north end of the lot. The road to the cigar makers' cottages was privately owned but it did have a line of telephone poles to the smaller houses. The cigar maker's cottages were about 12 feet wide, 30 feet deep and contained a kitchen and bath and one front room.

The idea was intriguing. Friends had made unrealistic statements like, "If you ever find a large Victorian house on the water for $5,000 ..." and no one ever did. There was a market for Miami people and Key West people.

The compound would be called Conch Grove; conch for the local people who may be interested, grove for Coconut Grove, the artsy section of Miami. Each person would own his/her own home and one 12th of a mysterious 13th piece of property in the very middle, each owner sharing equally in what we hoped would be a swimming pool.

Reality moved in. The houses would have to be expensive; the four small houses would be $6,000 each, and the other eight houses would be $8,000 each. Could we sell them?

As per agreement, each original house owner put $1,000 into a kitty, which was to be used to build a swimming pool on the 13th piece of property; $12,000. Everyone wanted a deep pool, one without a shallow end. At one meeting it was decided by vote that it was senseless to have a pool without a bar. There were no votes against. Danny Stirrup drew the plans for the poolhouse bar, and the shed at the other end of the pool had to go.

Then came the problem of finding a contractor who would build the pool. At that time, there were no swimming pool companies in town, but each contractor knew precisely how to do it. Halfway up the coral hole went four or five rows of concrete blocks. That cracked. Screening and cement and steel rods for the bottom. That cracked. Concrete blocks with steel rods and concrete. That cracked. Two years later, Conch Grove did not have a pool.

One local contractor knew the secret; blow wet cement. He borrowed the fire department's hose, spent half the day, and the technique was working perfectly. They never thought when they went to lunch that the hose would set up and harden. Conch Grove paid $600 for a new fire hose. The pool was finished.

Should Key West ever have a hurricane, go to the Conch Grove pool. Tons of cement, concrete block, bricks, iron bars, chicken wire, and construction wire went into the building of the pool. After that, the building of a poolhouse bar was easy.

Each house owner was responsible for fixing his/her own house. Some built additions. The school teacher in one of the cigar-maker's cottages stepped incorrectly in his attic and came crashing through his living room ceiling. He decided to leave the beams exposed over his one room and built a loft space over the kitchen and bath.

Regardless of the project of the day, around three o'clock in the afternoon, particularly on weekends, it was cocktail time around the open hole and eventually around the pool. Hammers and saws were put aside for fear that something would be decided at the meeting which had not been heard by all the owners. The rest of the day was unproductive.

One person had a young friend from the University of Miami that would come down with him on weekends for the purpose of painting the cottage. They would arrive in Key West around three o'clock on Fridays, cocktails at the pool, and dinner at a fine restaurant. The young man would paint on Saturday morning, slowly, but the summer sun was hot and the pool was inviting. The three o'clock meeting. Cocktails. Dining at a fine restaurant. Hitting the bars. Sunday morning. Lunch. In order to avoid the heaviest traffic, it seemed better to start back to Miami early. This procedure went on week after week. Finally the owner said "I could have had this house painted cheaper by Van Gogh."

It got a little risky after midnight and swimming nude in the pool. One owner would whisper loudly, "psst. Keep it down," from behind closed doors.

One owner brought home a young Marine of very questionable character but who freely admitted that he was a virgin and had never had any sexual experiences at all. A midnight swim. Drinks. Refills. This homeowner was the first person to whom the Marine had ever given gonorrhea.

It was at one of the three o'clock Conch Grove meetings that Danny Stirrup came up with another fantastic idea: "Let's have an enemy party tonight". The procedure was to call enemies of someone and invite both people while implying the other person would certainly be there. In a small town there was bound to be some friction. We all knew people that had not spoken to one another in weeks or years. Everyone knew.

There was one woman who tried to put the death notice of her enemy in "The Key West Citizen", a seemingly factual report that he had died from lack of oxygen to the brain, but the announcement was caught before publication. The information was viciously false.

One large homeowner had a baby-pink toilet, tub, and wash bowl delivered to his house. In the pool, another home owner commented "Can you imagine so-and-so's fat butt on that pink toilet". They were not talking.

Big controversy started over one of the large homeowner's houseguests. The guy was shaving his legs in the pool. The list of potential enemies was drawn, and the phone calls were made. The party was called for six o'clock poolside, and practically everyone showed on time, which rarely happened on the island. It was stiff at first. Then a second and third drink. Couples talked. Misunderstandings were clarified. Some admitted to wrong doing. The third drink. Someone accidentally fell into the pool. Too many cocktails. The party was a great success with many, but certainly not all, fences mended.

Most of the friction of the Conch Grove residents was minor and soon forgotten. Few held grudges, and if they held a grudge, they would just have to get over it. There were more important things to do.

Thirty-some years later, about half of the original owners of Conch Grove still own their original purchase in the compound. Others have sold, but the energy of the original owners is still with the people who live in Conch Grove.

There was a wild rooster that for some reason had a very awkward sense of timing and would start his announcing the new day a couple of hours prior to sunrise. One homeowner was particularly annoyed by this early sunrise announcement and tried in vain to capture, harm, poison and murder the wild rooster, but to no avail. Calls to the Humane Society, the police department, the Animal Shelter were fruitless. Poisoned corn. Pellet gun. A "45". Nothing seemed to work.

The frustrated homeowner was given good advice, "I have an idea. Go to the costume shop and rent a hen costume. Put it on. Make wooing chicken noises and when the rooster gets close, grab it and strangle it."

He responded "I can see the headlines now: 'Two-martini drunk in hen costume hit by beer truck while crossing the road'".

The rooster eventually died of old age.

The calendar of events of the small island was full. If you wanted to go to a party every night, it would have been possible in the town of 23,000 people that grew to 65,000 during season in the 70s. It would have become more possible to attend each nightly event if you were very wealthy, or you could have gone just to the bars for happy hour where a party would have happened.

Increasing real estate costs

The wooden houses of Old Town Key West have been here 80 or more years, and attempts have been made to modernize the basic structure of the house. Some of the old houses had no electricity, and that had to be added. Many did not have plumbing, and that was solved by adding an additional structure, usually at the rear of the house, and the new bathroom or kitchen often had a roofline different from the original house.

Some structure work was modern and not consistent with anything. Wooden pillars were removed; wrought iron supports were added. Wooden six-over-six windows were modernized to jalousie windows. Concrete slabs were laid, first for parking cars, then for easy lawn maintenance. The wooden balustrades were substituted with decorative concrete blocks, and many had rotted and were never replaced. Fences of all kinds were built. Wooden triangular supports held second- story porches where pillars once were. The pillars were cut back so they would not interfere with automobiles that seemed less manageable than the horse-drawn carriages.

Some changes in the architecture were wanted by new tenants and some were very positive. Windows were converted to French doors. Cisterns were turned into pools. Patio yards were bricked. False widow's walks were added. Gingerbread could compliment practically any turn-of- the-century basic construction.

Many of these modernizations were accomplished by going back to the original look of the house, while adding the modern touches that made the house more livable. All kept in mind that Key West was not a restored town like Jamestown, but that we had to live in the houses we were restoring, and that we were demanding more comfort, and that we had different guidelines for esthetics than in the years before.

There was much more emphasis upon plantings, and the tropical climate was compatible to many plants that were not indigenous to the island. A photograph of Key West in 1900 shows little vegetation in the town. Some trees and tropical bushes were planted that were not indigenous to the island. Many plants died in the strong sunlight. Others adjusted. All added to a tropical setting for small and large houses alike.

Many of the houses beyond Old Town were modern houses of the

50s and 60s, concrete block structures. Little attempt was made on these houses to moderrnize and reflect the appearance of the Victorian homes of 1900. Attempts that were made often failed. The new scale, construction ideas, proportions, windows and doors were wrong for the 1900 period. Many conchs who had once lived in Old Town and received profits from the sale of their real estate moved eagerly to New Town. The comfort of a more modern building had many advantages.

Advertising on commercial buildings in 1900 was painted with large letters in bright colors on unpainted or white-washed wooden buildings, and the homes were either the natural wood or white washed. Strict sign ordinances were imposed by the governing Old Island Restoration Commission ((OIRC), but they fell lax. New rules including only wooden signs were ignored. There was no one to implement the laws. Some felt they could ignore the rules, and some angry homeowners were fined for building without authorization. OIRC was changed to Historical Architectural Review Commission (HARC). Although historically accurate, we would not have wanted to live with the advertising of the l900s. We are still fighting City Hall for permits to do about anything to our private homes.

One thing that changed significantly was the color of the houses of Old Town. Some have said that if you painted your house, always with white-wash, the city tax assessor would re-evaluate your house. Others have said that the boat builders were proud of their carpentry skill and did not want their finished product hidden under paint. The original Old Town buildings were either a natural sun-bleached color or some were painted white houses, most with dark green shutters.

In the early 70s of renovation, the Caribbean colors of the homes came in fashion with painting of the Artist's House in subtle yet clear Caribbean colors. Many objected, but the fad kept on. "We're going to look like Disneyland" was a common cry. The paint was refined so it could better hold without fading against the sun and salt air. Natural or white houses were painted pastel colors and that gave way to brighter shades of pastel colors, brighter purples, greens, and blues.

I should have tried to make a fortune out of stupidity, but I didn't know how. I called a local lumber-yard to ask about getting some wood chips to spread in the yard and help the vegetation. Wood chips were $14 a truck load. I ordered two loads, $28, and I sent a check. A few days later, there was a mountain of wood chips in my yard. It took three weekends to finally spread those chips over the yard, and it took four months of walking on a yard that felt like walking on a water mattress for the chips to settle into the ground. But, the plants grew. And grew. And grew. Everything, including building mistakes, was hidden by lush, tropical plants.

The insides of the original houses of Old Town were usually the same. Since many were built by shipbuilders, the horizontal stacking of boards, particularly Dade County pine which was impervious to termites, with similar ceilings was used on the mansions as well as the shot-gun houses, and the cigar-rollers' cottages. The small rooms usually contained two windows, one on each wall, no closets, and a main hall from the front door. That was the period's standard.

Current detailing of construction

Currently, new construction of Victorian-style houses in Old Town makes it difficult to tell when a structure was built, with the new construction so much like the remodeled houses. We added closets in new construction. The doors between bedrooms were blocked for privacy. Blank walls hid undesirable views. We added air conditioning and soundproofing.

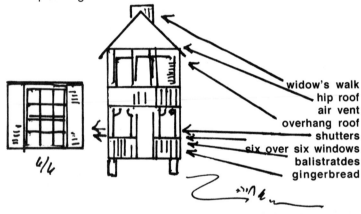

widow's walk
hip roof
air vent
overhang roof
shutters
six over six windows
balistratdes
gingerbread

two-story conch house terms

The two-story conch houses had many specific characteristics that could be easily duplicated with more modern technology. The gingerbread around porches used to be handmade; now it can be done by machines. I fear that someone will try to incorporate all of the characteristics of a conch house, making it much too "authentic", a mettle of shapes and forms. Conch houses designs have been bkuilt out of Oldtown, even at the golf course, on Tank Island, and at Duck Key

There were very few widow's walks in town in the l900s, mostly reserved for the large formal houses. The perch would be used to look out at the sea, as much for wives spotting husbands as men looking for grounded boats.

Some new widow's walks hide roof-top air conditioning units. I know of no original 1900 one-story house with a widow's walk, as should be. The widow's walk usually had the same shape of gingerbread trim as on the first and second porch railings.

The hip tin roof was common, easy to install and it lasted a long time. We seldom see owners painting their roofs the aluminum color, but that is because of a superior protected metal that fights rust. Roofs were often mended with black tar and painted aluminum.

There were air vents at the side points of the house, obviously to let out warm air. Ceiling ventilation holes similar to portholes in boats accomplished about the same thing, but were difficult to keep water-proofed. The ceiling holes were simply kept open by a stick. Air conditioning has eliminated their necessity.

Houses usually had six pained windows over six, making twelve separate panes. There were often two pairs of shutters on the windows, a pair outside for weather protection and a pair inside for light and breeze control. Although most houses were painted white or left natural in the l900s, today the shutters are an accent and painted a contrasting color or a complimentary darker color of the house.

The front door of the first level of the larger homes was centered on the four post porches, often with a complimentary door on the second floor off the center hall leading to the porch. The bedroom windows on either side looked out onto the porch for ventilation. Every exterior wall had a window in every room. Inside walls without windows usually contained a door even if it were to an adjoining bedroom. At night, the doors and windows were left open.

simplicity of a conch house

The porches were trimmed in gingerbread, but only the "grand" houses because the gingerbread served few purposes except for advertising (such as in the gambling house by "La te da"). The trim was of conservative design, not fish, paper-dolls, or flamingos. If painted, the ceiling of the first floor porch was usually green, the second story ceiling was painted blue. There was sufficient roof over-hang to protect against the tropical winds. The early shipbuilders did build porches that wrapped around two sides of the house, the sides most comfortable for breezes, but porches were considered a luxury although even the conch cigar rollers' cottages had porches, a social center.

The houses sat close to the road (or the road came close to the houses) for easier accessibility. The structures were on stone pillars a few feet above the ground level. The breezes blew under the house, and the under-the-house was a protection for the animals.

Modern technology and construction has outgrown cisterns, cook houses, out- houses, salt houses and barns. Two local builders did convert their privy into running water and hooked to the sewer line, expanded it with shower and steam room, and used it by the pool.

The 70s brought an influx of gays from New York, California and the mid-west, and with them the trimming, remodeling, and painting of many of the wooden conch houses. Along with the gays, straights, both singles and couples who were tolerant of the gay lifestyle followed. With the growth of motels and hotels, the building of high-rise condominiums and time-shares, the small amount of vacant land on the island gave way to new building. Private-home, waterfront property became more expensive. The beaches and ocean-front property rose in value. Large private homes were rebuilt into guesthouses or replaced with condominiums or hotel rooms. Property prices rose.

Flaming Maggie's, Books, Art, and Coffee
At the corner of Fleming and Duval take a right (east) and walk down several blocks of guesthouses and private homes to Margaret Street, where on the corner is the town's largest and most popular gay book store (830 Fleming). Get the paper, have a cup of coffee and sit at a table and "people watch". Paul runs the store, and you are almost guaranteed to meet someone you know. It's great cruisin'. It's also very relaxing and very Key West. Flaming Maggie's has the largest and most up-to-date collection of gay magazines, books, and interesting paintings by local artists.

THE 400 BLOCK
Fleming St. to Eaton St.

In the middle of the 80s, money started to get tight. There was less home entertaining and more large-function entertaining. Some people with second homes in Key West put their properties for sale to a non-buying public. The dollar started to get smaller, and much of the high living was out of reach for many. There grew a new kind of judgment, a new perspective of what Key West should be.

It was reported that Mary and John Spottswood bought the seven story La Concha Hotel, erected in 1924, and the Casa Marina building for $650,000; a millionaire's fund in 1966 or 1967. They bought the two buildings from Sam Hyman.

"The Mermaid Room"

The bar off the registration desk of the La Concha Hotel in the large lobby was called "The Mermaid Room". Although the hotel was closed, the first-floor bar remained open in the 60s. Patrons were the city's local characters, politicians, and many higher-ranking military who would gather nightly for cocktails. A blond woman named Tre le Roque waited on the men and women sitting around the bar, and she knew most of them.

It was Paul's, an adventuresome Pennsylvania bachelor, first trip to Key West, and only through the grapevine did he end up at "The Mermaid Room". He was nervous, unsure of this strange group of men and women, and he was not known by the bartender. He sat apart from the group and ordered a drink.

An attractive younger man came into the bar and sat a couple of seats away and said to Paul in a voice the whole bar could clearly hear "Sure. Don't speak to me today. It was okay for you last night. I suppose you want your five bucks back?"

Paul sank to the floor. "Who was this fool?" From that awkward introduction, Paul stayed on in Key West for the rest of his life.

Two young men in their 20s, Chuck Lamb and Steve Richie, arrived in Key West from Minnesota, fell for the city, got jobs as waiters, which required a white shirt and black tie and pants, and they would carry the black restaurant check receipt books. The guys would meet after their restaurant shifts at "The Mermaid Room" around three o'clock in the afternoon. They were quiet and reserved with the older crowd until Tre le Roque yelled "Are you two Bible salesmen here again?"

"The Mermaid Room" was a circular bar with a large plate glass window and door on Duval Street. A second entrance was from the lobby of the closed hotel. The bar's surface was a series of shells, sunken model pirate ships, fish, and sand embedded in two inches thick of epoxy. It had yellowed over the smoke-filled, liquor-spilled happenings. It was a favorite spot for the military brass. Carrie Trumbo managed the bar for a couple of years, and then it went through all kinds of phases including a little go-go dancer named Pygmy. It was popular. A common phrase during hurricane season was "If I'm going to be blown to death, let it be in the Mermaid Room." "I always said if I had a choice of death, I wanted to be screwed to death. I think I was." Eric Bogosian in "Special Effects".

"The Miami Herald" on November 5, 1980, headlined "A Reagan Landslide".

Miami had grown significantly. The Cuban community had stretched from Eighth Street through Coral Gables, South Miami, Miami Beach and in every part of Dade County. The city grew to have 52% of the population from Latin backgrounds, truly a bilingual city. In 1980, some 800,000 of Dade County's 1.7 million people were Latins by background.

The Miami boatlift from Cuba in 1980 assisted nearly 1,000 gay people according to the Coalition for Human Rights. The gays had swung into action with new organizations and the attention of the country's government to the problems facing patients with AIDS. Miami Crisis Network was established in 1983 and soon many other groups sprung up, often duplicating services and spreading the funding out very thin.

Key West did not have the same problems. The AIDS organization's responsibilities were strictly outlined under AIDS Help, and it became the leader in seeking the financial help for the care of the patient. With a giving community effort and the volunteer work of many people, AIDS Help soon owned its own living quarters for many suffering from the disease, and the public support with dollars was unbelievable. The churches, the social organizations, the bars and restaurants, the clubs and the part-time residents as well as the conchs supported those suffering. Benefits, art sales, penny banks, fund raising through marathons, beauty contests, drag shows or whatever added money to the cause.. Key West's care for AIDS patients was so outstanding that many who were ill somewhere else traveled here, the Paradise Island, and the community took in and supported even the visitors. They continue to give outstanding care.

Of course there was some racial friction; this type of growth practically assures complexity. In Miami, the McDuffie Case left 19 dead and 216 hurt when the "Herald" announced "Cops Freed in McDuffie Case". There was racial reaction to the killing of a black biker by a white cop. Since Key West had experienced few racial difficulties, we did not face this situation here.

In 1981 Hurricane Donna passed over the keys. Key West reported only 35 mph winds, the speed of a good tropical storm. The hurricane of 1985, Kate, was a mild hurricane, but it came at the time of the runoffs of the city's political elections, which had to be rescheduled for two weeks later.

A technique of how to survive a storm, a list of storm survival tips, was distributed. It is called a recipe for hurricane survival in Key West.

I. Set alcohol on drainboard.
2. Gather children and mate into house.
3. Point out major bearing wall out of range of flying glass. (Under stairwell or closet or bath are often good protection.)
4. Take one ounce of alcohol.
5. Board up or close shutters over windows.
   Open window opposite side of the house from the rain direction.
6. Take another ounce of alcohol.
7. Remove all objects that could be swept up by the wind including furniture, potted plants, the animals.
8. Refill glass.
9. Fill bathtub with water.
10. Make sure Bunsen burner and food is available. Have some other can opener except electric. Get matches for candles.
11. Glass.
12. Let her blow.

This is guaranteed to help you through the majority of hurricanes with minimal damage, except to your liver.

La Concha Hotel - Holiday Inn
"You cad! You swine! ... You make me sick when I had to let you kiss me. I only did it because you begged me. You hounded me. You drove me crazy. And after you kissed me, I always used to wipe my mouth --- wipe my mouth!" Bette Davis in "Of Human Bondage".

All hotels and motels had their problems. Months of hard labor went into the restoring of the La Concha Hotel by the Holiday Inn Corporation. Not only was a large addition built onto the existing hotel, but the old hotel had to be completely revamped, as they joined two long and narrow hotel rooms into one unit. There was one other solvable problem. According to the design of the old hotel, the new showers of the old hotel would have a large plate-glass window in the shower which overlooked the pool area, but a new technique of one-way glass easily solved the problem.

The opening of the Holiday Inn Hotel was attended by a mass of Key West locals and, like every other major venture, everyone who had worked on the building, those responsible for the design, carpet, or tile had to be thanked in a public ceremony. The hotel was beautiful and the mob of people gathered upstairs around the pool close to the two bars looking toward the six-floor structure, to hear the dedication speeches.

A light appeared on the fourth floor. A naked woman appeared in the light, a woman taking a shower and eventually shaving her legs. Attention was drawn away from the speakers as a low mumble went through the crowd. All attention was drawn to the fourth floor. The woman finished and her boy friend or husband came into view and took a brief shower. The installation of the one-way glass window had been reversed, and the bathers could not see out, but others could see in. The guests were never told. The next day the plate-glass one-way window was properly installed. An oversight.

There were many oversights in the keys. The couple who bought the two story eyebrow house to find before closing that the owner neglected to build steps from the first to the second story. The man who bought the large brick store on Fleming Street to restore it to condos only to find the brick was only veneer and hid a wood frame. Most oversights were handled peacefully or with gusto.

going to a party

John and Carol Wesley wintered in Key West from their home in Detroit and the successful retired medical doctor and his wife fell into the island rhythm. Their friends included a large group of single males and they entertained and were entertained often because they were compatible with everyone.

At one particular party hosted by one of their male friends, John and Carol were not invited. Oversight? The future host explained to John and Carol that this party was just for the guys.

The night of the party, John and Carol were having drinks with two other couples when John got an idea. Although he had a large, hairy chest, and was a very masculine man, he squeezed into one of his wife's dresses, and found shoes, hose, gloves, and a going to a party wig. He was not glamorous, a gross understatement. The two-and-a-half couples hid across the street from the party behind cars while uninvited John, probably the most ugly, completely dressed drag, rang the doorbell and went in. Silence, then laughter. A few minutes later, the host called the hiding couples into the party, and then the straight, next door neighbors, and it was another Key West social affair.

St. Paul's Church

The Reverend Alvah Bennet opened the first religious school in 1832 in Key West on the property which eventually became a church, St. Paul's Protestant Episcopal Church, built in 1840. It was destroyed in 1846 by a hurricane but was soon rebuilt. Forty years later, 1886, it was burned but then rebuilt. Again in 1909, it was destroyed by hurricane, but the present building has remained in place since 1912. There is a parsonage beside the church on Duval. A schoolhouse was built in 1842 called The Baldwin House, and, although it was a private school, it was subsidised by school taxes.

Somehow the Episcopal Church in Key West seemed to serve as the correction center for priests that had misbehaved at another place. There was an Episcopal priest from Coconut Grove named Eric that we used to kid who turned German Shepards into dachshunds by walking the dogs in public to the extent the dogs begged to be left home. He was a muscular, well developed, physical-fitness type who particularly liked to walk the dog at night around the cruisey area of the Grove. He was transferred to Key West. He walked new dogs in Key West where the street trafic was sailors. After a couple of years, he was transferred to Hawaii where he died.

Metropolitan Community Church

As a result of the strain of the times, six or more people who would sit at the Women's Club on Sunday morning working toward creating a better life for many of the gay people of the island by organizing a Metropolitan Community Church in 1980. Coconut Grove had started a gay church in 1970. A gay synagogue group, Etz Chaim, was founded in 1975.

Many gays had been brainwashed and discouraged by their family's religion into considering homosexuality a sin. The gays wanted something of their own. Two years later, the few had grown to 60 members. They bought the old Salvation Army building on Petronia Street and converted the building into a church. But the church attendance was not just made up of gays; it was a variety of people: married couples, straight singles, individuals all who were looking for more in the troubled times of confused values.

Some of the confusion of being gay was that so many religions felt being gay was not consistent with the teachings of a particular religion. Being religious people, the gays felt they had no place to worship and feel comfortable being themselves. The Metropolitan Church helped that lacking in a gay's lifestyle.

It was not that many gays lacked religious training. It is surprisng how many have been deeply involved in religious training, but have felt it would be better to step aside from their early religious training when they realized they had actively gay impulses.

Frank T. Hirons, STM, Ph.D.

Born in Massachusetts, Frank served as a Chaplain in the military where he was assigned to serve Harry Truman in Key West. He fell in love with the island. After being married for 31 years, and having one daughter, Nancy, he retired from the ministry, became a consultant and helped develop the National Condominium Act while he was with the Condominium Association Institute where he taught. He divorced, and retired to Key West ten years ago with Floyd Davis, his friend of 20 years. He continues writing and is now a grandfather. He is still very active in the Key West activities.

Many groups banded together to raise money to fight AIDS and to help those who found themselves in that position of being HIV positive. The Metroolitan Community Church grew. Hospice grew. AIDS Help grew. In the early 80s, there were virtually weekly events scheduled to raise money to fight and care for those afflicted, and to support those activities of the gay lifestyle.

Our understanding of the disease ran through every extreme. A local politician remarked in a public meeting "AIDS. Another Infected Dick Sucker." We were so ignorant of the problem. Even through this dreaded crisis, there was the sense of looking on the lighter side, maybe born from the tension and the desperate helplessness of the times. We joked out of ignorance and frustration. Some swore never to cut back on sex.

Robbery

No one likes the vulnerability of being robbed, but it is a common factor of the fast lane. Most will take precautions to protect themselves, but even the individual fouls up. Particularly the gays have an appreciation for the "finer things of life", and diamonds are probably one of those finer things.

Ken had a beautiful diamond ring that he willingly showed around the bar. One person would try on the ring and give it to another, then eventually back to Ken. He got drunk during this display and took an ugly-while-sober, handsome-while-drunk man back to his house for a nightcap. The next day Ken called one of the people who had admired his ring and asked him if he had kept Ken's ring. The man assured Ken that he had gotten the ring back from all the people that had admired it at the bar, and he advised Ken not to report it stolen until he had searched the house. Ken seemed to only half believe the friend.

Six hours later Ken called his friend to report "... the way I must have figured was to hide the ring where no one would ever look and in something that no one would ever steal. I found my ring in the middle of a knot in my underwear drawer". A drinker's perfect reasoning.

Chuck on Truman Avenue had a huge diamond set free-standing in a gold Tiffany mounting. Naturally he was quite proud to display the handsome and unique, very large diamond. When he died and his estate was settled, it was found that the ring's setting was from Tiffany, and its value was $240. However, the stone was glass and worthless.

The local owner of "Billies' Restaurant" had a New York apartment, and he would generously loan it out to friends. He loaned the apartment to Jim, who returned to Key West with a tragic story of how he had been mugged, losing his wallet, all money and identification, credit cards and, strangely, one shoe.

Two weeks later, the manager of the restaurant borrowed the apartment, and he found a strange thing. Stuffed between the ice cube trays was a shoe with wallet and all. The mugging had been a lie.

Most characteristic of the early 70s were the many small-home parties. Just meeting a person in a bar for a drink could start a party. Preconstruction parties for ideas. Finished-the-pool party. I'm bored blasts. Divorce parties. Locals admitted that they would use any excuse for a party, either in mass or small group or privately.

During one summer, a large house was being moved down Duval Street, and business was not brisk. The shop owners or managers closed their front doors, mixed some drinks, and sat on the curb to watch the large house being moved to its new location. Store patrons had to call to the curb for service. The house became the "Bagatelle Restaurant".

The town was losing the tackiness as new businesses opened weekly. There were few vacant shops on Duval Street, and the southern end of the business district grew up to Petronia Street. The northern end shops designed to take advantage of the tourist trade soon to be enhanced by the cruise ships. There were recognizable bars, tourist traps, and t-shirt shops.

In a small town little is secret. Those afflicted with AIDS knew the community was trying to do all that was possible. Rather than hide, many faced their problems openly before the public. We had gone beyond "... you can get it from a water glass". They knew the community understood.

Fantasy Fest

The idea of a Mardi gras parade was the economic trick that made a bad season successful. September and October were the months to vacation away from the islands. As the idea of Fantasy Fest and the reputation grew, each year more and more tourists would come to Key West, so the small town's partying became news that attracted even more tourists.

The early parades were filled with locals and kids and the high school marching band. (Later, to the wisdom of the school board, the high school band was not allowed to participate because of the questionable morality of the parade. Many full-time residents do not support the band being in the parade to this day. Most of the band members were at the parade, but not marching.) All would line the streets with their folding lawn chairs to watch the parade of crazy costumes, crooked lines of marchers, the four-and- five-year-old Twirlettes with dominating parents attempting to keep the lines straight, all marching down the main street of town.

Local block parties were organized too. Ladies sold brownies and conch fritters to the meandering locals. Local artists painted faces. Everyone was in costume. Every local drag was dressed for the occasion. A top-heavy young lady road bare-chested across the hood of an automobile; she was a hood ornament. The bars became crowded too, of course.

In the coming years, Fantasy Fest became more commercial, attracting more marchers and performers, more professional floats and professional costumes, and the parade was extended to a week of events, costume competitions, a lavish parade with lights, and the impossibility of finding lodging during the week without a many-months' reservation. The hometown parade of a quiet, poor business period became a hugh Mardi gras Parade.

Easter hat party

The Easter bonnet parties followed the same pattern. A local man held a party on Easter Sunday afternoon and requested the guests to wear hats. The couples, maybe 30 in all, tried to create something unusual, and the event became competitive. From baseball caps, hats with dangling beer cans, fresh flower hats, the group made a strange appearance of weird-looking men and women enjoying an excuse for a party. After the original party, the whole group went to the bar at 'La te da'.

The commercial advantages of the Easter Day Hat Party was obvious in the following years, and restaurants, bars, and galleries took over the event. Skillfully planned in the 90s, it was possible to go from one party to the second to the third with the same hat; a total day of partying.

Prior to this period, the small, sleepy town had tourists which were more interested in the quiet and lack of activity. With the influx of people from all over, their was the realization that many made money from more tourists, and the reputation of the laid-back party town continued to add tourists. The town was casual, but it was not laid back without activity. When to hold an event became paramount. Competition increased the full schedule of Key West.

Some events were tried and never repeated the following year. Many became yearly events. Four major events became annual standards: the Queen Mother Contest, the beer run, the bed race, and the best bartender competition.

Queen Mother contest

There was the Queen Mother contest. Babe had run "Delmonico's" Bar in the 60s, and she was voted the first Queen Mother. Babe ruled with a strict hand, until she would get a little into the sauce. Babe married a Canadian, Duckie, a fovorite bartender, and he could obtain American citizenship.

The Queen Mother contest was held the next Monday after Mother's Day. Each year a contest would be held and someone would be chosen to represent the gay life of Key West. When the gay cruise ship comes into Key West, the Queen Mother is there. She would host an annual tea party and attend many fund raising events. She is "the hostess with the mostest", spending many dollars on gowns and appearing as a representative of the alternate lifestyle of Key West. Regardless if she has won because she is beautiful, or "campy", or wicked, or talented, she has been selected each year since 1982.

Babe	1983-84
"Ma" Evans	1984-85
Nexxus DuCum	1985-86
Charlie Moeller	1986-87
Joe Lahey	1987-88
Parquesa	1988-89
Rusty Rhodes	1989-90
DDT (twice)	1990-92
DD Sharp	1992-93
Charlena Sugerbaker	1993-94
Judy (J. L.)	1994-95
Hellen Bedd	1995-96
Alma Jean	1996-97
La La Belle	1997-98
Diamonque	1998-99

One of the contestants and winners of Queen Mother ran a wonderful little hidden motel off the main street and nestled in a private home area. It was called the Sea Isle. Cocktails were served daily around the pool. The motel was filled with tourists that had come for years to the island for a couple of weeks of relaxation. Locals called the motel the Senile.

The beer run

Usually held on the Saturday closest to the Irish St. Patrick's Day celebration was the town's yearly beer run for all eager participants. The beer run was organized so, for a small fee, a person could join runners from one bar to another baar on the other side of town, downing a glass of beer, and on to the second, the third, the fourth until, if he or she lasted, to the fifth, sixth, seventh or eighth. Observers watched the slow deterioration of the runners and cheered them on. First to the finish line was the day's hero. The victor often got very ill.

In the 80s, the rules changed and the event became the beer walk. All the bars were in one line not having to run from one side of town to the other, and there were many more volunteers. Much less messy.

The bed race

The bed race was a competition of two or more beds per race and often ten or 12 races, and a run-off competition. Four people would push a bed with a rider in the bed for a specified distance of five or six blocks. The five-man-or-woman teams were sponsored by local hotels, restaurants, bars, or shops. A bed on wheels. A bed on skis. Four ladies from the Red Barn Theatre production, in nuns' habits and tennis shoes, pushed a four-poster bed and rider down Duval. The curbs of Key West cannot sustain the impact of a moving bed and rider. There are always crashes into the awaiting audience, but all crashes have been without casualties. The bed is pushed back into the street to continue the race.

The Best Bartender

The Best Bartender was a competition, but it was not a foot race. Each bar would have ballots, and the local patrons could complete these ballots for their selection of the ugliest bartender, the most efficient, the most employed by different bars during the year, the most liked, the most likely to get fired, the most often drunk. The categories changed yearly. At a late-evening party, the winners were announced to humorous charges of ballot packing, cheating, payoffs, and cheap politics.

The bartenders even had their own organization, CHUBS (Caya Hueso Ugly Bartender Society), and their own bar on the second floor over the Bull Bar. Only bartenders could join the club and only club members were allowed in the bar.

There has always been concern for the best bartenders in Key West, and this rides closely with who is making the most money. Actually, the most secure jobs are probably the jobs in the large hotel bars or chain bars that provide social security, hospitalization, dental insurance, etc. Most of the gay businesses are the smaller, privately owned restaurants and bars that do not have these luxuries. Don't mention "union" in any of these places for fear of being without a job.

Of the bartending jobs and bar-backs in bars and restaurants, the waiters and waitresses in heavily gay eating establishment, the desk people and housekeeping of the guesthouses, most of the gay labor of Key West has to have a job or two or three, at least two roommates, and live conservatively, and most still think living in Key West is worth the insecurity. Everyone blames everyone else. If rents were not so high ... If wages were better ... If it were not so expensive living here ... If I were rich ... Yet, labor doesn't often leave Key West.

Getting a job is usually not difficult if you realize you must start at the bottom and work your way up. However, living here is different from being here on vacation. It's more difficult to keep a gay relationship because we thrive on "temptation". Alcohol and drugs are common, and it's expensive.

What has developed is a group of about two dozen gay bartenders, several hundred gays as waiters who work side by side with straight waiters, many gay kitchen help whose sexuality isn't important unless they make it so, a few cooks or chiefs, many guesthouse owners who last three or more years, and a whole host of housekeepers, repair men, etc. They constantly change the growing number of jobs.

The worst I can do is to list the gay bar and its major bartender because it will be out-dated before printing. They are often products of the domino effect; one quits for an opening, creating changes up and down the chain of jobs. However, it is often nice to know your bartender, so a partial list includes

1. Nancy Wozniak was at "La te da" upstairs at "Tree Top Bar", now "Cafe Blue"
2. Rusty Rhodes and Constance at "Diner Shores"
3. Heather Ann at "Club International"
4. Travis was at " Cafe Blue", now at "Donnies' Place"
5. Patric and Sharon at "Square One"
6. Trish, Buckets, and Shar at "801 Bourbon Street"
7. J. R., Dawn and Chuck (Sylvia) at "Diva's"
8. Mat at " Saloon One"
9. Dish at the "Epoch"
10. Scotty Ann, Jerry and Mable at "Numbers"
    This list has probably changed twice since I've written it.

Along with all this frivolity were also yearly events that took a more serious direction: the Heart Fund, the blood drives, United Way, Mark House, a home for mentally challenged adults, and many more. All were supported by this community.

The town celebrated all of the traditional holidays also. Someone asked why the houses in Key West are so small, and the answer was "We're rarely home".

At a New Year's Eve party, rather "blast", in front of "Sloppy Joe's Bar", the police department was perplexed as to how to handle the larger than expected crowd that was pouring onto Duval from all the parties, beer cans in hand. A local woman who had a reputation of being in the thick of things felt the police action of getting out fire hoses was a violation of her rights, and she loudly told the policemen that she was a longtime, outstanding member of the community. Then she dared the policeman to use the hose on her. She found herself blown back, wet, against a picket fence.

But strange things happened even at events that were quite serious. The humor of the laid-back attitude was felt in all events.

At a fund raiser at the back pool of Duval House in the 800 block, which was an elegant combination of two turn-of-the-century homes made into a guesthouse in the 70s, one woman was loud, insulting, and irritating to most of the guests. They had come to the party to raise money for an AIDS-related function. She insulted the wrong person, and with a bump of his hip, the woman went into the pool and came to the surface yelling "I'll sue you."

I guess the service people of Key West have become so used to dealing with the individualistic personalities, the unique personal flairs of their clients, they have developed a great degree of tolerance. The waiters, bartenders, and back-ups also remember when there were not so many tourists in town. They are patient, but even patience can be broken. Patrick of "Square One" banned a woman "... for her lifetime and a day" in a previous job. The same woman said to a waiter that she eats breakfast at his restaurant every morning, and on one particular morning she said "I just don't feel like paying." He suggested she pay, and not return. The bar owners always back thier bartenders and, usually, their waiters.

Key West artists

When the weather is beautiful, lifestyles a little loose, and attitudes accepting, you'll always find a group of painters who try to capture the local color as well as the local attitudes on canvas. Key West has always had an in-house group of artists, some born on the island and some born anywhere else and finally settled on the island. They often gather at the coffee stands, and they are daily sprinkled throughout the city sketching and painting.

During the Depression, the WPA sent a group of artists to Key West, and a couple of the public schools as well as government buildings have murals that were completed showing the people of Key West with their Cuban heritage. "Sloopy Joe's" has a large WPA painting of a cock-fight, and East Martello has exhibited some of the paintings done during the Depression and the contribution of the WPA.

Not only were there artists that had the motivation to paint, there were many who pretended to be artists. Writers have the same way out. There are still many who will be "working on a book" and have not written a word. Hiding under the pretense of a creative person is an old trick, and it can be discovered when a product is demanded. Where's the painting? Where's the book? (Amusingly, some people are trying to "... find themselves", and some never do.)

Many people have used Key West to re-vitalize their direction, the attitude being one of having the temperment to find a direction. Thus, many real artists and writers have passed through Key West, and some have stayed. Our best known artists have been a local wood-cutter/painter Mario Sanchez and junk sculptor, Stanley Pappio, both having received national and international fame. The list of writers would be much longer, Hemingway leading in local popularity, Williams not far behind.

The value judgments of the artist have been demonstrated in the several bookstores in the community, the amount of books being read on the beaches and coffee houses. Where there was only one major private gallery in the 50s run by Marion Stephens, there are now 50. There are art scholarships, prizes, competitions, and public art galleries.

THE 300 BLOCK
Eaton St. to Catherine St.

Across Eaton Street is one of the most impressive blocks, the 300 block, that contains the Women's Club, the oldest house, The Red Barn Theatre and a couple of very famous, new, and very popular bars.

Two major large organizations became the center of the social scene of the island in the 60s: East Martello Museum and the Women's Club. The Key West Art and Historical Society of East Martello charged a fee that everyone could afford and featured ten free booze and munchies parties for $15, which was later dramatically increased to $25. The Women's Club, which usually had as many active men as active women, was usually free. Party attendance was often a couple of hundred people. In 1998 men were allowed to join The Women's Club, with the understanding that the organization's name would not change.

The Women's Club
In the red brick building halfway down the block houses the Women's Club. The men of the Women's Club were not all husbands but many volunteered for the club's fund raising activities. The monthly activities at the Key West Art and Historical Society, the Women's Club, and the monthly meetings of the City Commission meeting using the crime report from the "Key West Citizen" supplied the humor for most conversations and gossip.

The volunteer bartenders poured heavily at events of both organizations. The Women's Club did not serve liquor for years, and, in a very close vote, the organization approved the use of liquor. Attendance improved dramatically.

At the first approved liquor party, a little old lady in a neatly ironed gown came to a middle-aged volunteer bartender and stated, "Kid. Give me a scotch. No ice. No water. No stick. No napkin." The bartender was cautious. She was one who had voted against serving alcohol at the Women's Club, but he poured her half a glass of scotch anyway.
A half hour later the old lady returned and replied, "Kid. Give me another" and pushed forward the empty plastic glass. He obeyed. Thoughts of many empty bottles of scotch under her bed ran through his head, although she had voted against drinking, but she never did return during his shift.

Nancy, a thin widow well into her late 50s, liked the advantages of very young men, and she was often seen in their company. She kept herself in the latest fashions, her hair was perfect, and a great deal of time and money were spent on redoing what God had given her. She looked terrific. The natural question came up at a Women's Club meeting: "Nancy, how do you keep your youth?" She answered, "You never introduce them to anyone." According to Michael MacLiammoir in "Tom Jones", "We are all as God made us, and many of us much worse."

Not only did the Key West Women's Club decide to allow men to join in l998 without changing the name of the organization, Sara Fowler was voted the first black president of the organization to serve l998-2000. They were certainly not little old ladies that did nothing. They were very active in the community.

The Red Barn Theatre

Accurately, the red barn theatre was a barn, one of the few saved from the changes of transportation from the horse and carriage to the horse-less automobile. Behind the Women's Club and belonging to that piece of property, it has been converted into a theatre which is strongly supported by the locals. The productions are excellent with many retired writers, actors, and artists still very active in the community. They often do seldom-produced plays and also new theatrical productions.

Southern Cross Hotel

A young woman reporter, Windy Tucker, was attempting to modernize the language of the local newspaper in a story about Sarah Clevantes. She had taken a young man to her room at the Southern Cross Hotel (the 200 block) "to smoke a jay". While he was there he "... stole $150. from her pants and split". I sent Margaret Foresman, the editor, the clipping with a note that said "never carry money in your split". She had the wonderful ability to laugh.

It is not unusual that, in front of the Southern Cross Hoel a report that started, "A couple was arrested on Duval Street Thursday while having sex on the sidewalk ..." should be headlined, "Police see couple coupling on Duval". Another report that told of a "couple copulating on the hood of a car" was titled "The rape that wasn't". "I have no curiosity about the working classes." Gladys Cooper in "Separate Tables".

Guy Sauders had the Heron House on Simonton in '75 or '77 and sold it to buy the Southern Cross Hotel. Saunders ran it for years, appealing to a "cash conservative" tourist who wanted a clean and convenient place to stay. As the city grew even the fold-back windows of the lobby were attractive to jewelry sellers who did not want the expense of a store, and some rented the window space. Guy sold to David Axtell in 1996, but Guy had no intention of moving from the heartbeat of Duval Street, and he bought a large home behind "Diva's".

The Oldest House

Across the street from the Women's Club is what is considered to be the oldest house in Key West, backed and supported by the Old Island Restoration Society (OIRC).

The original house was built in 1829. It was moved from Whitehead Street in 1832 and owned by Richard W. Cussans, a carpenter of ships. It was built on limestone piers three feet high and measured 40' by 45' at the base. The mortise and tenon, joiners of ships, and even a ship's hatch in the bedroom aided ventilation. It had five bay facades with dormers. The three different size of dormers in front were simply adaptations over the years for controlling comfort.

A Capt. Francis Watlington from St. Croix, a New Yorker by birth, arrived in Key West in 1828 as a harbor pilot and married Emiline and had seven (of nine) surviving girls He bought the property from William H. Wall in 1839 who had bought it from Cussans in 1834, and Cussans moved to Texas. Now the stories differ. Some feel the house had not been expanded after Watlington with seven daughters moved in. Others argue that the house was originally very small and would have to be expanded. (5)

One of the amusing aspects of the house is that if the Waltingtons bought the house in 1836, an unmarried daughter of Captain Watlington and his Emiline lived in the house until 1936.

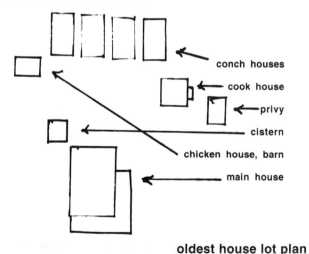

conch houses
cook house
privy
cistern
chicken house, barn
main house

oldest house lot plan

No one should start remodeling a Key West house in Old Town without going through the oldest house on Duval Street. This visit will give you an appreciation for what was and why. The trip is worth 25 "Architectural Digests"

The "Elks' Club" to the "Hard Rock Cafe"

The building on the other side of the driveway to The Red Barn Theatre of the Women's Club used to be the old Elk's Club, complete with a metal elk standing in the front yard, and a concrete-block hall behind the building matching nothing. It was the Elk's bar. The buildings were sold to a shell company that filled all with various kinds of shells, from practically everywhere in the world except Key West. (We've never been known for our shells.) It was sold again to the "Hard Rock Cafe" and the large, un-matching concrete building in back was put to good use as a bar. They took the time and money to paint the house in the multi-colored Caribbean style.

Beside the "Hard Rock Cafe" on the narrow street or alley that leads to the concrete hall also leads to Simonton Street. On the other side of the street is "Fat Tuesdays" on what used to be the back yard of a rooming house, restaurant and bar called "Tradewinds".

The Tradewinds Guesthouse to "Fat Tuesdays"

At the end of this Duval Street block, the "Tradewinds" was a large wooden Victorian rooming house and bar on the corner of Duval and Caroline Street across the street from the Fogerty House (now "Hooters"). It was a piano bar, and Betty French and Viola Viet were often there. Coffee Butler played the piano in his self- taught manner, and Viola would sing in her Marlene Dietrich interpretations of "Falling in Love Again" and "La via Rose". Bill Divins was the bartender. I had never seen the bar, but I've been told it was a Bohemian bar of the early days with such faces as Truman Capote and Tennessee Williams (the latter having roomed there). The "Tradewinds" burned down many years before I came to Key West.

the once majestic "Tradewinds"

The lot contained a brick insurance building at one time, but was later transformed into a series of one-story buildings up a flight of steps. One was a street-open bar called "Fat Tuesdays", currently quite popular for people watching.

The Pigeon Poop

On the little street running from Duval to Simonton Street beside "Fat Tuesdays", on the south side of the "Hard Rock Cafe", at the end of the block on Simonton Street is a very large, four-story building once housing a 46 room hotel. Tennessee Williams stayed there as did Ernest Hemingway. It also burned down. Mary Ann and Joe Worth bought the building in 1978 for $26,000 and with his construction knowledge, they rebuilt the gutted building for eight years into a single, private home, one with a pool and jungle atrium like few others. It is called the "Casa Antiqua".

The first floor contains "The Pigeon Poop", a store built from Mary Ann and Joe's traveling and buying some of the most unusual gifts imaginable from Mexico to Haiti. For a small fee, you can also view the magnificent pool and garden. Since Joe's death, Mary Ann lives in the many rooms with her son, Tom Oosterhoudt, and the home is the scene of many social gatherings. Well worth the one block walk to see the jungle and the unusual merchandise.

If you were to turn left (west) at the next intersection at Eaton Street and Duval and walk down in front of some elegant homes one block to Whitehead Street, you would find "Kelly's".

"Kelly's Caribbean Bar & Brewery" 303 Whitehead Street

The "Pigeon House" was a sales company called the Trading Post when I first came to town, but it was soon changed to the "Carrier Pigeon House" because of pigeon lofts (boxes) in the side yard. It boasted its history as being the first home of Pan American World Airways, and it was for a couple of months.

In theory, the pigeons were to be used on the 90-mile trip to Cuba to return to their nests with a message if there were trouble. No records have indicated the pigeons were taken aboard or released.

I remember the "Pigeon House Restaurant"; locals used to call it the "Pigeon Shit", at the time when "Delmonico" and the "Monster" were at their height. There was always one thing wrong with it, that of being too far off the beaten track (in reality, one block). It was a favorite to many.

Once finally there and past the dinner hour, it became a piano bar for Vaudeville types and theater people. Billy Nine Fingers (who really has nine fingers) and Jay Foote (both feet) would play, and the piano bar was filled with many that would sing along. Larry Harvey, Denys Fitzpatrick, Stell Adams, Marion Stevens. The locals would be there. Tourists from the Pier House loved it. The big discussion, aside from local politics or maybe including local politics, would be, "What's going to happen across the street?" Across the street was Truman's entrance to the Naval Base. "What was Mr. Dent going to do?"

The "Pigeon House" had years of different managers with new ideas. It kept going in and going out of business. It was simplified, re-organized, re-arranged, and re-adjusted. At one time it was filled with antiques. At another time it was managed by women. The house next door became the kitchen, then dining room, eventually a sunken bar between the two buildings run by Nancy Lowey.

In 1986, Pritham Singh bought the Navel property, The Truman Annex, for $17.25 million, and sold pieces of it. Developers were building a very large house across the street from the "Pigeon Shit", one designed like the Audubon House. I had not seen Nancy, the bartender, in awhile and decided to stop in for an early afternoon cocktail.

"Sorry I haven't been in. I've been so busy building the house across the street."

"Are you bringing down the whole staff?" She was willing to play at my joking.

"No. Just the butler and maybe a couple maids and, of course, my valet."

"Have you had any problems with construction?" She had sucked me in.

"A terrible time. The contractor put on these two guys to lay the brick for the up-stairs fireplaces, and they are terrible. All talk and no work. You know how labor is down here, even if you have lots of money. You just can't get anything done properly." A guy sitting three down from me lifted his head.

Without hesitation, Nancy exposed my lie. "I'd like you to meet the contractor", and she motioned to the man sitting three down. When you're caught, you're caught.

In the early 90s the original "Pigeon House" property included the house next door. Ther were two pieces of property were combined by Nancy's bar in the middle. Months of renovaton went into combining the two pieces into one. Today, it is called "Kelly's". The beautiful house sits across the street. I still have not moved in.

Fred Tillman and his actress wife, Kelly McGillis, bought the "Pigeon House" and through months of renovation combined the two quite-separate houses into appearing as one building, a major accomplishment complemented by a huge patio, a combination bar and restaurant. Tourists still ask where the old "Pigeon House" is.

Settled in Key West, the Tillmans also bought a building at 314 Duval across from the "Hard Rock" where they have announced plans to open a restaurant and includes one of the most outstanding pieces of Victorian architecture at 425 Caroline Street that they now plan to make their personal home, a beautiful home in which to raise a family.

Denys Brian Fitzpatrick

The son of Irish Royalty, Denys' mother was related to the English Queen and grew up his mother's manor house in Hailcroft. He attended Stowe Academy and would have matriculated to Eton had he not gotten tuberculosis and taken to Switzerland and South Africa, before returning to England.

Denys met Dorthy Dixon and he played in Flo Zigfield's "Cassinova" as Catherine's lover. He was too tall for Hollywood, and he was discharged from the military because of his previous bout with tuberculosis.

With an artistic flair, he bought and sold antiques in Houston and New York, and became a magazine designer, and a painter. Denys also designed labels for Fletcher Richard. His stamp decopague creations are outstanding.

He came to Key West at the time David Wolkowsky was building the Pier House and stayed at the La Concha Hotel for $165 a day. Denys has been in Key West since around 1962, and he is an entertainer at the "Key West Classics" each year. He remains very elegant, handsomely dressed, talented, and a pleasure in amusing his audiences. He is very interested in the many social events of the island.

The change

Among all groups of people with a limited knowledge of AIDS, there was a change in attitude of many people at the time with the intermixing of gays and straights. There was less physical contact, fewer hugs, less kissing, and more cleaning of glassware. In the gay community there were more people becoming couples, more relationships being established, fewer promiscuous acts, safer sex, associations for gay couples only. The bookstores were closed. The baths were raided.

Year-round Key West

Something else was happening in the early 80's in Key West. We had the influx of the gays in the late 60's and 70's and with it brought a level of sophistication and money not previously known. Houses sold for large profits. Shops and stores were beginning to stay open more than from December to April. Rents and keeping trusted employees demanded the shops, restaurants and bars be open more than just during the most popular winter season. Black integration had worked. The women's movement was getting stronger. The gays were popular. The locals, particularly those with property, were making money. The drug traffic changed, but certainly didn't go away.

It just went more underground. Political corruption was less obvious. Key West was becoming a self-sufficient place.

The corporation take-over

What happened of real significance although it's seldom talked about is the individual gave way to the corporation. At one time, it was possible for a man to own his own property and single-handedl create a business and run it. As prices grew, this procedure became more and more impossible, and the financial gamble demanded collective money and collective risks. We see the corporation of restaurants, hotels, and bars move into Key West. Where the Pier House used to be owned by David Wolkowsky, it became owned by a corporation. Also, more attention was paid to temporary fads.

When "Jimmy Buffet" opened, everyone recognized the name because of the popularity of his music. A whole list of other chainstores followed. Locals will say that the movement was started by Ed Swift and the building of the handsome structure to house "Burger King". Others feel it was just a natural progression. Others felt we have always had chainstores like Big Daddy's, Rexalls, and Dairy Queen.

There was no legal way to keep the corporately owned shops and complex ownerships out. The t-shirt shops started to infiltrate, and they became a major income for many foreigners. No one person owns Key West; not even the conchs. As free people, we may create our homes where we desire as long as we obey the rules. There was also a trend toward early retirement for people that dreamed of someday living in Paradise. Some made it come true. There was also the lack of respect for years devoted to a job, and the wisdom of the job was jerked from under the employee.

I've tried to avoid in this book the many chains in Key West that reflect other places without differentiating themselves to a Key West style. Some are accepted as "so what ...", the Eckerd, Walgreens, Subway, Sears, Pennys, and many others I have purposefully not pinpointed the many fine restaurants of the hotels such as the Hyatt and the Marriott, and those whose books and securities are owned by larger companies, and whose Key West operation is not unique to or characteristic of Key West. I've not reviewed time-shares which became cookie cutter models of any city. Most locals will complain that we are losing our uniqueness as they shop at Wynn Dixie and Publix rather than Fausto's.

But the gate has swung both ways. The typical "Sloppy Joe's" is now a chain of nine stores with former Republican Ron Saunders' bar of 260 seats in Tallahassee. Some others are in Coconut Grove, Ft. Lauderdale, Boca Raton, Orlando, Jacksonville Beach and Daytona Beach. The t-shirt shops of famous bars often make more money than the bars. There is the use of the name Key West in a restaurant/bar in Miami. "Captain Tony's" has opened in Coconut Grove, and a nightclub by that name in the Omni in Miami. There is a" Margaretaville" in New Orleans, and one planned for the new marina/stadium in downtown Miami.

There are certain places in any downtown that are characteristic of many images of long ago, the buildings that bring up the nostalgia of a period, those places close to quaint and that you remember for their being unique. These are the places which give a community a "charm" of being individualistic. The larger corporations can never duplicate that quality.

Of course, a corporation cannot get the same results. They establish a style they will sell, then they duplicate this quality in many cities. Travelers expect the same thing when they go into these places regardless of where they are located. If you go into "Hooters" in any city, you expect to see the scantly clad, beautiful waitresses with the same menu at about the same prices.

There was a run on breweries a few years ago.. I believe the first was "Kelly's", but now vats are obvious at what was "Hammerhead's Brewery (currently re-named "Irish Kevin's"), "Rum Runners", "Hog's Breath", "Hard Rock" and "Sloppy Joe's Bar" as well as many others have their own beer labels.

Key West has always fought "sameness" and the large corporate restaurants and bars give us their interpretation of what they have to offer and don't try to fit into the unique atmosphere of a place. Many tourists want something that is distinctively Key West, something of variety.

Unfortunately, most of the corporate restaurants and bars follow their formulas for success, which is the dollar. Their music is aimed at the 25-to-35-year-old, because that is who works there, and that is who is making the decisions. You can guess at the volume of music, the type, the quality of food, and the cost. Is the evening just another typical, expensive evening that you could have had in another town?

The gay bar and restaurant scenes suffer from the same problems, constantly recreating success, hoping to make the dollars. Most of the gay bars appeal to the 25- to-35-year-old and they are making the decisions. The music is deafening, already they are examples of it. The bartenders or DJs drown out the sounds of customers with loud music, and there is no one there to supervise.

"Square One" and, sometimes, "La te da" and "Cafe Blue" are exceptions. "Bourbon Street 801", "Bourbon Street", "Diva's", "Donnie's 422", "Number One Saloon", and the "Epoch" are all loud bars with the same volume of television or stereo. Even "Club International" screams. They attract the same age group as their music, and that's their financial game.

I can easily get the criticism that "you're just an old fart" and that is probably right. However, as a part of the older generation supposedly with disposable income, we go to a bar to talk with someone, not yell at them. We gays usually go to talk with other people of our own sex, not entertainers who are constantly hustling (unless we are looking for that). We are the group that is supposed to have money, but we want the quiet for our money. Please, anybody, open a "Papillon".

You would assume that with as many new businesses opening in Key West as we experienced, pre-opening business serveys would indicate that we have met our market, and that no more were needed. It is true that many of the restaurasnts and shops that have gone out of business have been privately owned and suffered from the lack of capital. It has also been true that many of the new businesses are repetitions of similar businesses on the island. How many ice cream shops, t-shirt shopes, gift shops, guesthouses can we have? We seem not to know.

Even the population of Key West is not growing much beyond the 23,000 residents. There is constant building of time-share, hotels, motels, and many new private homes. Stock Island is exploding with trailer parks and rentals. New homes flood the golf course and Junior College Road. There is expansion all around the airport with new apartments. There are few vacant lots left. There is building on practically every key through Shark Key into Marathon. Yet, Key West still has about the same amount of residents as in past years. We cannot deny the impact of the tourist industry on the residents.

If you take a right (east) onto Caroline Street, you'll see some fine examples of the large private homes that still maintain a yard. When the middle class began to gain some money, they often bought a chunk of the larger property, a desire to be close to neighbors in a respectable neighborhood. Scattered along Caroline are a series of nice houses, but not as grand or expensive as the large mansions. Many have been converted to apartments.

THE 200 BLOCK
Caroline St. to Greene St.

Fogerty House to "Hooters"

Notice the size of the Fogerty House across on the corner of Caroline and Duval. It was built in 1868 as a private home with 4,500 square feet of space, and it was in the residential section of Old Town. It is currently being redone, a house much too large and expensive for a single family, and it has become a "Hooters", one of 287 of the chain's holdings. The new tenants have leased and repaired the building owned by Ed and Joan Knight, and two of the Spottswood brothers. There was criticism of conchs turning property into commercial use, but few if any private person or family would spend the money to reclaim this huge, gorgeous house. The house will be saved. Its use has changed.

There was a period in the 60s when this building was an Italian restaurant with a small wrought-iron fence not three feet high around the corner, and we would sit outside on the open patio eating pasta and drinking red wine and listening to the music from "John Brown's Bar". The house was a kind of rooming house at that time with a restaurant on the first floor. There was also a little bar facing the house to the right which was filled with military officers and has since been torn down (and I'll never tell why I remember that.)

"Hooters" under construction

"Hooters" won their suit of equal opportunity concerning sexual bias against the federal government in 1997 and was able to continue hiring only female waitresses. (The advertising campaign of a half-shaven, big-busted man in drag won many gays' hearts, and would have easily fit in Key West. The corporate offices were against this move.) "Joe's Stonecrab House" in Miami Beach lost their suit of $1,000,000 of predominately male waiters, but it's back in court.

Caroline Street really marks the section of large homes that were built around the industrial docks in the 1900s, close in walking distance to the wharfs, but set back enough from the more commercial area. Looking to both your right (east) and left (west) for a few blocks in either direction are once grand homes. To the left, the large homes go back a block to the Navy Gate, but since this property was developed by Pritham Singh, he continued the large new homes in the Victorian detail beyond the gate. To the right from Duval along Caroline Street are several blocks of grand homes. The first block across the street includes the Curry House.

Amsterdam-Curry Inn

Milton Curry came to Key West penniless from the Bahamas and became the wealthiest person, a millionaire, in Florida before he died in l896. His son, William, built on his father's property in 1905 from where his father's home was carted away. The son opened William Curry and Sons Ship Chandlery and Warehouses. The house was the most luxurious mansion in Key West with inlaid floors, a magnificent staircase, and many porches.

Al and Edith Amsterdam bought the property, had additional guest rooms built in a separate building in the back, bought the property across the street and run a very successful guesthouse. They freely host parties at their elaborate guesthouse for fund raisers for the community.

"John Brown's Bar" to "The Bull"

Across Duval Street from the Fogerty House is "The Bull". It was one of those Saturday afternoons that I had escaped Miami to roam in Key West. I stopped in the "John Brown's Bar" at the corner of Duval Street and Caroline Street. (It has been "The Bull" for many years.) John had a particular passion for sailors and, while it was only my second time in the bar, John asked me to bartend because a particularly appealing military man had looked back at him while leisurely walking up the street. I expected John to be back within a few minutes.

I liked being behind the bar. People did not drink mixed drinks in the afternoon, at least the people who went to "John Brown's Bar". If you could read a beer label, and I could read, you could make it as a bartender. All the chit-chat conversations of "Where are you from? When do you get out of the Navy? How long have you been married? Is she your wife?" John Brown came back three hours later. I made seven dollars in tips that afternoon.

John had a friend or enemy, no one was quite sure, named Frank

Fontis and they fought back and forth for years, pranks that were half serious and half vicious. But they were friends in easier times. One day John Brown had parked his car around the corner from the bar. Fontis took a hammer and four large nails and pounded one into each tire, sinking the body of the car to the ground.

Frank Fontis

Frank Fontis was a good friend to Tennessee Williams, and he would help Williams with building projects. He somehow managed a small railroad museum that was in an old coffee house across a side alley on Greene Street from the brick courthouse. Whomever backed him, Fontis had collected railway cars, tracks, railroad memorabilia of all kinds, and turned a conch house into a train museum. Fontis had a large collection of letters, photographs, and junk he would find in Tennessee Williams' garbage can. Fontis smoked cigars, drove an old pickup, and wore women's jewelry including a huge deadly looking scorpion ring. He did a lot of yard work for various people.

Fontis had completed a large landscaping job up the Keys and was paid in cash, and told not to reveal the source of the money. Many made money from drugs. Fontis just couldn't keep a secret.

Not putting in his teet meant that he knew the person at his door, Fondis was murdered as he opened his front door. His ring turned up in Texas, but whomever murdered him was never caught. No one knew what happened to all the railroad stuff and other collectables that Fontis had gathered together.

"Delmonico's" to "Rum Runners"

One day Marion Stevens and Helen Chapman were sitting in "Delmonico's" in the afternoon enjoying their martinis, and Marion was starting to grumble to a placid Helen. They ordered a second drink and Marion left for the ladies' room.

Helen was frustrated by the conversation and took out her top false teeth plate and placed it in Marion's drink, to the amusement of the few people drinking nearby. As Marion started to return to her stool, Helen picked up the bridge from Marion's glass and replaced it into her mouth.

Marion continued to ramble on about something, sipped her drink to the amusement of those sitting nearby, and the group broke into laughter to Marion's bewilderment.

Perhaps one of the strangest marriages I had ever seen was a young man from South Africa, a caucasian that I had met in London and wanted to come to the United States for a visit. That was arranged and he loved the United States with all the gay bars, the activity and freedom. His vocation was a hairstylist, and it would be impossible for him to get papers from the limited immigration quota of South Africa. He made arrangements with an American attorney to meet a lady in Nassau, an American lady whom he would marry, get his citizenship here, and then divorce. Being gay, he married her, and they moved in together. Thirty years later, they are still living together, happily married.

An upstairs bar of "Delmonico's" opened that was called "Michael's". The path would be to start at the "Monster" and go to "Delmonico's" and/or to "Michael's", and stagger down the street to some of the newer bars, or maybe to the "Midget" or to "The Mermaid Room". "Michael's" even started drag shows with Rusty Rhodes in charge, but the drags at that time could not be held to a schedule and were undependable and, used to being treated harshly, the whole thing failed to draw the expected crowd.

Budweiser parking lot to "Irish Kevin's"

Four or five garages lined the back of the lot and only parking and turn-around space was available in the front on Duval. This was the Budweiser's storage facility owned by Charlie Ramos and it was one lot south of the old bank building close to the street. Over the years, the vacant property became important to the growth of the city. The lot was built upon in a series of small shops. A long hallway led to a furniture store (the original storage warehouse of Budweiser). The furniture store was rented by the daughter of Austin Labor, a developer of The Reach.

The building was redone in 1996 and opened as "Hammerhead's Brewery" with four huge copper vats visible from the street, and offering six different kinds of beer. In a way, there was continuity from being the Budweiser storage, both generously offering beer to Duval Street. It is currently going through a change of becoming an Irish Pub ("Irish Kevin's") to attract foreign tourists.

"Sloppy Joe's Bar"

Joe Russell was a friend of Hemingway and he appears as Freddy, a bartender and captain of a boat "The Queen Conch" in To Have and Have Not. The real Joe Russell rented a bar at 428 Greene Street called "The Blind Pig", later changed to "The Silver Slipper". Hemingway liked the name "Sloppy Joe's". Russell and the bar owner got into an argument concerning the rent. It was the Depression and the landlord wanted to raise the rent one dollar a month. Russell moved to its present location on May 5, 1937, and it remains "Sloppy Joe's".

One decor feature seemed to enhance the popularity of the bar. There was a hugh parachute hung from the ceiling that covered most of the room. Although eye-catching and unique, it served the purpose of catching the termite droppings from the wooden ceiling.

But there were many stories that did not make the evening paper. So the fable goes, the manager of "Sloppy Joe's Bar" at the corner of Duval

Street and Greene Street came into his bar early in the morning around closing time quite drunk. He sprawled out on the floor and fell asleep. His wife told the bartender, "He's probably dead", and she went home.

The manager slept comfortably and when the bartender was ready to close the bar for the remainder of the morning, he simply threw a tablecloth over the sleeping man, locked up, and left.

The manager was awakened the next morning, a little the less aware from his drunk, but he remembered his wife's comment. He called Lopez Funeral Home to deliver a casket in a hearse to his home. They did.

The "Midget Bar"

There was a bar on the east corner facing Greene Street at Simonton Street called the "Midget Bar" a block past the courthouse. It was not much more than a stained, yellow shack inhabited mostly by local fishermen and drunks. It was smelly and dilapidated, but I wandered in one afternoon for a beer.

Sitting beside me was a woman worn from previous alcohol talking with a white-rubber-booted shrimper. She would laugh and touch the sea-worn veteran, and I began to notice she would, from time to time, fondle him. He rose to the occasion. Cautiously, she unbuttoned his pants, un-enveloped his masculinity, and said to me, "Give me some room, honey". Her head disappeared from the view of the people sitting on the sides of the bar. When her head reappeared above the bar, he said "Give her 'nother beer".

Even the "Midget Bar" changed. When the gay movement caught on and places like "Delmonico's" and "The Monster" were raking in many dollars, other places tried to mimic the success. Patrick Calvin managed the "Midget Bar", which had been extended to include a large open area and a lean-to shed bar with dancing.

Dancing and drinking seemed to be the two most socially acceptable entertainments at the time. Men dancing with men was unique although two females could dance together without feeling awkward. The not socially acceptable entertainment was enjoyed by practically all, marijuana and poppers, and many took advantage of back room sex.

The "Midget Bar" was called "Dill Pickle", but it did not last long. The building fell into disrepair and was frequently used by local street people and drunks.

Key West Fabrics bought the long, brick warehouse across the street. The "Midget Bar" property stood vacant. It was bought by Strunk Lumber Store, and the building was demolished. It is now part of a parking lot of the new lumber store, soon to be a prime location on the bight.

the "Midget Bar"

"Captain Tony's Saloon"

As one of the most popular personalities on the island, one bar that reflects the old, unique characteristics of Key West is "Captain Tony's Saloon" because of the tales of smuggling, pirateering, drinking, and the fun personality of its owner. This many-time father can outstretch a sailor's longest tale to the complete amusement of the listener. Once the mayor of Key West, Captain Tony has always had the city, and the dollar, foremost in his mind. Some speculate which dominates.

There is some confusion as to Captain Tony once owning "Sloppy Joe's Bar" or where Hemingway really drank, but it depends upon what time of night and who tells the story as to the truth.

"Captain Tony's Saloon" remains the same as always, as far as I can remember, and that is a delight in a city that is constantly changing. For tourists or locals alike, it is a definite part of Key West's charm.

Audubon House

A block to the left (west) of "Captain Tony's Saloon" is the Geiger House. All conch train tours include passing by the Audubon House on

Greene and Whitehead Streets. It was built by a Captain John H. Geiger of Saint Augustine around 1830, and the house remained in the Geiger family generation after generation. Notice how close the house is to the wharfs.

When John James Audubon was in England in 1832, he wanted to return to the United States to paint the birds. It was winter in the north. Audubon realized that many birds had flown south, so he came south to the home of Captain Geiger. He was quite simply following the migrating birds.

Audubon was a bit of an egotist, claiming he was 52 years old, the right age to be related to some European family of high reputation and wealth. He was really 47. He was of modest income, a traveling woodsman.

He spent very little time, if any, at the house on Whitehead, for the city did not hold what he wanted to paint, and there were the many Geiger children. Audubon did not have a fondness for children. Some will say that there is confusion about Audubon staying at the Geiger House because Audubon slept on his boat, for the house was not yet built.

He found the swamplands to be the most intriguing, with rare and unusual birds whose images had rarely been published. He camped most nights in the swamps. He spent most of his time drawing the animals and bird life, certainly more time than he spent at the house.

What is seldom told is that James Audubon was a hunter as well as an artist. He would often shoot his models, studying the dead carcass to know more about the bird's structure. Bird feathers were also fashionable and brought a good price.

'

In 1958, the house, which was in bad repair was bought by Mitchell Wolfson and was restored as part of the Wolfson Family Foundation. The Audubon story was part of the sale of the house but it may be mostly myth. It is now a museum containing many Audubon prints, and a First Folio, now priceless.

The circumcision

Can oversight be as bad as a planned joke? As a 50 year old Catholic Chicago Italian, it was medically necessary for him to have a circumcision, and he checked into the local hospital and had the operation in relative secrecy.

In the Jewish religion, the ceremony of circumcision is called a Bris. Paul went to the card shop and bought a dozen of the same Bris cards, and Paul passed the cards out to the friends of the poor bedridden and sore man, and each person signed and addressed separate cards, later to send the card from their individual, local mailbox. After opening the fourth card, the wounded man realized he was the object of the joke.

Margaret's leg

Margaret had her leg amputated, and the prosthesis was a difficult fit. A friend gave her a false dummy leg laden with rhinestones, sparkles, and glass jewels, and they enjoyed the joke. Some years later there was a charity get-even auction with 12 unwanted things, a molting pink flamingo, a toilet and arbor, broken vases, where someone could bid and give the item to someone else who could either accept the item and up the bid, and he could give the item to another person who had the same choices.

Margaret gave her decorated dummy leg to the committee and when it came up for bids, she bid $500. and returned the leg to the original creator and gift giver. He refused the bid and Margaret had to pay $500 and maintain her own gift.

Some may say "how sick". Margaret had lost her leg, but she joked about it. Her friends were allowed to joke about it. The jeweled leg was taken as a joke. The donation of the leg, the attempt to get the maker to buy it back, the reverse of making Margaret pay for her own donation, all were jokes taken in good humor.

The Business Guild

A group of gay business owners got together to establish an organization that could deal with gay marketing in Key West, but the group continued to have straight members and being gay was not a prerequisite to membership. Built on principles not unlike the Key West Chamber of Commerce, the Business Guild is equally as powerful. They serve as a fund-raising organization with a board of ten directors. In 1998 Bruce Berkowitz of Marketech Marketing was elected president and Kent Henry, owner of Towels of Key West, was elected Vice President. Publishers, doctors, store owners, bar representatives, and local executive directors are active members. Not only is Key West a liberal city, but most people have to make a living on the island, and the Business Guild often leads.

There were names of places to which some of the people of Old Town referred, but that I did not remember because I was new to the town. "Remember when ..." and the storyteller would be off always closing with what a better town it was in the years before.

We are also caught with the experiences of the events that we, personally, have heard about or experienced. There are many events, impressions, activities, or stories that we know nothing about, not even by hearsay. A part of everyone's history of Key West will be personal to that person, and we can only hope we have enough common experiences to adequately identify Key West.

THE 100 BLOCK
Green St. to Front St.

From bank parking lot to "Planet Hollywood"

Back on Duval on the other side of Greene Street from "Sloppy Joe's Bar" seems to be a shopping block filled with interesting shops and topped off by a brick bank with a tower on the left (west) side, the old bank building. At one time the building stood alone with a large parking lot, eventually drive-through windows, and plenty of parking across the street around a corner of a brick building on which a seven foot tree had taken hold. There was parking around the bank.

David Tackett was retired from banking but hired to work a couple of days at the bank. Tackett was rather un-conventional and dressed often in leather and drove a Harley-Davidson. He really didn't need the job, but agreed, and in a few months he was working full time and became the President of this bank with the full support of the employees that he would not have to change his attire or mode of transportation. Tackett worked hard mending scars left from the Depression, and he wanted to restore the cupola that was striped in red and yellow brick, and the building was repaired. Tackett retired once again and left Key West. (The Jefferson Hotel became the parking lot of the bank. See the photo on page 204.)

However, the land had always been valuable beside the large Jefferson Hotel which burned, and it was too valueable for a parking lot and eventually drive-through windows of the bank. There was also additional parking across the street on a vacant chunk of land the bank owned.

the Jefferson Hotel

Once the tourists had arrived, a large two story building was tucked into the vacant lot which blended nicely into the architecture and nicely into the community. Facing the building from the Duval side, the left section contains the "Planet Hollywood" built in 1997. The building is very subtle with only the sign of "Planet Hollywood" in red, the rest quietly hidden. If the attraction is to feature the personalities of motion picture stars, Key West already has had experience at that.

The building on the east corner across from the bank remains a mystery to many. It was the old bank parking lot. In the early 90s, a hole was dug for underground parking although all knew the garage was close to the tide level. (Some said it was for parking and there wa no law that said parking had to be flood proof.) Seemingly over night, a building went up, incompatable to everything. No one would claim approval. The plans could not be found in the Building Department.

A very prominent clothing designer bought a large house in Old Town and completely redid the house, Hollywood style. He claimed he came to Key West because he did not want to be in the constant public view, and he was not. We had the experiences of the Tennessee Williams, film producers, politicians, and even a President or two. No one paid much attention to him. He moved a couple of years later to Coconut Grove where people would recognize him.

"The Monster" to "Hog's Breath", 400 Front Street

The current "Hog's Breath" bar on Front Street is the original location of the "Monster Bar" 20 years earlier. The "Monster" was the most popular bar in the city, although it was located in an alley between the bank and a gift shop. There was constant building of new bars into and on the roof of the gift shop. within the "Monster" hallway at the side of the building. At the front gate was a bouncer who knew everyone and decided if you were or were not welcomed. Most, straight and gay, were welcomed to spend money. There was a parrot's cage which was the old cupola of the Catholic School that burned on Truman Avenue. A side bar called "B. J. Flats". The "Upstairs Bar" was thick with funny marijuana smoke. The "Disco Bar" and the smell of poppers.

According to "The Key West Citizen", "A man and a woman arrested for exposure of sexual organs Friday morning were doing more than discussing the birds and the bees when a police officer arrived on the scene ... we were surprised to see two naked people who appeared to be having sex behind the peacock cage in broad daylight ..."

Across the street from the "Monster" and eventually "Hog's Breath" was a converted gas station to a small, quick-service, white restaurant which later became "Billie's".

THE "O" BLOCK
Front St. to Gulf of Mexic

Across the street from the "Monster" and beside what would someday be "Billie's" were warehouses and wharfs and a two-story, brick, square building that was eventually occupied by Jim Russel and Peter Pell. They had come to Key West to retire after successful careers in the fabric business in New York. They became bored and opened the Key West Fabrics company, and would allow tourists to come watch them lay out huge sheets of cotton cloth and apply the hand blocking.

What was unusual at that time was that their designs were bold, colorful and very distinctive. You never mixed blue and green in the same pattern, but Jim and Peter did. You never used yellow with orange or pink with red. They did. They were wise to team up with a clothes designer named Lilly Pulitzer, who popularized their fabrics. They were also smart enough to hire a local woman named Suzi Depue who helped with their designs. She had been a locally recognized artist with her drawings and ceramics.

The Key West Fabrics was a drawing card of the 1950s and 1960s. Their trash barrels were raided at night, and soon there were Key West Fabric patchwork quilts. Their clothes were chic, in, somewhat expensive, and very popular.

As the two guys were having dinner one evening, one choked on a piece of steak and died. The business seemed never to be as spontaneous and wavered after that. The business was simplified, and taste had also changed.

Today, there is a Key West Fabrics store in the brick storage building wharf on the corner of Simonton and Green Street, the east corner. Lilly Pulitzer has a shop on the corner of Front Street and Simonton streets in what is called the old Coca Cola Building, which was built about 15 years ago. (The original Coca Cola building was torn down since it had been built in 1903. Antique stores still carry the old Coca Cola bottles.) Suzi Depue still works for Key West Fabrics.

Through the 80s, the fast food industries opened on Roosevelt Boulevard. There were many chains that opened and many that closed to fierce competition. The police had to be called to direct traffic on the opening night of Taco Bell.

Some say, the Old Town section for shopping was unaffected by the many large chain cooperatives until the early 90s when a Burger King went to Front Street, one housed in a compatible conch style building. The people of Key West feared an invasion of chain stores would ruin the atmosphere of the Old Town. Chris Belland and Ed Swift had been successful with taking over the marina building, building the taxi business, eventually operating the Old Town Trolley, and many other business and property transactions. (Strangely, we all want to be financially successful, but we have a tendency to criticize and dislike the people who obtain success if we do not. We often use the same excuse: "They are destroying the town." In reality, they may have made the town, or at least helped it. I guess we are just jealous.)

The end of the 80s led many people into the starting of a downward slide in the housing market. Many homes that would have brought outstanding prices were leveling in price; few were super buys. The recession caused many people who had used Key West as a second home to put their house in Key West for sale, but the prices held their own.

The recession in the United States also resulted in less travel to Europe, and brought more people to the Keys. The difference in foreign money compared to the dollar with the Europeans made the Keys a reasonable place to spend a vacation, so we attracted many Europeans. These travelers vacationed in the fall of the year, and that helped a slow season, a period usually not fully booked in Key West.

Many Canadians were gone from Key West, but we had an influx of Irish in the fall of 1990 complete with the British which seem to go hand-in-hand. Then there was the German tourist season in the fall of 1991, and many seemed to stay.

In the fall of 1992 there were many visitors from the Asian countries. Add to those tourists the cruise ships, and the hoards of tourists that arrived from Fort Lauderdale and Miami, particularly on the weekends, and Key West had lost its slow summer season. The Tourist Development Council (TDC) plan for advertising the Keys was working.

The Custom's House
The Richardsonian Romanesque Revival building was built by the government in 1891 at a cost of $108,000. Its red roof could be seen by incoming ships to be the Custom Service which taxed foreign goods. The explosion in Havana Harbor of the USS Maine, which plunged the United States into war with Mexico in 1898, had preliminary meetings at the brick building on the waterfront.

The building was vacated by the Navy in 1947, having been revaged by attempts at remodeling, pure neglect, and time. With the needed red roof replacement, and the fireplaces required by federal specifications, the building was bought by Pritham Singh in 1986 when he acquired the Navy property.

The building became part of the Resolution Trust Corporation in 1991; sold back to the State of Florida for $1,000,000.

The government of Florida leased the building to the Key West Art and Historical Society and supplied funds for restoration. The Key West Art and Historical (often called the Key West Art and Hysterical) Society also controls East Martello by the airport, and the Lighthouse on Whitehead Street. With the modern convenience of climate control, fire stairs, bathrooms, and elevators, the building will be completely renovated by 1999 with the aid of $8,000,000.

Plans are to open the building to the public as a museum and art gallery. It will present our history of Key West as well as traveling and local art shows, including the works of Mario Sanchez, our most recognized primitive wood-cut artist, and Stanley Pappio, our famous junk sculptor from up the Keys. Both collections are now owned by the Key West Art and Historical Society.

The bight
There are several large hotel chains that have found the financial advantage to Key West and built large motels, hotels, condominiums, time-shares, or suites along an area called the bight. This is the old warehouse section and includes the dock space within the first block from the Gulf of Mexico, that will run ten or more blocks through the old electric company. (This is not an unusual development. Many cities have developed tourist attraction areas from Atlanta's "Underground", San Francisco's "Chocolate factory", St. Augustine's "Old Town", Santa Fe's "Riverwalk", etc.) With five or more of the city's largest hotels, the corporate money, and knowledge, these major hotels will watch their investments closely, and the Key West bight will be a success, hopefully to be completed in 2000.

For years, the Pier House was the major hotel, and the discarded La Concha and Casa Marina got new life. Across from the Pier House grew the Ocean Key House, and The Galleon started as time share also. With Pritham Singh's development of Truman Anne, the Hyatt was built followed by the Hilton. All offer similar amenities. They have restaurants, bars, coffee shops, bicycle rentals, swimming pools, and easy access to everywhere. All compete with each other and they are of similar expense.

Key West Hilton Resort and Marina
Wrapping around the Custom's House is the newest of the chain, a complex combination of rental shops, a 178 room hotel with parking, condominiums and luxury resort accommodations. It is a full-service marina and offers a shuttle service to Sunset Key, their private island that includes private homes. A Hilton condominium is beside the hotel. At sunset, the performers

give their presentations on the gulf walk of red brick, the patio theme of the bight.

There is a small island offshore of the Key West Hilton that came with the package to Pritham Singh, a rather undistinguished little island called Tank Island. It was conspicuous because of large, metal tanks that were built by the Navy, probably in which to store fuel for some confrontation that never happened, and they were never used. Our military dollar at work.

As Tank Island came under the control of the Hilton, they removed the tanks, landscaped, cleaned the beaches and put the lots for sale, building excellent, luxury homes and/or selling the lots which eventually included a clubhouse, bar/restaurant, and eventually a golf course. Everything has to be ferried to the island, including the hired help. (The idea had worked in Miami where the island such as Fisher Island became exclusive second homes for the wealthy, but in a town without a social society and few crimes except purse snatching, sales must be to a very unique group of people, but they continue to build.)

Waterfront Playhouse

Outstanding theatre has always been one of the qualities of Key West. The converted warehouse-to-theatre overlooking the large cruise ships is dwarfed by the size of the floating cities. The theatre sets among the plants close to the sculpture garden and no one can estimate the amount of pleasure it has given the people of Key West. It is staffed by volunteers under the supervision of Florence Recher, and the quality is superb. The productions include experimental as well as classical plays.

Key West Follies

There was a great deal of talent in Key West, some professional and some just in front or behind the bar, old vaudeville performers and entertainers who had chosen other professions but who had grown through the early Hollywood days of ideas, make-believe, and pretend. They often performed at the "Pigeon Shit". However, the real, major production was at the Waterfront Playhouse for two or three one performance evenings.

A group of these senior showstoppers got together to perform the Key West Follies at the Waterfront Theatre, and it became an annual event. Viola Viet again singing "Falling in Love Again" like at the "Tradewinds" years before. Silvia Shelly playing the piano. Larry Harvey in drag and the dapper Denys Fitzpatrick, Dolly Martin, Clair Kelly at the piano. Sally Lewis was the master-of-ceremonies and announced the various acts. An evening to remember.

the cistern

Between the two major hotels and beside what used to be a warehouse turned into a theatre is a cistern. If you met someone very attractive and you wanted a few private words with him/her, the cistern was always a safe and rather sexy spot in which you could have privacy.

the sculpture garden

Directly behind the cistern is a new sculpture garden where the busts of various famous Key West people have been erected. Moving from one bust to another will give you the history of our island for free.

"Billie's Restaurant"

In the early 80s, there were a great deal of British in Key West, an economic solution for young Englishmen to leave England and work in the more profitable United States. Some had their "green cards" and many didn't, but the desire to work and the availability of a warm body to do the job in a tourist city turned many restaurant managers' heads away from the legal complications.

An Englishman got a job as a waiter at "Billie's Restaurant" on Front Street. A Georgian man and his wife came into the restaurant and in a heavy Southern accent ordered something to eat from the rather confused British waiter. After the sandwich, the waiter returned to the table and asked the couple if they would care for dessert. The man said "pa". The waiter was confused. The man repeated "pa, pa, pa". The waiter made his fist to resemble a gun, pointed it at the man and mimicked "pow, pow, pow". The angered man said "like apple pa, key lime pa", and the confused waiter brought his pie.

Into "Billie's" came a couple from Ohio who were seated, ordered, ate, and were out within an hour. From a cruise ship, they realized they would probably never be back this way again, or maybe they didn't realize. Regardless, they left a very small tip of only a couple of quarters although their bill was over 12 dollars.

The two waiters worked the table and were disappointed at their gratuity. A telephone call confirmed the couple had left their camera behind. The waiters checked the table and found the camera. The couple was told to come in and pick up the camera, and that it had been found and was safe. The waiters remembered the couple and took the camera into the men's room. Several "not too modest" photos were taken. The couple returned, picked up their camera, tipped the waiter one dollar and left. The waiters laughed that somewhere in Ohio soon would be a man trying to explain to the police why he was being arrested for filming pornography.

Ocean Key House Suite Resort and Marina

Facing the Gulf and walking right (east) are a whole series of gift shops, novelty shops, sales offices, an aquarium, the main station for the conch train to the hotel facing on Duval, the Ocean Key House. In 1988 it was sold to Noble House owners of Little Palm Island.

In looking at the front of the building on Duval, you'll assume the bricked front patio is part of the hotel property. It's not; it just happened to get bricked when they built the time-share. (We were worried about an over-abundance of hotel rooms, so less confusion was caused by building a time share most of which eventually became a hotel.) Next to Mallory Square, the "Sunset Pier Bar" also has a "Dockside" raw bar, excellent entertainment, with perfect views of the cruise ships.

The Pier House

Across Duval to the right (east) is the oldest of the major hotels, but only in years rather than modern convenience. Every hotel has constant renovations. Their advertising reflects their attitude of "Wake up and smell the margaritas" and it continues to boast the uninhibited, laid back attitude of the island.

David Wolkowsky had done a restoration project in Philadelphia, and he came well recommended to do a series of little shops called Pirate's Alley off the south side of Front Street in front of the the conch train station. This action was the basic starting of the trend toward restoration.

Another of Wolkowsky's projects was to convert a very unattractive lot on the Gulf, eventually to become the Pier House.

before the Pier House

One of the oldest hotels on the island is the Pier House, east on the Gulf. The original, large house was brought from somewhere else on the island in the late 50s. The added rooms of the motel are constructed of concrete blocks, mostly only painted. The Pier House was the most expensive and exclusive hotel/motel on the island in the 50s, because it was about the only modern motel and close to the fast action on Front Street, which shared its fame with Duval's 100 block

David Wolkowsky owned the Pier House when I first came to town in the late 50s, and it was the most perfect place to stay. It was close to the "Monster" and two blocks away from "Delmonico's". Many gays who visited Key West never left this area, and some never left the hotel.

There is a classic story of a man who entered the hotel having made arrangements through a helper to have an unknown prostitute up to his room. He heard the knock on the door. When he opened the door, there was his 23 year old daughter.

There was a row of double-story, concrete-block rooms overlooking a white sand beach and pool. The "Chart Room" was in this main lobby building. Later, for some such reason, they built a three-story building of suites between the original building and the Gulf, partially blocking the view of the water. The Pier House contains l28 guest rooms and l4 suites.

The "Chart Room" was a local meeting room for the wealthy and the politicians opened in l969. Any breaking city news would first be heard in the "Chart Room". Conchs, winter visitors, drug dealers, the wealthy, the locals and the visitors met there. Marriages and divorces were started there. It was the local center of gossip as well as fact. Old or young, black or white, rich or poor, everyone was welcomed. It still maintains part of its old flavor.

There is a bar at the Pier House in the original old gulf-side building that is right before the "Pier House Restaurant", a piano bar made popular by a local piano player and singer named Bobby Nesbit. Although not a great singer or a great piano player, he puts the two together in a manner that is entertaining and wonderful. You can not sit around the piano without thinking that somewhere in you is the Mario Lanzo, and with a couple of drinks, you'll try to prove it. A marvelous entertainer, a marvelous person, a wonderful room. Try it.

The Pier House features the Caribbean Spa. They have an excellent restaurant and the "Havana Docks Sunset Deck" in the bayside house which was moved there. In an adjoining beachside building is "Beach Club Bar" as well as the "Chart Room" off the main lobby.

The Pier House marketplace
You would not think that, in the middle of so many restaurants and bars, a half-outside marketplace would be a major center of attention. There is a coffee space where you can sit and watch people. The inside is full of unusual fruits, vegetables, and produce that cannot be resisted. Although perhaps expensive, they service many of the restaurants in town, always with fine quality. Their pastries are unbelievable, and the coffee is good.

The Hyatt
You cannot see the Hyatt from Front Street, hidden in back of a driveway and tropical plants. Built in l988, the 120 room hotel offers a 60 foot sailboat, the Floriday's, at the marina, perfect for watching the sunset. With typical Hyatt accommodation of excellence, it's pricey but very nice. There is Nicola Seafood for Caribbean cuisine and "Nick's Bar and Grill" for casual fare. "Scuttles" is a poolside bar. Very elegant. Obviously, very nice.

The Galleon
Next to the Hyatt is the Galleon which had a difficult time when first constructed. Again, as with the Ocean Key House, it was that time when our

politicians felt we were overbuilding hotels but that time-shares were acceptable. The Galleon is both a hotel and a time-share. Most important, it delights in being a marina. The Galleon Marina hosts the World Championship Powerboat Races, the Clearwater to Key West Yacht Races, and Yachting Magazine Races and Regatta.

The slow start for the building was probably because it was just a little away from the other major hotels on a street with an old "A and B Lobster House" and an empty Coca Cola Building series of shop. With the development of the bight, that has all quickly changed. The "A and B" is redeveloped and is a central point to the bight. The Coca Cola building has tenants including Lilly Pulitzer clothing. The one-block distance from Duval Street allows the Galleon to be more quiet, with less confusion, more laid-back. The services are, however, certainly not laid-back.

The bight continues

There are several more blocks of the bight property, including a large chunk called the Singleton properties. There are a variety of opinions of what the bight should include, and now have raw bars, stores, shops, and many pieces that have not yet been tied together, but that will be before the completion date. Singleton's bought Strunk Lumber and plan to build housing on a second level. There are now growing antique shops, art galleries, restaurants, a green turtle hatchery, bookstores, and so on. When completed, it will be a dramatic and dynamic walk, a sure tourist winner.

Sunset

A half hour before the sun sets over the Gulf of Mexico, many locals and some tourists or some locals and many tourists stroll leisurely toward Mallory Square, a two-block-long, concrete pier that had originally been the loading and unloading docks for this shipping island. If a couple were going to dinner, they may be finely dressed. Another couple would come directly from the beach in their swimming attire. Tourists would be in their Hawaiian shirts and shorts sprouting white armsd and legs. Young and old, rich and poor, class or street bums; all wander to Mallory Square to watch the sun set. Python Bill with his big snake is sure to be there. Cigarette Billy is panhandling. The cat jumps through the fire hoop. Parrots are common. A dozen entertainers are doing their individual acts for tips.

If it were a beautiful sunset and most are, the small gathering of 30 or 40 people would applaud when the sun hit the horizontal sea. If the sunset were not as sensational, the group would boo.

Sunset at Mallory Square was a direct line to God. After the sunset, the crowd would go in various directions to do what they had planned or what they had made up, or to wait to see what would happen. Only a couple of fishermen with the lines wrapped around spools that they held in their fists would be left on the pier.

Over 40 or more years, the Mallory Square Sunset grew from a religious ritual to a commercial sales and entertainment center, but with rules that the large cruise ships must leave the docks before the sun sets, the crowd protecting their rights and still being able, in mass, to talk directly to God.

The performers, from the sword swallower to the mime, had a type of union (a very bad word in Key West particularly to the restaurant group) who fought for their rights to perform for the crowd. They established their own rules and regulations and govern themselves. (Later when the large hotels invaded the Gulf shore, the time-share highrises, the hotels, the condominiums, the land was considered public, attracting tourists to the bight, a walkway of retail stores and shops. Some of the more successful entertainers at Mallory Square were offered contracts to entertain at the Hilton compound next to the Square, and the performers were bought out to do their acts and attract attention there.) In the 60s there would be a line of a lot of tourists and locals to go to watch the sunset at Mallory Square.

the cruise ships arrive

Although traveling by boat has always been a way to get into Key West, it was not until the middle 80s that there were so many, each carrying a couple of thousand tourists. In 1986 the Western Caribbean Company created an all-male cruise on the Bermuda Cruise Line. Names like Royal Viking Sun, Mercury, Ecstasy, Leeward, and Sovereign of the Seas bring in about 600,000 people yearly.

Cruise ships for lesbians booking organizations like Above and Beyond, Atlantis Events and Olivia grew quickly. Olivia has had over 35 cruises. It is part of their $17-million market for gay men and lesbians. In Key West, it is estimated the tourists spend about $41 each, plus the landing tax to enter the island. The gay men and lesbians spend more. Cruise ship passengers spend $73 to $106 a day less than the overnight visitors.

At first, the hotels were not particularly happy with the cruise lines because each sails before sunset, but they continue to make money from their restaurants, bars, gift shops, etc., rather than their lodgings.

Some of the cruise ships were filled with gay tourists, which Key West did not mind but which caused a little problem in the Bahamas. The Rt. Hon.

Hubert A. Ingraham, Prime Minister, put out a long response stating the Commonwealth cannot hinder gays' or lesbians' travel. He was obviously aware of the financial gain from the gay travelers.

Supposedly, the disturbance he was referring to was only with ten or so people on the pier opposed to a lesbian tourist ship. However, we have all found that people do not like what they do not understand, but the dollar seems to win out in the end.

A change in gays

There has been a steady change in the way straight American people look at gays and lesbians in relation to the way they look at themselves. There is the new "unapologetic gay" and the "normalizing of gays", where gays no longer are seen as suffering from being gay. In fact, most live productive, interesting lives.

The new understanding of the gays and the straights has given us another perspective on our life pattern. We have known married men who have wives and families, and realize their gay direction later in life, but do not want to leave the security, comfort, children and style of life to be actively gay. The spouse is understanding, and they can live happy lives. We know of fewer lesbians still married that don't want to confront the children with the possibility of their being gay, and live straight although not sexual lives with their husbands. More lesbians seem to live alone without sex, while the male is generallly more promiscuous.

Hollywood is responsible for some movies like Julia Robert and Rupert Everett of "My Best Friend's Wedding", made in 1997, and particularly "The Object of My Affection", with Paul Rudd as openly gay and Jennifer Aniston falling in love with him, a situation of her being pregnant by a straight dude, and a realistic conclusion. It was made by 20th Century Fox and was probably the first reasonably honest portrayal of the gay and straight relationships. The film even shows a new interpretation of family unit.

What the movies have taught us

Although I have quoted the famous lines from a variety of motion pictures which so influenced our gay lives when there were no other heroes or heroines with whom we could associate, the motion picture industry has taught us some important lessons that are useful to our lives.

I.   The hero always gets the girl (even if he may want the boy.)

2.   All police movies set in New York, Los Angeles or San Francisco

must visit at least one gay bar looking for the villain.

3.   Crashed cars always burst into flames.

4.   The hero shooting at I5 men has a better chance of killing them than the 15 men have a chance of killing the hero.

5.   A slight cough is a sign of an approaching terminal illness.

6.   Computer disks work in any computer.

7.   Heterosexual couples who hate each other will fall in love within an hour and a half.

8.   When in love, someone plays the violin, or sings, or dances, or all three.

9.   In science fiction, a well-stacked, 22-year-old, blond woman can be an internationally known nuclear fission expert.

10.   The proper place to hide a gun is in the ventilation system.

11.   The most innocent person in the beginning is the murderer.

12.   When foreigners are alone with each other, they always speak English.

13.   You can drive a car without looking at the road.

And Hollywood changed

Although the people of Hollywood claimed they were giving the American public what they wanted, they changed gears. Probably the depth of showing gays as contagiously afflicted with murderous impulses and campy, unrealistic behavior was "Crusing" in I980, starring Al Pacino as a serial killer preying on the gay community. The characterization of gays had deteriorated from the gay maitre'ds and butlers, the swishy hair- dressers, the drag queens of the beginning of film-making. It was not even Ellen DeGeneres coming out on television and real life. It wasn't the I992 film of "Basic Instinct" with Sharon Stone as a lesbian with an ice pick. It was probably the $100 million the films made in the United States alone.

William Hurt was the first actor to win an Academy Award for portraying a gay prisoner in "Kiss of the Spider Woman". Bruce Davison eanned an Academy Award nomination for best supporting actor in "Longtime Companion" in 1990 in a film about AIDS. In I996 Robin Williams' portrayed a gay man in "The Birdcage" which grossed over $100 million. The next year Greg Kinnear got an Oscar nomination for "As Good as it Gets". At last Hollywood puts over $30 million on "The Object of My Affection", hoping the gay boyfriend is accepted by other characters as a thinking, intelligent, and "normal" homosexual. It is not a film with graphic gay sex, but the script does have the character expressing physical affection for another male.

Do not assume that the complete change to the accepting of gays will not include every extreme of gay life and probably some we have yet to imagine. Remember the motivation was the same for denying the gay lifestyle as it is for accepting it. Money. It was and will continue to be the bottom line of profit. However, through all this, we are finally getting some role models, and relieving some of the guilt that has been placed upon us. (6)

A gay weekly newspaper - Celebrate!
We even have our own weekly gay newspaper. "Key West, the Newspaper", "Island News", "Solaris Hill", and "Celebrate!" are our four weekly newspapers aside from the daily, except Saturday, "Key Wet Citizen". "Celebrate" is owned by "Island News" and it is exclusively gay. It presents the weekly attractions, gossip, advertising, reviews and all the current buzz.

The Gulf of Mexico
When you stand on Duval Street facing the Gulf and see the tourist boats, the hotels around you, the water dancing to fascinate you, maybe the movie industry isn't much different from a tourist town. The films want to entertain you for a fee. So does a tourist town. But there is a difference when you stand at the Gulf and look back up Duval Street and remember what it used to be, and what it has become.

Duval Street, looking south

Boca Chica

In the 80s after the downtown bars closed around two in the morning, and when the atmosphere and comradeship were right, a whole gathering of party lovers and employees would continue to Stock Island's Boca Chica Bar that was open 24 hours. It was a dirty, drunken, urine-smelling, dimly lit bar that attracted all levels. with the common theme of drinking too much. Everyone wandering out of the bar with the morning sunlight hitting them wanted to repent. The bar owner's son took over the bar. A new county law stated that all bars had to close between four and six in the morning. The son closed the bar for good.

A community center

Many of the older gays and lesbians of Key West want a center that does not focus around the bar scene. They want a place where visitors can ask questions concerning the lifestyle, the housing, etc., that will attract many more to working and/or retiring here. Organized in a group called 49 Plus, the older residents are attempting to raise funds to establish a Gay and Lesbian Community Center, and they'll do it. They have been given by Square One Restauranteur, Michael Stewart, the shop two businesses east of the restaurant for their headquarters.

When Cuba is free

Many people have speculated that when Castro no longer controls Cuba and a democracy has been established, the tourist crowds will by-pass Key West to visit Cuba. Currently it is without question that the Helms-Burton embargo not allowing money or products into Cuba has had a tremendous effect upon the Cuban government and Key West. There are millions of dollars of Miami Cubans that are ready to be spent in Cuba once the country has established a democracy.

Will Cuba become a tourist destination? Of course. However, it may take a long time for the country to be able to match the conveniences now found in other places. The Cuban infrastructure is badly in need of repair. They need new buildings and repair of the old. They need hotels and food for restaurants, and skills to please the visitors from the United States as well as Europe. Legalized gambling may be one solution.

What Key West does have is a wonderful climate, now even tolerable with air conditioning in the summer. You can drive 160 miles from Miami to Key West. Key West is walkable; you don't need a car. It's emjoyable, with all kinds of hotels, restaurants, and bars. It's relatively safe. It is internationally known as a successful party destination, and it is under the protection of the United States. It has a party attitude.

For Cuba to be comparable, you would have to be able to drive the 90 miles to Cuba, or fly into Cuban airports that are not modern, or stay in less refined accommodations with limited menus. The cruise ship lines are never going to give up stopping in Key West so long as we do not price ourselves out of the market. There is one major reason. Key West is only a short distance from Miami, the central cruise ship headquarters. It is like no other place. Havana is only 90 miles away. Key West is on the way to the Bahama Islands as well as Mexico. The major operational cost of a cruise line is fuel. Stopping in Key West is another sales point in selling tickets to ship travelers, and the tourist economy of Key West is ready. (6)   It makes good financial sense.

There were no good days, no day out of the week, no week out of the month, or hour that the combination of people would not click together to make it a fun time. No one was accurate in trying to predict that special time when all people were ready. One Sunday night would be dead. The next Sunday night was wild. No one figured out the party system. It just happened. Even the full moon has been fooled in Key West.

Through the 80s, the fast-food industries opened on Roosevelt Boulevard and there were many chains that opened and many that closed to fierce competition.

Now, the shops stay open 12 months of the year. Their vacations become two weeks rather than closing for the summer. Even the restaurant and bar people will not be looking for summer jobs in a new location if they had any kind of job stability. August, when the weather is hot, and September, when the kids go back to school, are probably the most difficult months, but even that is questioned. Much, like not knowing when the bars will be fun, seems impossible to tell what months are weakest for business, but shop owners still complain.

The small shop owners complain that their goals, based on next year's projection of ten percent increase from this year's profit, often aren't met, that goal of an only-nine-percent increase in business means a business failure. I have never heard a small-shop owner say "This has been a great business month or year, enough profit". The excuses are "Rents are too high", "... there are not enough wealthy tourists", "The gays have taken over."

It might seem that the 90s would lead us into a period of manners, wealth, $100 dinners, the Palm Beach and South Hampton elegance, with full buffet tables, lots of big home parties, donations to charity, social climbing and "in" people, but it has not. There are too many people in Old Town that remember what brought them to the island in the beginning, the beauty of the island even with hotels and tall buildings, and a part of each person's story contains the craziness of the people.

In the late 90s, we are more concerned about President Clinton's sexual scandals and accusations than we were concerned with the economy, which seemed to be going well. Regardless of what happened in our personal lives, the American economy is good, unemployment is down, jobs and wages are plentiful, we are not at war, and the future looks bright. We feel even social security may make it.

But, there was a growing skepticism about the "honesty of things". Bill Gates is the richest, self-made man in the United States. The motion picture "Titanic" made more money than any other film before. Crooks are discovered in all kinds of business deals. Charity seemed to join big business in stealing a larger fee as the charity origination accepts a smaller fee. There are statements like "a percentage will be donated to AIDS Help ..." The sheriff's fund raiser, the Metropolitan Church's demands, the college fund, the home phones ring and the mail boxes are full of requests for money. Everyone wants the big event where charity gets a percentage, and there are changes in values, particularly changes in the freedom of the charity dollar.

There is also change in the attitudes of the gays at a bar. The medical "cocktail" for AIDS seems to satisfy some, and some of the younger gays had only heard about but not experienced the backroom sex with strangers, the game known to the previous generation. A couple of bars open or reopen their back sex rooms. The gay patrons eagerly take advantage of back room sex. It seemed hypocritical giving money to prevent AIDS and allowing the breeding ground for AIDS to exist on the same property. We have medicine but not a cure.

There are other changes. A whole group of people lead their lives apart from the carefree bars. There are more gay couples. Many singles can not afford the increased expenses of the drinks. Non-drinkers are not rare, and being alone is not the end of the world. Many do not drink as the new emphasis upon good health demands. There are many health fears.

A new sense of freedom had been born in Key West. With the added knowledge of the gay lifestyle comes greater acceptance of gay people, and the fear of the gay lifestyle competing and the straight lifestyle seems to lessen, and the gays are allowed and welcomed in all bars throughout the city. All this, gives us more choices.

There will be new people in town, here to enjoy the weather, the fishing, the water life, and, often, the bars. They will bring their values, their forms of identity. The island will continue to change not only because of them but with them. But with the acceptance of being gay comes other characteristics. Many straight-acting gays do not want to associate with the leather, macho gays or the drags. Smaller homogeneous groups form quickly. Although gay men and lesbians had mixed quite freely, the right not to mix is also recognized and respected.

The sale of real estate is increasing. The dollar, not yet if ever stable, seems to be better. You can now walk on the sidewalks without fear of tripping or stepping in something. Police ride bikes and walk their beats. There are even gay cops. Traffic lights usually work. Electricity goes off less. We register 'hate' crimes. But, there is always fear of when this will change.

There is a different attitude toward work. No longer did we believe the large corporation will take care of us. There are good businesses, but no more "Ma Bell". Skepticism keeps an attitude toward business as mostly monetary. It's difficult for a person over 50 to hold the job. It is difficult for young people to save money. There are new kinds of jobs making money replacing the wisdom of previous managers with business sense. Business avoids the humanitarian factors. We also realize that local elected government officials and politicians do not always make the right decisions.

There is the integration of blacks and women into the work force and a constant struggle for equality. Financial equalization for the female. More liberal benefits for the gay and his/her relationships. The word "pride" dominates over "fear" in the gay's vocabulary. We should coin the phrase "heterosexually handicapped", meaning the straights that will not accept any kind of lifestyle except the one they have chosen. We have accepted same-sex relationships in some of our laws and sometimes in our job benefits. Greater acceptance of the gay relationships without the fear of reprisals makes, couples want to share more with their friends and lovers, and there is a move to the more desirable physical locations. The tolerance of Key West is very appealing to many. "It ain't Kansas, Dorothy".

When a hurricane is spotted in the Atlantic off the coast of Africa, the radio, newspaper, and television give us plenty of warning of the possibility. A hurricane dominates the conversation; some say they are trying to figure a way to leave the island, others say they will stick it out. Some are not even concerned.

Most ambiguous of all is the wait that comes before every scare. What will happen? The lack of predictability of a hurricane makes us aware, once again, that we are small compared to a much greater God. Every hurricane scare has someone say "We haven't seen the big one yet". Ears turn to the conchs that say they can "feel it in my bones".

Some people leave at the first possibility of a storm, an excuse perhaps to visit friends in other places. Many drive north before the one road to Miami becomes too crowded. Others wait for more information and when this finally comes, if they were to evacuate, the road would be clogged with travelers. Most just wait it out, realizing the long wait would make it impossible to leave the Keys anyway. Our governor and road system administrators cannot understand why the people of Key West do not get hysterical at the possibility of tragedy affecting them.   Fortunately, of the several hurricanes that are reported each year, a very few hit the land or the small spot of land in the ocean called Key West. But, it only takes one.

In the middle of August, 1992, we got the warning of the

approaching storm with the same result that some people left, but most people stayed in Key West. The hotels emptied. On the evening of August 22, there was concern hurricane Andrew would hit Miami, and it would be stupid to leave Key West and drive into the storm. By the next morning the hurricane started hitting the Florida City area, south of Miami. Hurricane Andrew completely devastated the area by August 24, causing millions of dollars in destruction. It leveled buildings and trees, and brought death. Two years after Hurricane Andrew, the area has not been totally rebuilt.

During the storm, Key West had a pleasant, sunny day although there were clouds in the north. There was a heavier than usual breeze, but no drama. The nice day in Key West made the residents feal almost guilty since the storm so devastated the Homestead area 123 miles up the road. Telephone lines were down and the lack of communication implied Key West was gone.

The "wait until tomorrow" attitude is like redoing a house down here. If you are going to worry about the haste of getting a plumber or painter, you're going to be living in frustration. Unless it is an emergency, and an emergency is defined as "immediate death for many", you'll just have to wait until they get around to it. "Tomorrow" means a week, a month, or maybe more. That is why they call Key West the land of tomorrow. A sign in a bar reads "Free Beer - Tomorrow".

With the financial recession of the 90s and a depressed real estate market, many of the houses of Key West went up for sale. That was not unusual, for many people played the game of placing a piece of property on the market to see if there is a "taker", but there were few takers. After Hurricane Andrew there were even fewer. But property has always changed hands in Key West.

The island is attracting new kinds of buyers, often the affluent. Prices at the new hotels and restaurants are expensive, and there is constant competition for more elegance, finer meals, less expensive living accommodations. The direction has changed from the "in" places that were often funky but fun. When there is no war and financial stability, the real estate buyers come, and the buyers want something different, more exciting.

Business changed on the island also. There seems to have

always been an abundance of t-shirt shops, but slowly stores with better merchandise infiltrated. Fast Buck Freddies kept up with the pace. Strangely, whenever someone got a good idea and attracted the public, the idea would be duplicated. At one time there was one ice cream store, and now there are a dozen.

The businesses of Duval Street began to expand south toward the ocean as Front Street gained more and more tourists. As the industry blossomed and expanded, the southern end grew with restaurants, shops, and guesthouses. This was a period when the businesses of Petronia Street, the major street into the black section of town, began to make themselves more appealing to tourists. The "neighborhood watch" became involved and the people grew tired of living in the crack neighborhoods, and they called the police.

With the expense of the island, the new and elegant guesthouses and hotels like the Marquesa and Cafe, and the restoration of the Peggy Mills Garden, the building of the Sheraton beside Key West by the Sea, a new style of living developes. Charles Monroe held his 50th birthday party in an air conditioned tent on the lawn of East Martello in August of 1993, an affair with dance floors, bands, and catered dinner with an invitation list of 750 people. Black tie.

There is a great deal of difference in living full-time in Key West and coming here as a tourist. Firstly, when one day passes quickly into the next, the party spirit seems to fade. Drinking is a problem for many, unable to spend their time on something more interesting. I've seen many gay couples break up; temptation is everywhere. Living can be expensive. Rentals are expensive. Unless you are in a high empact, tourist-related business, there are limited jobs.

The current situation
Rents are rising. There are shortages of living space, particularly for the low income families. Key West considers itself a tourist industry. There is no other major manufacturing in town. Everyone seems to be related to the tourist industry in some respect. Guesthouses flourish. Restaurants are competitive. Hotels arrange special events for their selective guests. Mopeds. T-shirt shops.

The city thrives on its previous reputation of being a liberal place, a place for a party, a city that is free and open to everyone, a city of wider personal values, a place of creativity and energy. It is a place to relax and be yourself without explaining yourself. It has all kinds of people with all kinds of ideas. There is a strong Christian Crusade constantly challenging the gay lifestyle.

The lifestyle has changed for many. There is more hesitancy about accepting a different type of lifestyle by many straights and gays. There is more coupling, more staying in evenings and not hitting the bars, the bookstores, the beaches at night. The Metropolitan Church gained members, both gay and straight. But even the gay community is caught in the current tourist market. Not only are many in the market, but Key West has approximately 650,000 gay travelers a year. We are all aware that gay men and lesbians love to travel. One source says 37% of gay men and 36% of lesbians stayed in a resort in l997, and they had gone on vacation within the last three months. (1)

Most people realize that the heavy concentration of gays is in Old Town, and that the gays accounted for little more than the 15% predicted in practically all larger cities. Key West is definitely for straights. But, the way of life is liberal and understanding, not only for gays, but for all people whatever their lifestyles.

Many of the problems that had once affected the residents of the keys are being fixed. The quality of the water keeps getting better. We have television. Ask a conch about the electric shortages, the blackouts, and the number of people who had to return to where ever because the draw-bridges wouldn't go down. Ask about the mosquito problems, and the rotten politics.

Ask about the activities that grew. At the time we had three or four live theatres that gave us excellent performances. There were concerts sponsored by some of the big hotels. There was always a raffle or a drawing. There were children's days and family affairs. Fireworks. Boat racing. Swimming tournaments. There was always the ocean and the bay inviting you to swim, to hunt for lobster, to scuba dive, to fish, to sail, or just to relax.

The lovely, grand homes were turned into apartments during the wars, and these gave way to guesthouses and bed and breakfast hotels A street without any attention, which once was a local common occurrence, no longer exist. There are no "fix-er-up"s; no falling houses that did not have a large price tag on them. No Victorian mansions on the ocean with minimal down payment.

When Key West by the Sea was built, it was an investment in an idea that people would live in apartments and condominiums. New expennsive condos are on the drawing boards. There are many local compounds where people own their own home and usually have the use of the pool as a common element. Wolkowsky's Pier House proved the need, and more hotels and motels, more condominiums and compounds spring up rapidly.

People began to realize that to vacation in Key West and to live here is expensive, and continually getting more expensive. The common use of air conditioning in the late 70s and early 80s solved one problem. The constant flights to Key West from Miami solved another. The lifestyle of walking where you wanted to go, watching the sun set on Mallory Square, good theatre, island living, a remarkable lack of serious crime, and the wonderful people of Key West, not only the conchs, but also the hundreds of people that have settled here have made this vacation place different from any other.

The recipe for Key West? Take the competition from Miami. Take the farming and the turtle crawls, the salt bins, the adding of electricity, water, the airlines, the ships, the train and automobiles, World War I and II, Viet Nam, a change in American attitudes and values.

Before you try to make that recipe, order a piece of key lime pie, a grouper sandwich, conch fritters, black beans and rice or some Keys lobster or shrimp and sit back and enjoy it, and you can still hear the ocean breezes or the sound of rain on a tin roof, or the stillness of the night.

The constant complaint

Most locals and tourists complain that Duval Street looks tacky with its restaurants, bars, too manly t-shirt shops and other gimics to get the tourist dollar. The subject would probably be the only idea that would get a hundred percent agreement from locals and tourists. But who wants to clean it up? No one. Not the shop owners that are getting good rents. Not the merchants that are selling their goods. Not even the t-shirt shops.

Tacky Duval Street is like plenty of main street attractions. Bourbon Street of New Orleans, 42nd Street of New York, Castro Street of San Francisco are certainly not the Park Avenues of expensive specialty shops, antique stores and chic shops. Many towns have their questionable streets, and these are often the same streets that seem to be the most fun for many tourists. Locals like Duval also.

If not, you can walk a block or two away from Duval and meet a great variety of people who are willing and welcome your attention. Stop in a restaurant on Petronia Street. Talk with the guys reading out front at Flaming Maggies' Bookstore, an ice cream at Flammingo Crossing, watch the fishing boats unload, do a tour of the cemerery, swim at Higgs Beach, take a walk. The "real" people of Key West are all around you. Some are in luxury homes or condominiums. Others are in what appears to be shanties until you get inside. These are people who are here because they want to be here.

And the fakes
Some people say they come to a place like this for the "different", but they really want what they have always had. "I love the laid-back attitude of Key West". "Why doesn't that waiter hurry up?" "The cool breezes." "My air conditioner doesn't seem to work so well down here." "The people, conchs and tourists." "It's packed with middle class people. It has no sophistication. It is not like South Hampton."

There are always those that will complain that there are not enough fine restaurants, intellectual activities, or a special social class. There is not enough sophistication and things are not very chic. Thank God. There is an awful lot of partying. People seem to drink a lot. There's more activity around the bars than anyplace else. Thank God.

There are all kinds of people, blacks, gays, educated, hookers and whores, simple married couples, divorced men and women. And all these people are thrown together. The weather is wonderful. The town is friendly.

The pace is whatever pace you want to take. You can walk through the cemetery, ride your bike to the Atlantic or to the Gulf of Mexico, listen to nightclub entertainment or just the sound of the silent night.

What is the future to all this? We will never stand still. We'll continue to build, with or without the state's approval. We've developed a new animal called "affordable housing", whatever that means. Our homes will continue to be more modern. Eventually everyone will have air conditioning. We'll build front yard walls to hide behind and swimming pools in every imaginable space. We'll build second stories, then third stories. Our homes will be expensive, as they are now, but we will somehow manage to afford them.

But the hurricanes, the algae in the Everglades, the pollution from the mainland, the garbage and solid waste. "We'll manage." The increasing taxes. The cost of going to a restaurant or into a bar. We need new schools. We need more firemen and policemen. There are not enough jobs for our graduates. Wages are low. It's tough to live here. Where can we find a place to live or a job? "We'll manage."

We live and stay here because we want to, not to suffer the hardships, but to get that little piece of happiness that is so difficult to find, to get that little piece of happiness called friendship and loving. To wake up in the morning glad that you're here. To long for Key West when you are not in town. To find even charm in the broken sidewalks. To hear the quiet rhythm of the ocean. The shrill sound of a bird. But, we live here mostly because of the people. Those wonderful, crazy, wild, wacky people ... of which, we are part.

Key West? An attitude; not only a place. Key West. Population? 23,000. Number of liquor licenses? 300. Number of restaurants? 185l. Number of hotel rooms ? 3,410

. Sometimes, the old is more exciting than the new. I would like to live in a house on Grunt Bone Alley, Donkey Milk Lane, or Lover' Lane, but the names have often been changed. I find it amusing to know the Margaret Truman laundry is on the corner of Margaret Street and Truman Avenue. It's interesting to look at a conch house and know if it is historical or modern-made-to-appear-historical. I'm curious about "what used to be". Knowing Truman Street separated the town from the swamp makes me realize the size of old Key West was only several square blocks.

At the turn of the Twentieth Century, the small docks were the hub of activity for fishing, sponging, shipping and a gateway to the Carribbean Islands, including Cuba. The large homes of the wealthy were built only a couple of blocks away from the wharfs. Now what homes are left from these exciting Victorian years are in the middle of the congested downtown. The brick Women's Club is across the street from The Oldest House three blocks from the docks. Swamps were filled, land was added, and the city grew. Truman's Summer Whitehouse and the Lighthouse across from Hemingway's House used to be on the beach.

Even the numbering system for addresses progresses from the docks. The 100 block is one block away from the Gulf of Mexico; the 600 addresses are six blocks away from the wharfs. Odd numbers are on the east side of Duval, even numbers are on the west side. If you consider, Duval Street runs roughly south to the Atlantic Ocean (where much is properly marked "southernmost"), north to the docks and sunset strip and the Gulf of Mexico. (The direction is close enough, easy to remember although not exactly accurate)

What are you going to do?
There will always be someone who is bored. There are boring people. However, anyone with an ounce of inspiration can find plenty to do in Key West or, we like to say, do what you want to do. There is a whole ocean of swimming, sailing, diving, touring, kayaking, shell collecting, boating, water skiing, para-sailing, or just sitting by the ocean. Your time is filled with the many local events from the funny parades to the demonstrations. There are a few local theatres for live entertainment, movie houses for films. There are concerts, dances, and about any kind of evening entertainment. There's even a "scrub club" where a little clad young lady will scrub your body for a fee. But, above all, be friendly and polite, and don't be "phony". Just have a naturally good time. Above all, relax. It's your vacation. Read a book.

Undoubtedly, you can't see everything and every part of the city. The Navy yard is a totally different world, as are the shopping malls along route1, the county beaches, the salt ponds, the martellos, and the rows of New Town homes, condominiums, town houses, and apartments. Not only do the residents play in Key West, we also live here. Yes, we have schools, a community college, shops, a Salvation Army, the homeless, a few thieves, domestic abuse, and one or two murders a year. It is all part of island living.

[If you skipped the beginning history of Key West, go back to

[the beginning of the book and read those pages. Now you are relaxed and you can take as long as you want.]

Sure, Key West has changed in 40 years. Gone is the quiet of summer. Empty streets. Warm or hot days with a fresh ocean or bay breeze. Often rain in the early afternoon for an hour or so. The second home people moved away for North or South Carolina to avoid the heat. Parking spaces were available without parking meters. The dog barking or the rooster crowing. Little or nothing on the social calendar. The locals used to say that during the summer time, 75% of all gossip was false; 25% in the winter. There was nothing to do in the summer, and few new faces. Businesses opened late and closed early, and some were not open at all. Gone. The dull and wonderful summers changed to the sounds of hammers and redoing. Eventually, the sounds of automobiles, service trucks, and people.

Although Key West is a place where nothing is demanded of you, there is always a group who constantly work to make it a better place. Not based on financial status, although the gay movement did bring many of means into the community, nor social positions, many acquired it prior and had become dull. No one cares about family status. No one cares. They share a common thread of being able to laugh at themselves, their situations, and whatever the topic of conversation. They are here to live.

We heard on television of the possibility of a hurricane coming from the African coastline, but we paid little attention. It tore through many of the Bahama Islands, and hit the coastal areas of Cuba. We watched, but only with half attention. Five days before, Key West was told to evacuate, but there was the chance the hurricane would hit Miami, and some worried and left Key West, and many decided to "wait it out".

A local radio station announced the available shelters that were available to the 7,000 people who stayed. Some ran for the shelters. Others boarded up their homes, got food supplies and batteries, and decided to stand against Hurricane Georges. Someone called the radio station to announce the space under the Cow Channel bridge to Stock Island was full, and the space would not allow more people (a space previously home for the homeless) "... and we don't need no more Publix shopping carts".

228

Hurrican Georges headed directly for Key West during the evening of September 24, 1998, with 110 mph winds and slashing rain. About noon on Friday, Georges' eye went up Duval Street, from the South off Cuba to the North, cruisin' Duval. The eye lasted about two hours of calm, and the winds and rain hit from the back side of the hurricane.

The power was shut off, television was gone, curfews were called, bars were closed because of electricity outage as well as safty. We were under an emergency.

People waited in shelters or at their homes. They waited to see or hear what would next fall or sweep by. There was only a brief check outside as the eye moved across the island. The hurricane pounded the island for many hours and it continued to linger. The tree's calling out for help could not be heard over the sound of wind. There was fear and pain in many faces.

Many phone lines did not go out, and the phones rang with friends and relatives as well as homeowners who had left Key West, all wanting survival information. With it being dark at 7:30, there was not much more to do except to try to sleep on the sweat drinched bed, with the phone off the hook.

When people began to see other people, the major concern was if anyone were hurt. There was a report that a certain woman fell down a flight of stairs, "... but she falls down that flight of stairs every week". No one was seriously hurt.

The next three or seven days were of "inconvenience", but not harm. No electricity. No water. No showers or baths. No television. No air conditioning. Few bars could open. But, we did have the telephone. The Red Cross, FEMA, supplied food, ice and water.
Key West was a mess. There was 38 million pounds of tree garbage left, and the city manager said it would cost six million dollars in cleanup. The tree debris was about 19,000 tons stacked at the old fair grounds to be chipped and sent north. The total cost was close to seven billion dollars.

And the band marches on. The wild and funny people. The humor. The situations. The events. The gentle old homes. The weather, both good and bad. The attitude of the people. The state of mind. The caring.

This writing stops on September 30, 1998. History goes on, but to tell about history forces a writer to stop and tell some of the things that are known at that time. History is not stagnant. Writing about it may be. Changes will go on in Key West. Events, people, their attitudes, all stand under the limitation of time and place.

What I have told about the times, situations and people of Key West is based upon what I have experienced or been told, and there has been no intent to embarrass anyone. Fortunately, we have the ability to laugh at ourselves.

Thanks for enjoying it with us.

BIBLIOGRAPHY of HISTORY

Artman, L. P. Jr., *Key West History*, Key West: L. P. Artman, l969.

Artman, L. P. Jr., *Old Key West Stories*, March 1981.

Brothers, Betty, *Wreckers and Workers of Old Key West*, Big Pine: Litoky, 1972.

Dodez, Lee, *Memories of Key West*, Key West, l984.

Kaufelt, Lynn Mitsuko, *Key West Writers and Their Houses*,
     Englewood, Florida, Pineapple Press, 1986.

Langley, Joan and Wright, *Key West Images of the Past*,
     Key West, Key West Images of the Past, Inc., 1982.

Maloney, Walter C., *A Sketch of the History of Key West*,
     Facsimile and Reprint Series, Gainsville: Univerrsity of Florida Press, 1976.

Mart, Martin, *The Voyeur's Guide to Men and Women in the Movies*,
     Contemporary Books, Chicago, 1994.

Nichols, Stephen, *A Chronological History of Key West*,
     Key West Images of the Past, Inc., Key West , 1989.

Raymer, Dorothy, *Key West Collection*,
     Key West Island Bookstore, Key West, l981.

Sherrill, Chris and Roger Aiello, *Key West :The Last Resort*,
     Key West Book and Card Company, Key West, 1978.

Warnke, James R., *Ballustrades and Gingerbread*, Banyan Books, Inc.,
     Miami, 1978.

Well, Sharon and Lawson Little, *Portraits: Wooden Houses of Key West*,
     Historic Key West Preservation Board, Florida Department of State, 1982.

Westfall, L. Glenn, *Key West: Cigar City, U.S.A.*,
     The Historic Key West Preservation Board, Key West, l984.

Windhorn, Stan and Wright Langley, *Yesterday's Florida Keys*,
     Key West: Langley Press, Inc., 1974.

Windhorn, Stan and Wright Langley, *Yesterday's Key West*,
     Key West: Langley Press Inc., l973.

"The Key West Citizen" Newspaper, Key West, Florida.

BIBLIOGRAPHY of TEXT

1.   "The Miami Herald," "The Gay Vacationer. South Florida is 'in'"
Johnny Dias, March 8, 1998, p. 18A"

2.   Harry Benshoff, "Monsters in the Closet: Homosexuality and the
Horror Film", Manchester Univerity Press.

3.   Alex Caemmerer, *The Houses of Key West* , Pineapple Press,
Sarasota. Florida, l992.

4.   Eugene Patron, *Miami's Gay and Lesbian History*, "Out Pages",
Winter/Spring, l997-98, p.7.

5.   William Carl Shiver, University Microfilm International (UMI)
Doctoral dissertation, l991. Degree awarded in l987.

6.   Rene Rodriguez " "The Miami Herald", Herald Movie Critic, "The
Evolution of Gays in Film", April l2, 1998, p. 61.

7.   Frank Ramano, "Key West Citizen" (guest column), April l2, l998,
p. 9C.

Mart Martin, *The Voyeur's Guide to Men and Women in the Movies*, Contemporary Books, Chicago, 1944.

BIOGRAPHY of ILLUSTRATIONS

1. p. 41, "Papilllon's", photograph by Lee Dode', 1992.
2. p. 50, "Duval Street, south to north", Monroe County Library, Key West, Fla., 288.
3. p. 53 , "under construction", Southernmost House, photograph by Lee Dode' 1997.
4. p. 56, "Bird Cage Lounge" arches, Casa Marina, Monroe County Library, Key West, Fla., 590.
5. p. 63, "Living in Paradise", painting by Donna Hayes, @ 1983.
6. p. 74, "The elegant "La te da", photograph by Lee Dode', 1997.
7. p. 75, " a formal affair", Bill and Sue Seller, Sue Burford, Becky and Jerry Beaver, photograph by Ty Burford, @ 1990.
8. p. 85, "early two-story house floor plan", sketch by Lee Dode'.
9. p. 97, "Nesbitt at "The Affair", @ 1975.
10. p. 142, "Ripley's "Believe it or not", Strand Theatre, photograph by Lee Dode', 1998.
11. p. 147, "Home in Key West", photograph owned, @ 1973.
12. p. 166, " two story conch house terms", sketch by Lee Dode'.
13. p. 167 "simplicity of a conch house", photograph by Lee Dode', 1998.
14. p. 172 "going to a party", permission of and photographed by Carol Wesley, @ 1986.
15. p. 185 "old house lot plan", sketch by Lee Dode', 1998.
16. p. 186 "the once majestic 'Tradewinds'", Monroe County Library, Key West, 2099.
17. p. 193 "Hooters" under construction, Fogerty House, photograph by Lee Dode' ,
18. p. 198 " the "Midget Bar", woodcut by George Garcia, owned by author.
19. p. 202 "The Jeffferson Hotel", Monroe County Library, Key West, no. 2098.
20. p. 206 "the cistern", Monroe County Library, Key West, no. 665.
21. p. 208 "before the Pier House, warf space", Monroe County Libary, Key West, 7260.
22. p. 216 "Duval Street, north to south", Monroe County Library, Key West, 2329.

Cover photograph by Lee Dode'.
Cover by Dina Designs, Key West.

The Author's Background:

A midwesterner, Lee Dode', Ph. D., taught   at Ohio State University, University of Maryland, Florida Atlantic University and Miami-Dade Community College where he was an Associate Dean of Humanities, and a full professor. He found Key West and established a home in 1960.   An active artist, ceramist, Director of Key West Art and Historical Society, and writer, Dode' has watched and experienced the development of the gay movement.

He emphasizes selecting the right job, the right place, the most relevant time in which to be an individual and gay contributor to a dynamic lifestyle. He puts the responsibility on the individual: the outlook, attitude, sense of humor, and development of the happy and successful gay male or lesbian. "The gay person is responsible for making him/herself happy.   Where he/she lives, habits, attitudes, goals, and direction either help or hurt. If you are gay and not happy, it's your fault." This book is researched but also opinionated and maybe, controversial. You'll have a lot to talk about.

There is a serious side to facing the gay lifestyle.   You better know it.

Gay Happiness, How to get it

Lee Dode', Ph.D.

... a more serious side of the gay lifestyle.

If you thought you may be "different" 30 or 40 years ago, what would you have done? Who directed you? Who were your idols? Where would you go? What would you do? What would you become?

The subject of **Gay Happiness, How to get it** puts the responsibility of decisions on the individual gay by learning to handle gay and straight acceptance. He/she can be healthy, wealthy and successful during each of the five periods of the gay man or lesbian's life. In agreement with the 1973 conclusion of the American Psychiatric Association that homosexuality is not a disease, the book reflects the problems and possible conclusions, and answers some questions many gays face, how they approach a gay lifestyle , and what the gay man or lesbian should do to be happy. Telling your parents, finding a lover, building a life, preparing yourself to be important is intentional. Understanding the gay movement is important. You must be aware of your family, religious groups, alchohol and often yourself. A coffee-table book for gays and their parents, friends and lovers. (234 p.) Published May '98.

$ 14.95

ORDER FORM

Gay Happiness, How to get it $14.95 plus $4.00 postage

Gay Key West Cruisin' Duval $14.95 plus $4.00 postage

by Lee Dode', Ph.D.

Both books SPECIAL $25.OO plus $6.00 postage
(valid with this coupon).

To: _____

Address_____

City_____ State_____ Zip_____

Telephone (_____) _____

Shipping: Please add $4.00 for one book, $2.00 for each additional book shipped to the same address. Books will be sent in a plain, book envelope without book description within seven days. Please send a check; no C.O.D. or charge card. Do not send cash. I understand that I may return any book for a refund.

Make check payable to **Arete Publishing.**

Thank you.

Arete Publishing
Post Office Box 4382
Key West, Florida 33041-4382